Excel 97
SmartStart

DONNA M. MATHERLY, PH. D.
TALLAHASSEE COMMUNITY COLLEGE

An Imprint of Macmillan
Computer Publishing

D1410060

Excel 97 SmartStart

Library of Congress Catalog No.: 97-65620

ISBN: 1-57576-816-X

01 00 99   4

Interpretation of the printing code: the rightmost double-digit number is the year of the book's printing; the rightmost single-digit number, the number of the book's printing. For example, a printing code of 98-1 shows that the first printing of the book occurred in 1998.

Screens reproduced in this book were created using Collage Plus from Inner Media, Inc., Hollis, NH.

Excel 97 SmartStart is based on Microsoft Excel 97.

Publisher: Robert Linsky

Executive Editor: Kyle Lewis

Director of Product Marketing: Susan L. Kindel

Managing Editor: Caroline Roop

Development Editor: Sally A. Yuska

Copy Editor: Sydney Jones

Team Coordinator: Ken Schmidt

Technical Editor: Ed Metzler

Cover Designer: Anne Jones

Book Designer: Gary Adair

Production Team: Trina Brown, Dan Caparo, Aleata Howard, Linda Knose, Christy Wagner

Indexers: Sandra Henselmeier, Nadia Ibrahim, Tim Tate

Composed in *Stone Serif* and *MCPdigital* by Que® Education and Training

About the Author

Dr. Donna Matherly teaches in and coordinates the Introduction to Computer Literacy program at Tallahassee Community College. She has written many articles on office automation and more than a dozen software instructional manuals and workbooks. She has also conducted training programs for private businesses and state departments.

Acknowledgments

Que Education and Training is grateful for the assistance provided by Ed Metzler, for his technical edit of this book.

Trademark Acknowledgments

All terms mentioned in this book that are known to be trademarks or service marks have been appropriately capitalized. Que Education and Training cannot attest to the accuracy of this information. Use of a term in this book should not be regarded as affecting the validity of any trademark or service mark.

Preface

Que Education and Training is the educational publishing imprint of Macmillan Computer Publishing, the world's leading computer book publisher. Macmillan Computer Publishing books have taught more than 20 million people how to be productive with their computers.

This expertise in producing high-quality computer tutorial and reference books is evident in every Que Education and Training title we publish. The same tried-and-true authoring and product development process that makes Macmillan Computer Publishing books bestsellers is used to ensure that every Que Education and Training textbook has the most accurate and most up-to-date information. Experienced and respected instructors write and review every manuscript to provide class-tested pedagogy. Quality-assurance editors check every keystroke and command in Que Education and Training books to ensure that instructions are clear and precise.

Above all, Macmillan Computer Publishing and, in turn, Que Education and Training have years of experience in meeting the learning demands of computer users in business and at home. This "real world" experience means that Que Education and Training textbooks help students understand how the skills they learn will be applied and why these skills are important.

A Smart Start to Learning Excel 97

Excel 97 SmartStart provides a hands-on approach to one of the most popular spreadsheet programs available. The design of the text is flexible enough to meet a wide variety of needs. The text includes both basic and advanced features of Excel 97. This text can introduce a student to Excel 97, or it can supplement a student's previous learning. The abundance of step-by-step, hands-on tutorials enables the student to learn either independently or within a large lab setting.

Before presenting the step-by-step tutorials, *Excel 97 SmartStart* explains the purpose and practical use of each feature. Within this context, students quickly learn how to use Excel 97. The explanations and many tutorials enable students to remember how to apply the particular skill and to transfer their knowledge easily to other Microsoft applications. This approach ensures that students will use their skills in a practical manner.

Organization

Excel 97 SmartStart uses a logical, simple-to-complex organization. Features that are easy to use and understand are presented first. The student can quickly master basic features and develop a framework for learning more complicated features. In addition, features that students can use to improve efficiency as they are learning are introduced very early in the text.

Each chapter begins with an introduction explaining why the features in that chapter are used. Learning objectives are listed after the introduction and then repeated at the appropriate points within the chapter.

Each chapter contains an abundance of hands-on tutorials, tables, and screen illustrations to facilitate learning. Each chapter ends with a summary to help the student absorb and remember the chapter skills. The end-of-chapter exercises include objective questions and hands-on projects to help students check and apply their skills.

Distinctive Features

Excel 97 SmartStart provides many distinctive features to ensure student success, including the following:

- For convenience and easy reference, key terms are defined in the margin where a new term is first used.

- Each tutorial consists of concise, clear steps. These steps are highlighted in the book design for ease of use and later reference.

- Notes, shortcuts, and other helpful hints provide additional information to enhance learning.

- "If you have problems..." sections act as a teaching assistant in the lab by anticipating where common student errors occur and offering practical assistance.

- Each project is realistic and designed to appeal to a wide variety of business skills and interests.

- The numerous end-of-chapter exercises focus on developing and applying critical thinking skills—not on rote memorization.

- Continuing projects are provided throughout the text. The continuing projects help learners "pull the pieces together."

- A glossary is provided.

- An index helps users quickly locate information.

To the Student:

Although this *SmartStart* provides a step-by-step approach, it is much more than a button-pushing book. In response to your requests, we have included a short explanation of the purpose for each feature. Our focus is on teaching you to use Excel 97 effectively rather than on simply listing its features. We want to make certain that you remember how to apply your knowledge of Excel 97 long after you have taken this course.

You will not spend a great deal of time simply typing documents. We have provided you with a data disk containing the files needed to complete the tutorials and end of chapter exercises. You can then spend your time completing interesting projects with real-life scenarios.

To the Instructor:

The Instructor's Manual includes a Curriculum Guide to help you plan class sessions and assignments. Each chapter in the Instructor's Manual contains a list of objectives, a variety of tips to facilitate teaching and learning, answers to Checking Your Skills questions, Applying Your Skills exercises, PowerPoint slides, additional hands-on projects, and test questions and answers.

The disk that is packaged with the Instructor's Manual includes electronic files of the Instructor's Manual text, the student data files needed for completing the tutorials, solutions for the instructor, and a PowerPoint presentation.

The Instructor's Manual is available to the adopters of *Excel 97 SmartStart*, upon written request. Please submit your request on school letterhead to your local representative or to Que E&T Sales Support, Macmillan Computer Publishing, 201 W. 103rd Street, Indianapolis, IN 46290-1097.
Fax 317-581-3084.

Look for the following additional *SmartStarts* in versions for Windows 3.1 and Windows 95, as well as Microsoft Office 97.

Access

dBASE

Excel

Lotus 1-2-3

Novell NetWare

Paradox*

PowerPoint

Quattro Pro*

Windows

Word

WordPerfect

For more information call:

1-800-428-5331

*Available in versions for Windows 3.1 only.

Contents at a Glance

Table of Contents

Introduction

Welcome to *Excel 97 SmartStart*. Whether you are new to Excel or upgrading from an earlier version, this *SmartStart* tutorial is one of the fastest and easiest ways to get started and become productive.

If you are experienced with Windows 95, you may be familiar with many of the concepts used in Excel 97. If you are new to Windows 95, you will discover that Windows 95 is a much easier and more intuitive operating environment than the traditional character-based environment.

All aspects of Excel 97 contain improvements, including enhanced analytical capabilities, greater flexibility with database management, increased charting options, and the capability to automate tasks and customize Excel with Visual Basic macros. Excel 97 also includes many new features designed to enhance its presentation capabilities. All Excel 97 features focus on ease of use and increased productivity—which is why Excel 97 is considered the spreadsheet of choice by many users.

What's New in Excel 97?

A considerable number of new worksheet features have been added to Microsoft Excel 97. The following list summarizes many of the new features that are presented in this textbook.

Basic Features

- Multiple Undo enables you to undo up to the last 16 actions
- Row and column headings indicate the active cell; as you move the highlight for the active cell, the row number and column letter "light up"
- Yes to All option is now available when closing multiple files
- Toolbars, graphics, and integration with Microsoft Office
- More customization capabilities of toolbars and menu bars
- The addition of the Drawing toolbar
- Integration with Microsoft Outlook
- More graphic filters (GIF and JPEG)
- Formula palette makes it easy to create formulas by automatically correcting common mistakes

- Paste Function Command incorporates features of the Microsoft Excel 5.0 Function Wizard

- Range Finder—as you edit a formula, all cells and ranges to which the formula refers are displayed in color, and a matching color border is applied to the cells and ranges

- Natural-language formulas enable you to use row and column labels in formulas to refer to cells without using cell references or creating range names

- Data validation enables you to specify the type of data allowed in a cell, such as text, whole numbers, or dates

Formatting and Layout

- Page Break Preview offers an intuitive way to set your worksheet up for printing

- Merged cells enable you to achieve the alignment and appearance you want on forms

- Indented text in cells enables you true indenting of text within cells. You can now indent up to 15 steps in a cell

- Rotated text in cells enables you to rotate text to any angle in a cell

- Conditional formats enable you to apply different formats to cells whose values fall outside or within the limits you specify

Microsoft Excel on the Web

- Hyperlinks enable you to jump to other Office files on your system, your network, intranet, or the Internet

- URLs in formulas can be used in formulas the same as other file names and network addresses

- Web queries enable you to create and run queries to retrieve data available on the World Wide Web

- The Web toolbar makes it easy to browse Microsoft Excel 97 and Office files that are connected by hyperlinks

What Does This Book Contain?

Each chapter in *Excel 97 SmartStart* focuses on a particular Excel feature or set of features. At the end of each chapter, the student can work through the questions in the Checking Your Skills section and the projects in the Applying Your Skills section. Overall, the book's movement reflects the steps typical in guiding you through the required mouse actions or keystrokes.

Who Should Use This Book?

Excel 97 SmartStart is a tutorial developed with easy-to-follow, step-by-step instructions. Because *Excel 97 SmartStart* concisely covers only the most important concepts, your time on the learning curve is greatly reduced. Each chapter begins with a set of objectives. You learn by following the hands-on tutorials in each chapter. Exercises and questions at the end of each chapter give you a chance to practice what you have learned and to check your understanding of the objectives.

If you are a new spreadsheet user, *Excel 97 SmartStart* will help you become productive quickly. If you are an experienced computer user who is new to the Windows 95 environment, *Excel 97 SmartStart* will give you a head start on learning other Windows applications, such as Microsoft Word 97, Microsoft PowerPoint 97, Aldus PageMaker, or any of the many Windows applications you might use.

How This Book is Organized

Each chapter of this book follows the same format. A chapter overview comes first, where chapter objectives are listed. Next, procedures are presented in tutorial steps to guide you through the required actions. In most cases, illustrations show how the screen should appear during and after a certain action. Each tutorial is set off on the page by a different color background. Key terms are defined in the margin when they are used for the first time in the chapter. Chapters include questions and check your mastery of the chapter objectives and end with exercises in which you apply the skills learned in the chapter. Special "If you have problems…" boxes point out possible trouble spots and give you simple solutions to these difficulties.

The early chapters provide an understanding of Excel worksheet basics. The rest of the chapters discuss more advanced features, including functions, charting, database management, macros, linking and embedding data, and using hyperlinks.

Chapter 1, "Excel Workbook and Worksheet Basics," explains the main components of Excel. The information includes how to start Excel and review the basics of the screen, menus, keyboard, and commands. You learn how to enter data, move around the worksheet, access commands, and save and print a workbook.

Chapter 2, "Building a Worksheet," covers naming and labeling ranges; moving, copying, and clearing cell contents; inserting and deleting cells, columns, and rows; and changing column width and row height. This chapter introduces Excel 97 online Help, the Office Assistant, and ScreenTips.

Chapter 3, "Formatting Worksheets," shows you how to use various formatting commands to enhance the appearance of your worksheets. A new Excel 97 feature, conditional formats, is introduced, and you learn to use this feature. This chapter also explains how to check the spelling in a worksheet.

Chapter 4, "Using Functions," describes many of Excel's built-in functions, explains the types of functions used for a variety of calculations, and demonstrates how to enter functions into a worksheet. Also, the Paste Function (formerly known as the Function Wizard) is used to develop many functions.

Chapter 5, "Managing Workbooks," explains how to name, move, copy, and delete a workbook's worksheet. You also learn to use the Zoom and Page Preview commands, and how to set up a worksheet for printing by adding headers and footers and identifying the print area.

Chapter 6, "Creating Charts and Maps," teaches you how to create charts and maps, change chart types, and enhance, format, modify, and print charts and maps.

Chapter 7, "Managing Data," explains Excel databases (lists) and tells you how to build one. You learn how to add data to the database, view the data, delete records, and sort records. This chapter also covers how to search for records in a database using the AutoFilter feature.

Chapter 8, "Using Excel Macros to Automate Repetitive Tasks," shows you how to create a macro using the Macro Recorder, run a macro, create a button to run a macro, and how to delete a macro you no longer need.

Chapter 9, "Linking, Summarizing, and Consolidating Worksheets," explains links between worksheets and shows you how to create, change, and restore links between two Excel worksheets. You then learn how to link an Excel worksheet to a document in another Windows application. Creating summary reports with subtotals and consolidated reports is also demonstrated.

Chapter 10, "Analyzing Worksheet Data," shows you how to set up one- and two-input tables, introduces forecasting worksheets, and explains how to use the Scenario Manager.

Chapter 11, "Hyperlinks in Excel 97," discusses the relationship between the World Wide Web, hyperlinks, and Excel 97. You learn to create hyperlinks to other Excel 97 workbooks and to other Microsoft Office 97 documents. In addition to creating text and button hyperlinks, students learn to edit and delete hyperlinks.

Appendix A, "Working with Windows 95," gives you the basics for working with Microsoft Windows 95 and any Windows 95 application.

The Glossary, which defines the key terms used in each chapter, serves as a valuable reference for the reader.

Conventions Used in This Book

The conventions used in this book have been established to help you learn to use Excel 97 quickly and easily. As much as possible, the conventions correspond with those used in the Excel 97 program and documentation.

In this book, selecting means highlighting text or an option, and choosing means executing a command from a menu or a dialog box.

The keys you press and the text you type appear in **boldfaced** type. Key combinations are joined by a plus sign: ⁺Shift+F5.

The key combination ⁺Shift+F5 indicates that you are to press and hold down ⁺Shift while you press and release F5. The key combination ⁺Shift, F5 indicates that you are to press and release ⁺Shift, and then press F5.

Any on-screen text appears in **boldfaced** type. Any hot keys within boldface type are underlined. *Italic* type font is used for new terms when they are first mentioned.

CHAPTER 1

Excel Workbook and Worksheet Basics

One of the most valuable computer programs for businesses is the electronic spreadsheet. Spreadsheet programs are used in the financial and scientific analysis of numeric data. Spreadsheet programs perform calculations, illustrate relationships in data by displaying charts, and can also help you organize data. VisiCalc (VISIble CALCulator), the first electronic spreadsheet program, was developed in 1979. It was easy to use, and performed repetitive bookkeeping-type calculations quickly and accurately. This program helped justify bringing the microcomputer into the work place. Soon thereafter, other programs, such as word processing and database applications, entered the office environment.

Microsoft Excel 97 is the latest in a long line of popular and powerful spreadsheet programs developed for users at all skill levels. Excel is easy for beginners to learn and use; yet it provides powerful features for programmers and high-level users. Using Microsoft Excel 97 has become an essential skill for many office workers and managers.

Worksheet
One page (or sheet) of your work in an Excel workbook consisting of columns and rows in which you enter text, numbers, and formulas.

In Excel, you work with electronic *worksheets* that contain values (numbers), formulas, and text. An electronic worksheet is organized in lettered columns and numbered rows. The intersection of a row and column is called a *cell*. You enter data into cells, and Excel uses this data when it performs calculations. In Excel 97, up to 32,000 characters can be in a cell.

Cell
The intersection of a column and a row in a spreadsheet.

Typical uses of electronic worksheets include the calculation of budgets, expense accounts, and accounting problems. Excel worksheets are also used for business plans, financial analysis, list management, and data analysis. Because relationships within large volumes of numeric data can be confusing, Excel also gives you the capability to create graphs, or charts, and maps from worksheet data. Related Excel worksheets, charts, and maps are stored in the same data file, called a *workbook*.

Workbook
A collection of related worksheets in a single file. A workbook can contain 1 to 255 worksheets.

In this chapter, you learn the worksheet basics—how to move around in the rows and columns of the worksheet, as well as enter data, formulas, and functions into a blank worksheet. As you work on a project, you learn to use commands, print, and work with the individual worksheets in a workbook. In addition, you become familiar with commands that open, close, name, save, and delete a workbook. Finally, you learn to exit Excel.

Note

If you have not used Windows 95 before, you need to read Appendix A, "Working with Windows 95." It provides basic information about working in Windows 95.

If you need to leave your computer before you complete your work in this chapter, be sure to save your work and close the file you have been using. You can then reopen the file with the saved changes when you want to continue this chapter.

Objectives

By the time you have finished this chapter, you will have learned to

1. Start Excel

2. Be Familiar with the Excel Screen

3. Understand Excel's Toolbars

4. Move around in a Worksheet

5. Enter and Edit Text, Numbers, and Formulas

6. Name and Save a Workbook File

7. Print a Worksheet

8. Open and Close a File

9. Exit Excel

Objective 1: Start Excel

Because Excel 97 is a Windows 95 program, you must have Windows 95 loaded on your machine before you start Excel. If Windows 95 is running on your computer, you will see the Windows 95 desktop on your screen. If Windows 95 is not running, your instructor can explain how to start Windows 95.

After Windows 95 is loaded, the Windows 95 desktop is displayed. (If you are unfamiliar with Windows 95, refer to Appendix A.)

Starting Excel

The best way to learn the basics of Excel is to dive in and start exploring. To start Excel, follow these steps:

1 Make sure that Windows 95 is running on your computer and that the desktop is displayed.

Default
An automatic setting that the computer uses unless you specify another setting.

2 Point to the Start button located at the left edge of the Windows 95 taskbar (by *default*, the taskbar is located at the bottom of the desktop). Notice the ToolTip that indicates you should Click here to begin.

3 Click the Start button.

4 Point to **P**rograms in the Windows 95 Start menu.

The programs available on your computer are displayed in the Programs submenu. If Microsoft Excel is not in the menu, point to the folder that contains Excel (check with your instructor).

Excel icon
A small picture representing the Excel program in the Programs list.

5 Click Microsoft Excel (the Microsoft *Excel icon* resembles a large X).

The Excel program window opens (see Figure 1.1) and a Microsoft Excel button is displayed in the taskbar at the bottom of your screen.

> **Note**
>
> The Microsoft Assistant also pops up when you launch Excel from Office 97.

Objective 2: Be Familiar with the Excel Screen

Toolbar
A bar across the top of the Excel window containing a series of icon buttons used to access commands and other features.

When you start Excel 97, numerous *toolbars* and other spreadsheet screen features are displayed. You don't have to master everything at once. This chapter presents an overview of the Excel screen. Throughout this textbook, you learn about Excel one step at a time. See Figures 1.1 and 1.2 and Table 1.1 for an overview of the major features of the Excel screen.

> **Note**
>
> Your screen may not look exactly like the screens in this book.

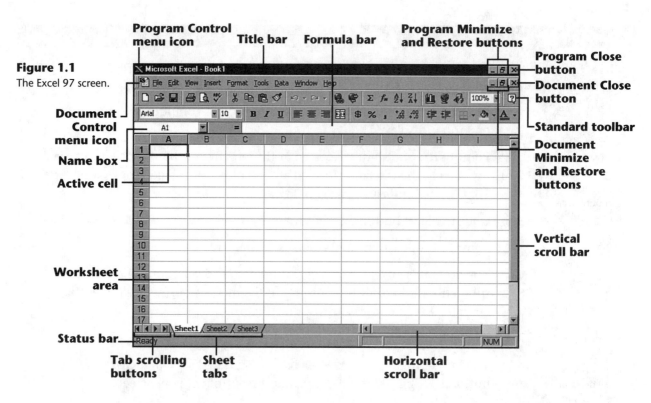

Figure 1.1
The Excel 97 screen.

Table 1.1 contains a brief description of each screen component. More detail about certain components is covered later in this chapter.

Table 1.1 The Excel 97 Screen	
Component	**Description**
Program window	Excel runs in this outer window.
Document window	The inner window. Contains the workbook, enclosed by numbered row headings and lettered column headings.
Program Control menu icon	Located in the upper-left corner of the program window (looks like a large X), which you use to close, resize, move, minimize, maximize, or restore the program window.
Document Control menu icon	Located in the upper-left corner of the document window (looks like an X on top of a sheet of paper), which you use to close, resize, move, minimize, maximize, or restore the document window.
Title bar	Displayed in the top portion of the window and lists the program or document name; the title Book1 will be replaced by the name of a spreadsheet when you save the file to a disk.
Minimize button	Located in the upper-right corner of the window. Looks like a single horizontal line; the Program Minimize button reduces the program window to a button on the Windows taskbar. The Document Minimize button reduces the document window to an icon at the bottom of the program window.
Maximize button	Located in the upper-right corner of the window. Looks like a box; the Program Maximize button enlarges the size of the program window so that it fills the entire screen. The Document Maximize button enlarges the size of the document window so that it fills the entire screen.

Component	Description
Restore button	Located in the upper-right corner of the window. Looks like two overlapping boxes; it replaces the Maximize button when the window is maximized, and restores the window to the size between minimized and maximized positions.
Close button	Located in the upper-right corner of the window. Looks like an X; the Program Close Window button exits the program and the document. The Close Window button exits the document.
Menu bar	Located directly below the title bar and contains the names of the nine main Excel 97 menus. Each pull-down menu contains a list of commands that display when the menu is activated.
Standard toolbar	Located between the menu bar and the formula bar and contains buttons, represented by icons, for quick, graphical access to commands.
Formatting toolbar	Contains buttons that enable you to change and enhance the appearance of your worksheets; it is located below the Standard toolbar.
Formula bar	Located directly above the document window and displays cell contents. It is used to edit cell contents.
Name box	Located at the left end of the formula bar; it contains the address of the active cell.
Scroll bars	Located along the right side and bottom of the document window and are used to move the screen display horizontally or vertically.
Sheet tabs	Located at the bottom of the worksheet area. The highlighted tab tells you which worksheet you are using; you also use these tabs to move among worksheets.
Status bar	Located at the very bottom of the program window and displays a prompt line to tell you what a command will do or what to do next to complete the execution of the command. The Status bar displays the word Ready when Excel will accept data entered into a worksheet. Other information will display as needed.

Learning the Parts of the Program Window

The program window is the outer window, with Microsoft Excel and the name of the open workbook displayed in the title bar. This window contains the menu bar, formula bar, toolbars, and any open workbook windows. To minimize, maximize, or restore the program window, use the sizing icons in the upper-right corner of the window, or use the Program Control menu icon located in the upper-left corner of the window. When minimized, the window disappears but the Microsoft Excel button remains in the Windows taskbar. You can restore the program to its previous position and size by clicking the Microsoft Excel button on the taskbar.

The Menu Bar

The Excel program window has a menu bar that displays nine menus. The **F**ile, **E**dit, **V**iew, **I**nsert, **F**ormat, **T**ools, **D**ata, **W**indow, and **H**elp menus are listed across the menu bar. When selected, each menu displays a list of commands (see Figure 1.2). You can access a menu by using the mouse or the keyboard. You learn how to use menus later in this chapter.

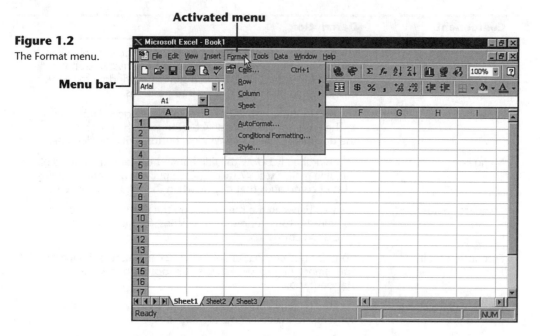

Figure 1.2
The Format menu.

Menu bar

Activated menu

Objective 3: Understand Excel's Toolbars

Dialog box
A window that opens on-screen to provide information about the current action or to ask the user to enter additional information to complete an action.

Excel displays the Standard and Formatting toolbars below the menu bar across the top of the screen. A toolbar is a group of buttons or icons, representing commonly used menu commands. Toolbar buttons offer more efficient, faster methods of executing Excel commands than the menus. For example, to boldface an entry, click the Bold button on the Formatting toolbar rather than choose the Format, Cells command, click the Font tab; select the Bold option in the Format Cells *dialog box* and then choose OK.

If you place the mouse pointer on a toolbar button and don't click, Excel displays a ToolTip—a small label that displays the name of the button.

Table 1.2 lists the functions of the buttons on the Standard and Formatting toolbars. These buttons are explained in later chapters as you use them.

Table 1.2 The Toolbar Buttons		
Icon	**Button Name**	**Purpose**
Standard Toolbar		
	New	Opens a new workbook.
	Open	Displays the dialog box for opening an existing file.
	Save	Saves the active file; displays the File Save As dialog box if the file has no name.

Icon	Button Name	Purpose
Standard Toolbar		
	Print	Begins printing the active document.
	Print Preview	Displays the current worksheet as it will appear when printed.
	Spelling	Performs a spelling check on the current worksheet.
	Cut	Cuts selection and places it in the *Clipboard*.
	Copy	Copies selection and places it in the Clipboard.
	Paste	Places the contents of the Clipboard into the worksheet at the active cell.
	Format Painter	Copies and pastes cell formats only.
	Undo	Undoes up to the last 16 actions or commands.
	Redo	Repeats last action or command.
	Insert Hyperlink	Creates a link to a file or an Internet address.
	Web Toolbar	Opens a start page or a search page in your Web browser.
	AutoSum	Inserts the SUM function and adds numbers directly above or to the left of the active cell.
	Paste Function	Aids in the creation of functions.
	Sort Ascending	Arranges selected rows from smallest to largest value.

Clipboard
A part of memory set aside for storing information or formulas you want to move or copy to another location.

(continues)

Table 1.2 Continued

Icon	Button Name	Purpose
Standard Toolbar		
Z↓A	Sort Descending	Arranges selected rows from largest to smallest value.
	Chart Wizard	Aids in the construction of a chart.
	Map	Creates a map of your data.
	Drawing	Shows or hides the Drawing toolbar.
100% ▼	Zoom Control	Increases or decreases the visible worksheet area.
?	Office Assistant	Provides Help topics and tips useful for completing a task.
Formatting Toolbar		
B	Bold	Boldfaces selected text.
I	Italic	Italicizes selected text.
U	Underline	Underlines selected text.
≡	Align Left	Left-aligns text.
≡	Center	Centers text.
≡	Align Right	Right-aligns text.
	Merge and Center	Merges cells in a row and centers the cell contents.
$	Currency Style	Adds a dollar sign, commas, a decimal point, and two decimal places to selected cells.

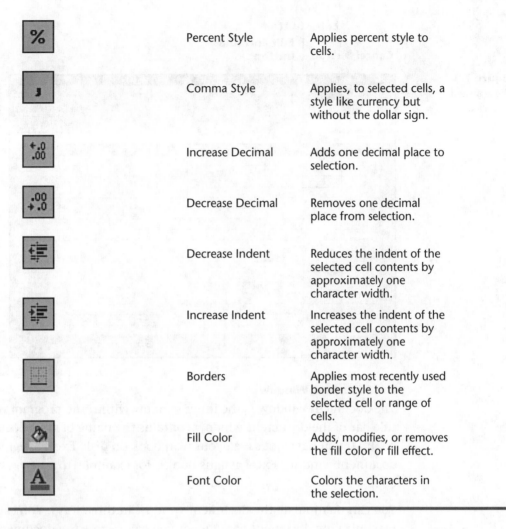

	Percent Style	Applies percent style to cells.
	Comma Style	Applies, to selected cells, a style like currency but without the dollar sign.
	Increase Decimal	Adds one decimal place to selection.
	Decrease Decimal	Removes one decimal place from selection.
	Decrease Indent	Reduces the indent of the selected cell contents by approximately one character width.
	Increase Indent	Increases the indent of the selected cell contents by approximately one character width.
	Borders	Applies most recently used border style to the selected cell or range of cells.
	Fill Color	Adds, modifies, or removes the fill color or fill effect.
	Font Color	Colors the characters in the selection.

The Formula Bar

Formula bar
Area near the top of the Excel screen where you enter and edit data.

Active cell
The worksheet cell receiving the data you type surrounded by a thick border.

The *formula bar* is located directly above the column headings in a worksheet (refer to Figure 1.1). The address of the active cell is displayed at the left end of the formula bar in the Name Box. The formula bar becomes active when you enter data into a cell. When the formula bar is active, a Cancel button (looks like an X) and an Enter button (looks like a check mark) appear to the left of the area displaying the entered data. You click the Cancel button to cancel the entry, and you click the Enter button to enter the entry into the cell. The button to the right of the Enter button is called the Edit Formula button (looks like an equals sign) and activates the Formula Palette, explained in Chapter 4, "Using Functions." The formula bar displays the formula (calculation) or data contained in the *active cell*, and the cell itself displays the number that results from calculating the formula (see Figure 1.3).

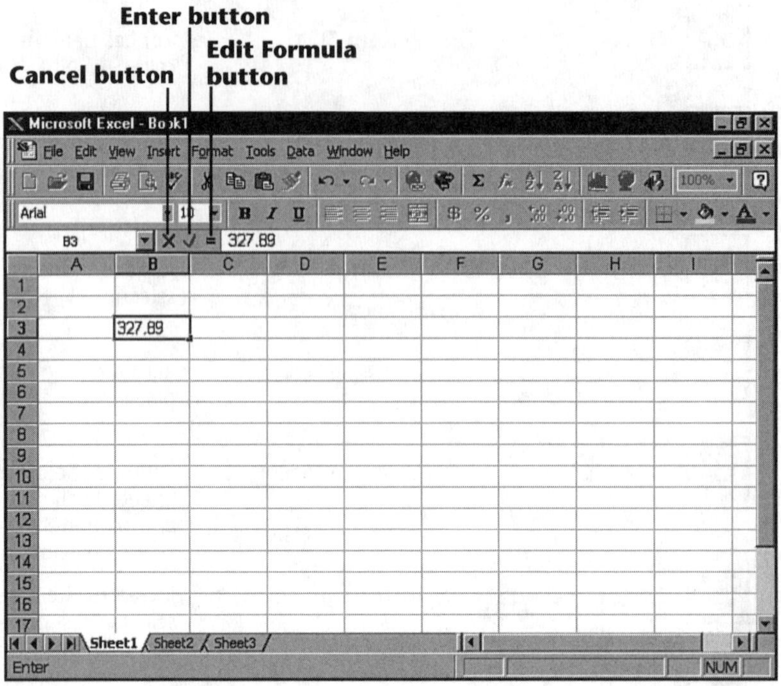

Enter button

Edit Formula button

Cancel button

Figure 1.3
The activated formula bar.

Figure 1.3
The activated formula bar.

The Document Window

The document window is the inner window within the program window. The title bar of the document window contains the name of your document (workbook). If you have not saved your workbook on disk, Excel assigns a name to the document window. Excel assigns Book1, for example, to a new, unnamed workbook.

You can manipulate the document window in three ways. You can minimize or maximize the document window, or you can restore the document window to its previous size. If the window is maximized, the document window title appears in the title bar of the program window, as indicated in Figures 1.1, 1.2, and 1.3. Figure 1.4 displays the document window before it is maximized. Most people maximize the document window to see as much as possible of a worksheet.

To restore a maximized window, click the Restore button, which looks like two overlapping boxes and is located in the upper-right corner of the document window.

The Worksheet Area

The worksheet area (also referred to as the worksheet window) is a grid with labeled columns and rows. Columns are labeled with letters across the top of the worksheet; rows are labeled with numbers down the left side of the worksheet. The intersection of a column and a row is called a cell. An Excel 97 worksheet has four times the number of rows available for use in previous worksheets, (65,536 rows for each worksheet instead of the traditional 16,384 rows). The standard number of worksheet columns, 256, is available in Excel 97. The grid created by the intersection of columns and rows makes more than 16 million cells available for entering text, numbers, or calculations. Usually you use relatively few rows and columns, those in the upper-left corner of a worksheet. By default, a new workbook contains three worksheets; worksheets can be added or deleted. A workbook can contain a maximum of 255 worksheets.

Figure 1.4
The document window before being maximized.

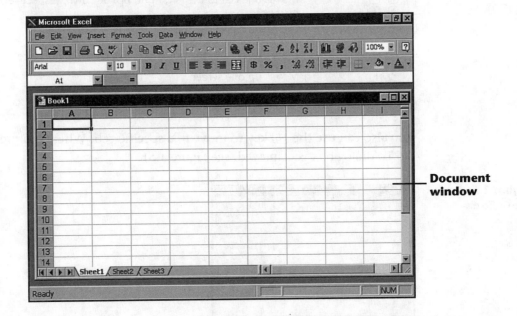

Document window

Cell address
Location of a cell based on the intersection of a column and row.

When referring to a particular worksheet cell, you use the *cell address*, which is determined by the column and row intersection. Cell C3, for example, refers to the cell at the intersection of column C and row 3.

Objective 4: Move Around in a Worksheet

When you start Excel, a blank worksheet is displayed in the document window (refer to Figure 1.1). This worksheet is the first of three blank worksheets in a workbook titled Book1. Excel automatically assigns the name Book1 to the workbook until you save the workbook in a disk file and give it a file name. The workbook is the document Excel uses for storing and manipulating data.

Cell pointer
A cross-shaped white marker; the shape the mouse pointer takes when it is on the worksheet.

In a new worksheet, the cell at the intersection of column A and row 1 is outlined with a border darker than the other cells' borders. The darker border indicates that cell A1 is the active cell. If you start typing, data is displayed in this cell. To enter data into another cell, you must activate that cell. You activate another cell in the worksheet by clicking the cell or by using the mouse or the arrow keys to move the *cell pointer* to the cell. Moving to different locations in a worksheet is the first skill you should master.

You can easily accomplish many tasks in Excel with a mouse. If you are using a mouse to move in a worksheet, you can make a cell active by placing the cell pointer, a white cross, on the cell and clicking the left mouse button. Using the keyboard, you can press the arrow keys, (PgUp), or (PgDn) to move to another cell and activate that cell. The keys used for moving to new locations are listed in Table 1.3.

Table 1.3 Moving among Cells with the Keyboard	
Key(s)	**Description**
←, →, ↑, ↓	Moves one cell to the left, right, up, or down, respectively; activates the new cell.
Home	Moves to column A of the active row.
Ctrl+Home	Moves to cell A1, the home cell; activates the home cell.
PgUp	Moves up one screen.
PgDn	Moves down one screen.

You also can use the F5 key to move to a specific cell. When you press F5, the Go To dialog box is displayed (see Figure 1.5).

Figure 1.5
The Go To dialog box.

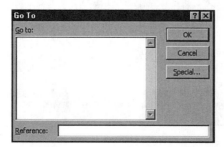

When the Go To dialog box is displayed, type the address of the cell you want activated in the **R**eference text box, and then press ↵Enter. If, for example, you want to move to the cell in column B, row 5, type **B5**, and then press ↵Enter or choose OK. Cell B5 becomes active.

Changing the Active Cell Using the Mouse

To activate cell E10, make sure that you have started Excel; then follow these steps:

1 Place the cell pointer on cell E10.

2 Click the left mouse button. A dark border is displayed around cell E10 indicating that it is the active cell, and the Name Box displays the address of the active cell.

You can enter data more efficiently into a worksheet if you keep your hands on the keyboard and use the movement keys on the keyboard. You practice using the keyboard in the following tutorial.

Changing the Active Cell Using the Keyboard

To make cell C7 the active cell, follow these steps:

1 While E10 is still the active cell, press ← twice.

2 Press ↑ three times.

To go directly to cell H16, follow these steps:

1 Press F5.

2 When the Go To dialog box is displayed, type **H16** in the **R**eference text box and press ↵Enter. Cell H16 is activated.

3 To return to cell A1 of your worksheet, press Ctrl+Home.

Leave this workbook open for the next tutorial.

1

Using the Mouse

With the mouse, you can efficiently perform a variety of actions. The mouse pointer shape indicates what you can do with the mouse. The shape changes as the mouse pointer is moved to different areas of the Excel window.

Objective 5: Enter and Edit Text, Numbers, and Formulas

You can enter text, such as a row or column heading, values (numbers), and formulas into a worksheet cell. The headings show what the values represent. Some worksheet cells contain (store) values. These values are data you enter, and they change only when you enter a different number into the cell. In other cells, you place formulas that use the data cells to produce and display calculated results. The value displayed in a formula cell depends on the numbers you type in the data cells. The power of using a worksheet for financial reports, income statements, budget forecasts, and other business applications comes from Excel's automatic recalculation of formulas when you change data in the worksheet.

Understanding Formulas

Formulas can calculate data using numbers or the addresses of other cells. A formula starts with an equal sign (=) and uses mathematical symbols to describe which type of operation the formula performs, then uses cell addresses to identify the location of the data the formula calculates. As you create the formula, it is displayed in the formula bar. The numerical results, however, are displayed in the cell itself. In Figure 1.6, cell A4, the active cell, shows the results of the addition of the values in cells A1 through A3, and the formula bar displays the formula used to sum the cell values.

Figure 1.6
A formula to sum
cells A1 through A3.

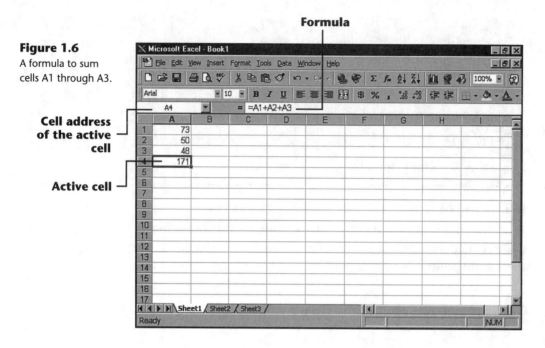

**Cell address
of the active
cell**

Active cell

After you enter a formula, Excel automatically performs the calculation. If you change a number stored in a cell address used in a formula, Excel automatically recalculates the results of the formula. The use of a formula enables you to test outcomes by using different numbers in the cells referenced in the formula. For example, if a formula in cell C5 includes cell B10 and you type a new number in cell B10, the cell containing the formula (C5) automatically recalculates and displays the new result.

Entering a Formula

To enter a formula in the active cell, first type = (an equal sign). Next, type the formula. If, for example, three numbers have been entered into cells B1, B2, and B3, and you want to display the total in cell B4, you type the formula =B1+B2+B3 in cell B4. Both the active cell and the formula bar display the formula as you enter it. Do not type spaces in the formula.

Because the entry in cell B4 starts with an equal sign, Excel recognizes the entry as a formula. After the formula is complete and you press ⊣Enter, cell B4 displays the result of the formula. The formula bar shows the formula whenever cell B4 is activated. In the first review exercise at the end of this chapter, you set up a business worksheet. In the following set of tutorials, you practice the skills you need for this project.

Entering Text and Numbers into Cells and Adding the Numbers Using the Keyboard

To enter numbers into the top three rows of column B and then add them, follow these steps:

1 In the open worksheet, make cell A1 the active cell and type **BUDGET**.

2 Make cell B1 the active cell and type **5**.

3 Make cell B2 the active cell and type **8**.

4 Make cell B3 the active cell and type **9**.

5 Make cell B4 the active cell and type the following formula:

>   **=B1+B2+B3**

6 Press ⏎Enter. The number 22 is displayed in cell B4.

7 Make cell B1 the active cell; type **200** and press ⏎Enter. This entry replaces the old contents of cell B1. Notice that the result in cell B4 changes to 217 because cell B1 changed.

8 Make cell A4 the active cell and type the following label for your result:

>   **SUM =**

9 Press ⏎Enter.

10 Make cell A12 the active cell and type:

>   **MY FIRST EXCEL WORKSHEET**

11 Press ⏎Enter.

12 Save the worksheet and keep it open for the next tutorial.

Errors can occur when you are typing cell addresses in a formula. To avoid making typing errors, you can choose to build a formula by selecting cells (pointing to the cells you want Excel to use), rather than typing cell addresses. Use either the mouse or the keyboard to select cells for use in a formula.

Building a Formula by Using the Mouse to Select Cells

Suppose that you want to insert a formula in cell D9 that subtracts the number in cell B2 from the total in cell B4. To build the formula with the mouse, follow these steps:

1 In the open worksheet, type an equal sign (=) in cell D9 to start the formula.

2 Click cell B4 to add that cell address to the formula in the formula bar.

3 Type a minus sign (–).

4 Click cell B2 to insert that cell address into the formula.

5 Press ⏎Enter to complete the formula entry. The complete formula is entered in cell D9, with the result displayed in that cell (209). The formula is displayed in the formula bar when D9 is the active cell.

6 Save the file and keep this workbook open for the next tutorial.

Using Mathematical Operators in Formulas

The following mathematical operators are used in calculations:

+	Addition
–	Subtraction
*	Multiplication
/	Division
^	Exponentiation

Order of precedence
The order mathematicians have established for performing arithmetical operations in a formula.

Errors will occur in your worksheet if you do not remember the *order of precedence*—the mathematically defined order of calculations. Excel always follows the correct order of precedence. The order of precedence for mathematical operations is:

^	Exponentiation
*, /	Multiplication, division
+, –	Addition, subtraction

Exponentiation occurs before multiplication or division in a formula, and multiplication and division occur before addition or subtraction. If a formula includes mathematical operators that are at the same level of precedence, calculations are done from left to right. For example, if a formula includes only addition and subtraction, and the addition operation appears in the formula to the left of the subtraction, Excel performs addition first. The computer always performs exponentiation first, no matter where it appears in a formula.

To alter the normal order of precedence, use parentheses around one or more mathematical operations in the formula. Any operations enclosed in parentheses are evaluated first; then the order of precedence is followed.

Editing Formulas, Text, and Data

When you are setting up a worksheet, you sometimes need to make a change to the formula, number, or text in a cell. To replace a cell's contents, activate the cell containing the data you want to replace. Enter the new data in the selected cell. The new data replaces old data in the cell.

Cursor
The blinking line in the formula bar, indicating the point of insertion.

To edit (rather than replace) the contents of a cell, first activate that cell. Next activate the formula bar by pressing F2 or by using the mouse. To activate the formula bar using the mouse, move the mouse pointer to the formula bar. The mouse pointer becomes an I-beam. Position the I-beam in the formula bar and click the left mouse button. A blinking bar is displayed in the formula bar indicating the location of the insertion *cursor*. To move the cursor, use the arrow keys. Pressing +Backspace deletes characters to the left of the cursor. Pressing Del removes characters to the right of the cursor. Pressing Ctrl+Del deletes to the end of the line. The Status bar shows that you are in Edit mode rather than Ready mode.

After activating the cell into which you want to enter data, you can type text, numbers, or formulas in that cell. As you enter data, the data appears in both the active cell and the formula bar. The cell address of the active cell is displayed in the left end of the formula bar. The Cancel button, Enter button, and Edit Formula button all appear at the left end of the formula bar (refer to Figure 1.6).

In the formula bar, typed data appears to the right of the Cancel, Enter, and Edit Formula buttons. To have Excel accept your entry into the active cell, click the Enter button, or press ↵Enter. To have excel reject your entry, click the Cancel button, or press Esc.

Using the Edit, Undo Command

Excel has a built-in safety net that enables you to reverse many commands or actions. In the **E**dit menu, the **U**ndo command reverses up to the last 16 commands chosen or the last actions performed. To undo a command or action, choose the **U**ndo command from the **E**dit menu or use the Undo button on the Standard toolbar.

Although the **U**ndo command can reverse many actions, it is not available for all commands. For example, if you choose the **F**ile, **C**lose command and close a file, the **E**dit menu displays the dimmed command Can't Undo.

To reverse the **U**ndo command, open the **E**dit menu and choose the **R**epeat command. This step is necessary only if you undo a change that you want to keep.

Caution

Although Excel 97 retains in memory the last 16 actions or commands you have performed, you should choose the Undo command immediately after you choose a command or perform an action you don't want to perform.

Using the Edit Undo Command

To practice undoing an action, follow these steps:

❶ In the open worksheet, make cell B3 the active cell.

❷ Type **123** and press ↵Enter. 123 appears in cell B3.

❸ From the **E**dit menu, choose **U**ndo Typing. The content of cell B3 reverts back to what it was before you entered 123—19.

❹ Save the workbook and keep it open for the next tutorial.

In the following tutorial, you edit a formula that you have already entered in a cell.

Editing the Contents of a Cell

Edit the formula (=B1+B2+B3) in cell B4 so that you first double the contents of cell B3 and then perform the addition. Follow these steps:

1 In the open worksheet, make cell B4 the active cell and press F2.

The blinking insertion cursor is displayed at the end of the formula in cell B4.

2 Type *2 at the end of the formula; then press ↵Enter. This formula multiplies B3 by 2 and then adds the result to the sum of B1 and B2. The answer 226 is displayed in cell B4.

3 Save the workbook and keep it open for the next tutorial.

Remember that in the new formula (=B1+B2+B3*2), multiplication has a higher order of precedence and is performed before any addition.

Correcting Mistakes in Formulas

The purpose of this tutorial is to show you how to enter a formula and correct mistakes in a formula, as well as illustrate the importance of the order of precedence. To find the average of the numbers you entered in the worksheet, follow these steps:

1 Make cell B5 the active cell; type **=B1+B2+B3/3** and press ↵Enter.

The result is 211. The formula apparently instructed Excel to find the average by adding the three numbers and then dividing by 3.

But notice that cell B5 obviously doesn't contain the average because Excel follows the established order of precedence and divides B3 by 3 before the addition occurs. You must use parentheses to cause the addition to occur before the division.

To correct the formula, you must place parentheses around the addition operation so that the formula is =(B1+B2+B3)/3.

2 Double-click cell B5 to begin editing the formula.

When in edit mode, the values in the cell addresses referenced in the formula display colored borders. The cell references in the formula are displayed in the same color as the borders.

3 Press ← to move the insertion point to the right of the = sign; then type **(**.

4 Press → to move the insertion point to the left of the /; then type **)**.

5 Press ↵Enter. The result in cell B4 is 72.33333.

6 Save the workbook and keep it open for the next tutorial.

Note that the parentheses force the addition to be completed before the division. Always check your worksheet's formulas to be sure that they are working the way you intended.

Editing and Formatting Commands

Every Windows 95 program has a menu bar directly below the program's title bar. (Appendix A reviews the use of Windows 95 menus.) Excel's menu bar has nine menus, starting with the **F**ile menu on the left and ending with the **H**elp menu on the right. In Excel, you can quickly access some of the more commonly used **E**dit and F**o**rmat commands by using a shortcut menu. **E**dit commands—such as Cu**t**, **C**opy, **P**aste, Clear Co**n**tents, **I**nsert, and **D**elete—and F**o**rmat commands—such as Number, Alignment, Font, Border, and Patterns—are displayed on a shortcut menu when you click the right mouse button (see Figure 1.7). Excel has several shortcut menus. The shortcut menu that appears when you click the right mouse button varies depending on where the mouse pointer is located.

Figure 1.7
The Edit shortcut menu.

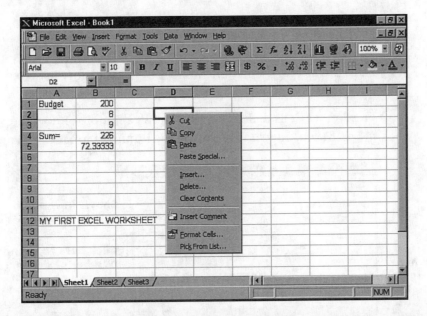

Using a Menu Command

To use the F**o**rmat menu command to change the way numbers are displayed in cell B1 of the worksheet you have created, follow these steps:

1 In the open worksheet, select the cell you want to format by placing the cell pointer on cell B1 and clicking the left mouse button.

2 Place the mouse pointer on F**o**rmat in the menu bar, and click the left mouse button. The F**o**rmat menu drops down (refer to Figure 1.2).

3 Choose C**e**lls to display the Format Cells dialog box (see Figure 1.8).

Note that the dialog box contains six different tabs. By default, the Number tab is selected.

(continues)

Using a Menu Command (continued)

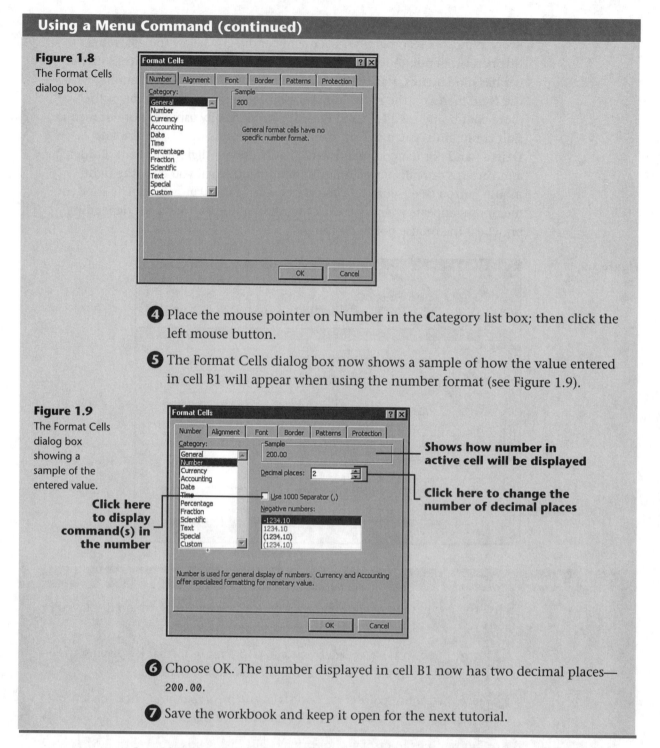

Figure 1.8
The Format Cells dialog box.

Figure 1.9
The Format Cells dialog box showing a sample of the entered value.

Click here to display command(s) in the number

Shows how number in active cell will be displayed

Click here to change the number of decimal places

④ Place the mouse pointer on Number in the **C**ategory list box; then click the left mouse button.

⑤ The Format Cells dialog box now shows a sample of how the value entered in cell B1 will appear when using the number format (see Figure 1.9).

⑥ Choose OK. The number displayed in cell B1 now has two decimal places— 200.00.

⑦ Save the workbook and keep it open for the next tutorial.

In addition to using one of the nine menus and their options to execute commands, many commands can be completed using toolbar buttons. In the next tutorial, you use a toolbar button to format values.

Using a Toolbar Button

To use the Currency Style button on the Formatting toolbar to change the way numbers are displayed in cell B2 of the open worksheet, follow these steps:

❶ Make cell B2 the active cell.

 ❷ Place the mouse pointer on the Currency Style button (on the Formatting toolbar) and click the left mouse button.

The number in cell B2 is now displayed as currency.

❸ Save the workbook and keep it open for the next tutorial.

Objective 6: Name and Save a Workbook File

RAM
Random-access memory is a temporary memory area in a computer.

File
The area on a disk in which workbooks are saved.

Some of the most frequently used Excel commands involve files. When you are working with a worksheet in a workbook, the data you enter or edit is actually stored in a temporary memory area of your computer called *RAM* (random-access memory). If a power outage or computer failure occurs while you are working, the temporary memory is wiped out, taking all entered or edited data with it. To avoid losing your work, save it frequently to a disk. Also, save your workbook before exiting Excel. Items saved on disk are stored in a permanent memory area called a *file*. Each file must have a unique name. When you need to use a workbook already on disk, you must open the workbook's file.

Naming and Saving a Workbook File

Your internal hard drive or floppy disk permanently stores data. To place a file in a permanent storage area, you must issue a command to save the file and indicate to which disk drive (A:, B:, or C:) you want the file saved. When you save a file the first time, you must give the workbook a file name. The file name enables you (and Excel) to identify your file in the permanent storage area on disk. When you save a new workbook, give it a name different from the other workbooks already on disk; each file name in a directory folder must be unique. The complete path, including drive letter, server name, folder path, file name, and three-character extension can contain up to 218 characters. In addition, file names cannot include any of the following: forward slash (/), backslash (\), greater-than sign (>), less-than sign (<), asterisk (*), question mark (?), quotation mark ("), pipe symbol (|), colon (:), or semicolon (;).

Understanding the File, Save Command

To save a new workbook in Excel, you open the **F**ile menu and choose the **S**ave command, or you can click the Save button on the Standard toolbar. The Save As dialog box is displayed on-screen when you are saving a file for the first time or when you choose the **F**ile, Save **A**s command (see Figure 1.10).

Figure 1.10

The Save As dialog box.

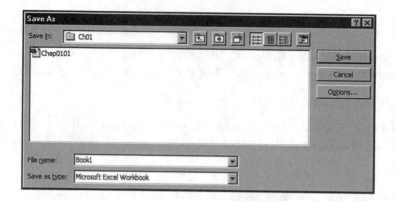

In the File **n**ame text box, enter a name that will help you identify the workbook in the future.

You can also save a file to another drive or folder. Select the drive and folder from the Save **i**n drop-down list. When you choose the **F**ile, **S**ave command to save changes to a file already saved and named, the Save As dialog box does not appear. The **F**ile, **S**ave command overwrites the named file with the changes made.

Saving a Workbook File

If you are saving files to a floppy disk, make sure that you have a formatted disk in the proper drive (A: or B:). Then follow these steps to save the worksheet:

1 Open the **F**ile menu by clicking the menu name.

2 From the **F**ile drop-down menu, click the **S**ave command. The Save As dialog box is displayed (refer to Figure 1.10).

3 Type **My File** in the File **n**ame text box.

4 Click the arrow to the right of the Save **i**n drop-down list. Select the disk drive and folder in which you want to store your file by moving the mouse pointer to the designated drive or folder and clicking the left mouse button.

5 Choose **S**ave. The workbook is saved on disk in the workbook named My File. The document window title bar should now display the name My File.

By default, workbooks in Microsoft Excel 97 are assigned the file name extension of .xls. When using Windows 95, you have the option of having the file name extension display on the document title bar and in various dialog boxes, such as the Save As dialog box. To have file name extensions display, click the Start button on the Windows 95 Taskbar, choose **P**rograms, Windows Explorer. When the Windows Explorer appears, choose the **V**iew, **O**ptions command. To display file name extensions, make sure that there is no check mark to the left of the Hide MS-DOS file **e**xtensions for file types that are registered option box. To hide file name extensions, make sure that there is a check mark in the option box.

Using the File, Save As Command

Sometimes you may want to keep different versions of a workbook. For example, if you need to build a workbook for this month's budget, many of the formulas will be the same as those in last month's budget workbook. You can work most efficiently by starting with last month's workbook. When you want to refer to a previous version of a document and keep the original, you will want to have two copies of the document: one containing the changes made and one without changes. The **F**ile, Save **A**s command enables you to keep the original document and assign another file name when you save the changed document. The Save As dialog box looks like the dialog box that is displayed when an unnamed document is saved (refer to Figure 1.10).

Saving a File with the File, Save As Command

To save your workbook in a second file named My File 2, follow these steps:

1 Open the **F**ile menu and choose the Save **A**s command. The Save As dialog box is displayed (refer to Figure 1.10).

2 In the File **n**ame text box, type **My File 2**.

3 Select the correct drive and folder from the Save **in** drop-down list.

4 Choose **S**ave to save the workbook as My File 2.

5 Check to see that the document title bar now displays the name My File 2.

> **Note**
>
> The .xls extension may or may not display, depending on the Windows 95 view options.

Your workbook has been saved in two separate files—once as My File and once as My File 2.

Keep this workbook open for the next tutorial.

Objective 7: Print a Worksheet

When you are building your worksheet or making changes to it, the worksheet must be in the computer's internal memory. When the worksheet is in internal memory and on-screen, you can print it. As you learn later, you can also use the **F**ile, **O**pen command and Settings command to print a file.

> **Note**
>
> To print, a worksheet must contain data.

If your worksheet has data in more columns than can print on one page, the column(s) on the right side will be printed on the second page.

Printing a Worksheet

In this tutorial, you print the first worksheet in the My File 2 workbook. (If My File 2 is not on-screen, use the **F**ile, **O**pen command to open the workbook.) If your computer is not connected to a printer, you cannot complete this tutorial. (Ask your instructor for assistance in this case.) Follow these steps:

❶ Make sure that your printer is turned on.

❷ Click the Print button on the Standard toolbar. The worksheet begins to print.

Note

If you are not hooked up to a printer, you can get an idea of what a printout will look like by choosing **F**ile, Print Pre**v**iew.

Objective 8: Open and Close a File

You have already learned how to name and save a file on disk. You now learn how to retrieve a file stored on disk and how to close a workbook.

Opening and Closing a File

A workbook file must be open before any of its worksheets can be used.

To open a workbook file, click the **F**ile menu, and choose the **O**pen command, or click the Open button on the Standard toolbar. The Open dialog box is displayed (see Figure 1.11).

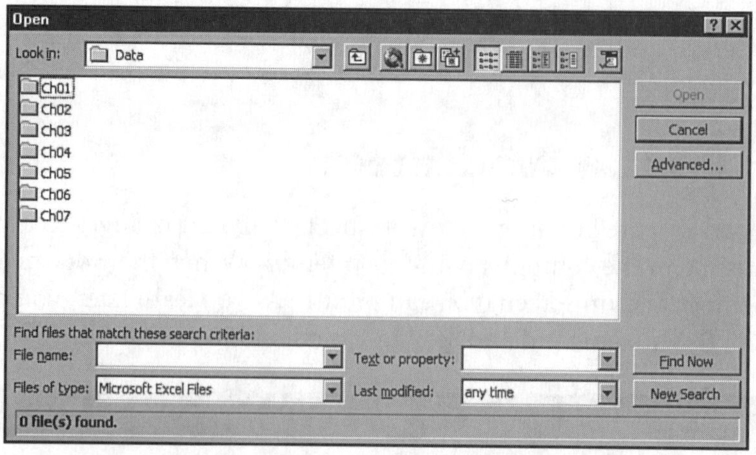

Figure 1.11
The Open dialog box.

Open	? X
Look in: 📁 Data	

Ch01
Ch02
Ch03
Ch04
Ch05
Ch06
Ch07

Open
Cancel
Advanced...

Find files that match these search criteria:

| File name: | ▾ | Text or property: | ▾ | Find Now |
| Files of type: Microsoft Excel Files | ▾ | Last modified: any time | ▾ | New Search |

0 file(s) found.

Using the Options in the Open Dialog Box

The Open dialog box enables you to open a workbook; you can specify its file name, folder, and the drive on which it is stored. The Look **in** text box appears when the Open dialog box is displayed. Open a file by selecting the drive and folder in the Look **in** text box, the file name in the file name list box, and then choosing **O**pen or pressing ⏎Enter.

The Open dialog box displays an alphabetical list of all Excel files in the current folder, and the folder is displayed in the Look **in** list box. To select a file with the mouse, place the mouse pointer on the file name; then double-click the left mouse button or choose **O**pen.

The Look **in** list box displays all available folders, enabling you to locate a file in another folder. To change to another drive or folder with the mouse, click the downward-pointing arrow at the right end of the Look **in** list box to display available drives and folders. Move the mouse pointer to the folder name; then double-click the left mouse button, or select the folder name and choose **O**pen. (To view choices not visible in the list box, use the scroll bar.)

Using the Close Command

When you finish working on a worksheet, close its workbook file. Open the **F**ile menu and choose the **C**lose command. If you have not saved changes made to the file, Excel prompts you to save before closing the workbook (see Figure 1.12).

Figure 1.12
The Excel prompt for saving a file.

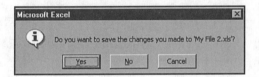

To close the workbook and save changes, choose **Y**es. To close the workbook and not save your changes, choose **N**o. To close the dialog box and keep the workbook open, choose Cancel. If you saved all changes before choosing **F**ile, **C**lose, you do not need to save again; the window closes without prompting you to save.

Closing a Workbook

Follow these steps to close the active My File 2 workbook:

❶ Open the **F**ile menu and choose the **C**lose command.

❷ If the Save Changes dialog box is displayed on-screen, choose the **Y**es button to save any changes you made since you last saved the worksheet. Choose the **N**o button to close the worksheet without saving changes you made since you last saved. Either choice can be used in this tutorial. The Workbook window disappears from the screen, and menu choices are limited to **F**ile and **H**elp.

Notice how your screen looks when no workbook is open (see Figure 1.13).

Figure 1.13
The Excel screen when no workbooks are open.

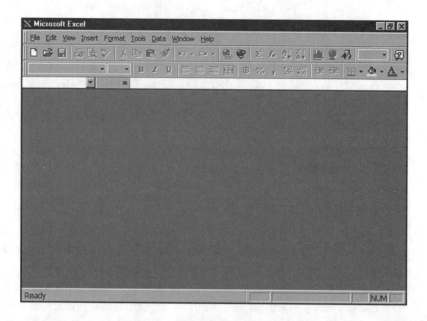

Opening a Workbook File

To open the My File 2 workbook, follow these steps:

1 Choose **F**ile, **O**pen. The Open dialog box is displayed (refer to Figure 1.11).

2 Check to see that the drive and folder listed in the Look **i**n list box in the upper-left corner of the dialog box shows the correct drive and folder. If not, click the arrow button to the right of the Look **i**n list box; then click the letter of the correct drive. Also, check that the Look **i**n list shows the correct folder. If not, select the correct folder by clicking its name in the Look **i**n list.

3 Names of the workbook files in the folder on the disk are displayed in the Look **i**n list. Place the mouse pointer on the file name My File; then double-click the left mouse button. The My File workbook opens in the document window, and the title bar displays My File.

You can now use the worksheets in My File.

Objective 9: Exit Excel

At the beginning of this chapter, you learned to start Excel. This section shows you how to exit, or quit, the Excel program. You can exit Excel in the following ways:

- Open the **F**ile menu and choose E**x**it

- Click the Program Control menu icon and choose **C**lose

- Double-click the Program Control menu icon

- Press Alt+F4

If you have forgotten to save any open documents, Excel prompts you with a dialog box (refer to Figure 1.12). Choose **Y**es to save any changes made to the document(s). Choose **N**o to lose the changes. After Excel closes, you return to the Windows 95 desktop.

Exiting Excel

Follow these steps to exit from Excel using the Program Control menu.

① Place the mouse pointer on the Program Control menu icon (represented by a large X in the upper-left corner of the Excel program screen).

② Click the left mouse button.

③ Choose **C**lose from the Control menu by placing the mouse pointer on the command and clicking the left mouse button.

You exit Excel and return to the Windows 95 desktop.

Chapter Summary

This chapter covers many concepts imperative for using Excel, including starting and exiting Excel. You have learned to move around in a worksheet, enter and edit data and formulas, use toolbar buttons, menus, and dialog boxes, and to print worksheets. Additionally, you learned procedures for opening, saving, naming, closing, and deleting workbook files.

If you feel comfortable with the information in this chapter, you are ready to learn more about building Excel worksheets. In Chapter 2, "Building a Worksheet," you learn to use worksheet ranges, change column widths and row heights, move cells, copy cells, and insert and delete columns and rows.

Checking Your Skills

True/False

For each of the following, circle *T* or *F* to indicate whether the statement is true or false.

T   F   **1.** The active cell in an Excel 97 worksheet is outlined with a border that is darker than the other cells' borders.

T   F   **2.** To insert the formula bar entry into the active cell, you can click the Cancel button on the formula bar or press ⏎Enter.

T   F   **3.** If you turn off your computer, your Excel 97 workbook will be lost unless you have saved it to disk.

T   F   **4.** To close a workbook file, you must exit Excel 97.

T   F   **5.** To choose a command from a menu with the mouse, point to the command, and click the left mouse button.

T   F   **6.** By default, the Excel 97 screen displays the Standard toolbar across the bottom of the screen.

T   F   **7.** Excel 97 worksheet column headings are labeled with numbers.

T   F   **8.** In an Excel 97 worksheet, the intersection of a column and a row is called a field.

T   F   **9.** Before entering data into a worksheet, you must type the address of the cell in which the data will be stored.

T   F   **10.** By default, the formula bar is located directly above the worksheet's column headings.

Multiple Choice

In the blank provided, write the letter of the correct answer for each of the following.

1. The function key that enables you to go directly to a particular cell in the worksheet is _____.

   a. F1

   b. F2

   c. F5

   d. none of the above

2. To view an area of your worksheet not on-screen, you can use the _____.

   a. Minimize icon

   b. scroll bar

   c. =

   d. Range command

3. To change (edit) the contents of the active cell, you first press _____.

   a. F8

   b. F3

   c. F2

   d. F9

4. When you save your workbook on disk, the workbook is saved in a(n) _____.

   a. file

   b. active cell

   c. range

   d. extension

5. To move to cell A1, press _____.

   a. Ctrl+Home

   b. Home

   c. Home+Home

   d. PgUp

6. Excel 97 assumes that the content of a cell is a value or a formula if the entry starts with _____.

   a. =

   b. +

   c. a and b

   d. none of the above

7. An Excel 97 worksheet can consist of a maximum of _____ columns.

    a. 100

    b. 200

    c. 300

    d. none of the above

8. To move to column A of the active row, press _____.

    a. Ctrl + Home

    b. Home

    c. Home + Home

    d. PgUp

9. The cell address of the active cell is displayed in the _____.

    a. Standard toolbar

    b. status bar

    c. formula bar

    d. menu bar

10. The symbol used for multiplication in an Excel 97 formula is _____.

    a. x

    b. /

    c. >

    d. *

Fill in the Blank

In the blank provided, write the correct answer for each of the following statements.

1. To save a file on the A drive, select A: from the _____ drop-down list in the Save As dialog box.

2. To open a workbook you saved on disk, choose the _____ command from the File menu.

3. The formula used to multiply the contents of cell D5 by the contents of cell E2 is _____.

4. The formula used to add the contents of cell A3 to the contents of cell B3 and divide the sum by 4 is _____.

5. The order in which arithmetic operations are performed by Excel 97 is _____.

6. Scrolling does not change the _____ cell.

7. To activate a cell, place the cell pointer over the cell and _____.

8. A new workbook contains _____ worksheets.

9. An Excel 97 file name can consist of up to _____ characters.

10. The _____ window is the outer window with Microsoft Excel 97 in the title bar.

Applying Your Skills

Review Exercises

Exercise 1: Gaining Familiarity with the Excel Window

In this exercise, you become more familiar with the Excel window.

1. Start Excel by clicking the Excel icon in the Windows 95 **P**rograms menu.

2. Retrieve My File 2.

3. Minimize the document window.

4. Minimize the program window.

5. Maximize the program and the document windows.

6. Move the mouse around the screen to see the different mouse pointer shapes.

7. Use the formula bar to see what the formula is in cell D9.

8. Close the document.

Exercise 2: Entering, Saving, and Printing a Workbook

This exercise reviews information presented in the chapter and helps bring it all together. In this exercise, you enter and save an Excel worksheet, shown in Figure 1.14. Read all the steps before you begin.

Figure 1.14

The First workbook.

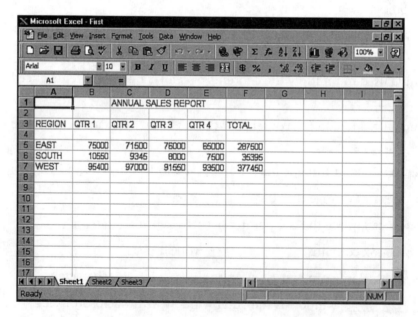

1. Start Excel, if necessary. If you plan to save the workbook to a floppy disk, make sure that a formatted disk is in your disk drive.

2. In the blank worksheet, activate cell C1 by clicking it with the left mouse button. Type **ANNUAL SALES REPORT**. Then press ↵Enter.

> **Note**
>
> If you make a mistake typing in a cell or selecting from a menu, press Esc to start again.

3. Activate cell A3. Type **REGION** in cell A3, **QTR 1** in cell B3, **QTR 2** in cell C3, **QTR 3** in cell D3, **QTR 4** in cell E3, and **TOTAL** in cell F3. Press ➡ after each entry.

4. Activate cell A5. Type **EAST** in cell A5, **SOUTH** in cell A6, and **WEST** in cell A7. Press ⬇ after each entry.

5. Activate cell B5. Type **75000** in cell B5 and press ⏎Enter.

6. Refer to Figure 1.16 to fill in the remaining sales figures for quarters one through four.

    Do not enter numbers in the TOTAL column; in the following steps, you insert formulas into that column so that changes in quarterly sales are reflected in the new total.

7. Now enter the formulas that calculate total sales for each region. Make cell F5 the active cell; enter the formula **=B5+C5+D5+E5** and press ⏎Enter.

8. Enter the formula **=B6+C6+D6+E6** in cell F6 and press ⏎Enter. Enter the formula **=B7+C7+D7+E7** in cell F7 and press ⏎Enter.

    Your worksheet should now look like the one shown in Figure 1.16.

9. Next, save the workbook. Do this either by clicking the Save button on the Standard toolbar or by choosing **F**ile, **S**ave.

10. In the File **n**ame text box of the Save dialog box, type **First**.

11. Select the correct drive and folder from the Save **in** drop-down list.

12. Choose **S**ave to save the workbook as First.

    Check to see that the document title bar now displays the name First. You could exit Excel now, and the workbook would not be lost.

13. If your computer is hooked up to a printer, print two copies of your workbook (one to keep and one to turn in to your instructor) by clicking the Print button on the Standard toolbar.

14. Close the file.

Exercise 3: Modifying an Existing Workbook

In this exercise, you add totals and averages to the First workbook.

1. Start Excel, if necessary. Open the First workbook.

2. Enter **TOTAL** in cell A9 of Sheet1. In cell B9, enter the formula to calculate total sales for QTR 1. Enter the formulas to calculate the respective total sales in cells C9 through F9.

3. Change the contents of cell C5 to 100. Do cells F5, C9, and F9 change? Should any other cells change when you change the contents of C5?

4. In cell G3, enter **AVERAGE** and in cell A11, enter **AVERAGE**. In cell B11, enter the formula to calculate the average sales for QTR 1. In cell G5, enter the formula to calculate the average sales for the EAST.

5. Fill in the appropriate cells in column G and in row 11 so that the proper averages are calculated. Do the averages change when the quarterly sales figures are changed?

6. Print two copies of the workbook—one to keep and one to turn in to your instructor.

7. Save the workbook as **Second** and close the file.

Exercise 4: Using the Formatting Toolbar

In this exercise, you use the Formatting toolbar to make formatting changes to the Second workbook.

1. Start Excel, if necessary; open the Second workbook.

2. Use the Bold and the Underline buttons on the Formatting toolbar to boldface and underline the contents of cell C1.

3. Use the Formatting toolbar to make the contents of cells A3, A9, All, F3, and G3 boldface and centered in their cells.

4. To indicate that a cell in the worksheet contains a formula, boldface each cell that contains a formula.

5. Print two copies of the worksheet; then save the workbook with the name **Third**.

Exercise 5: Using Mathematical Operators and the Order of Precedence When Creating Formulas

A good way to understand the order of precedence is to work with it! In this exercise, you enter several formulas, sometimes using parentheses to alter the order of precedence of the calculations.

1. Open Chap0101. The workbook contains formulas in column A. Enter the formulas into column B, preceded by the = sign to observe how the parentheses effect the order of precedence. Press ⏎Enter after each formula.

2. Save the workbook as **Operators**.

Continuing Projects

Project 1: Creating a Payroll Worksheet

Cape Enterprises, home-based at Port St. Joe, Florida, is a nation-wide real estate organization. In this project, you set up a worksheet for listing sales in each region and district.

The title should use the company's name. The four column headings are REGION, DISTRICT, DOLLARS, and EMPLOYEES. Enter the region, district, dollars, and number of employees, for five regions.

Your worksheet should calculate the total dollars sold by Cape Enterprises, as well as the total number of employees. Format the TOTAL dollars using the Currency Style and the Bold Formatting toolbar buttons. Include a label in your spreadsheet to identify the TOTAL row. Save this worksheet in a workbook file named **Real Estate 1**. Print two copies of the worksheet—one to keep and one to turn in to your instructor.

Project 2: Tracking Hours in a Worksheet

Worksheets are often used to maintain a record of employee hours worked and to produce productivity statistics. In this project, you set up a worksheet to maintain this information for yourself.

Set up your own worksheet to enter the hours you work each day during a typical week at Kipper Industries. Be honest. In your worksheet, include formulas that calculate total number of hours worked during the week and average daily number of hours worked. Make sure that you include labels such as TOTAL for any calculations in your worksheet.

Name the workbook **Employee 1** and save it to disk. If you have a printer connected to your computer, print two copies of your worksheet—one to keep and one to turn in to your instructor. Verify that when you change the value for the number of hours worked on Wednesday, your weekly total and daily average automatically change to reflect the new value.

Project 3: Keeping a Record of the Mileage of Vehicles in a Motor Pool

Coastal Sales, a small, independent company, possesses six company automobiles. Assume that you need to maintain a record of the vehicles' mileage for insurance, maintenance, and depreciation purposes. Set up a worksheet in which the miles driven for each day of the week (Monday through Friday) can be recorded for each vehicle.

The worksheet should show daily totals for miles driven and weekly totals for each of the six individual vehicles. Also, show the average number of miles per day each vehicle traveled. Make the cells with formulas boldface. Save the workbook as **Vehicle Mileage 1**. Enter sample numbers for each vehicle for every day of the week, check the results of your formulas, and print two copies of the worksheet—one to keep and one to turn in to your instructor.

Chapter 2

Building a Worksheet

In Chapter 1, "Excel Workbook and Worksheet Basics," you learned how to move around within a worksheet, enter data, save files, use menus and toolbars, and print a worksheet. Now that you are familiar with these basic concepts, you are ready to learn about setting up worksheets. The topics covered in this chapter include defining and naming ranges; creating cell comments, moving, copying, and clearing cell contents; inserting and deleting cells, columns, and rows; changing column width and row height; and using the Excel Spell feature.

If you need to leave your computer before you complete your work in this chapter, be sure to save your work and close the file you have been using. You can then reopen the file with the saved changes when you want to continue this chapter.

Objectives

By the time you have finished this chapter, you will have learned to

1. Start a New Workbook
2. Annotate a Worksheet with Cell Comments
3. Work with Ranges
4. Move Cell Contents
5. Change Column Width and Row Height
6. Copy Cell Contents
7. Clear, Delete, and Insert Cells
8. Insert and Delete Columns and Rows
9. Use Excel Help

Objective 1: Start a New Workbook

When you start Excel, you see a blank workbook in the document window. If you want to start building a new worksheet in your workbook, Excel is ready for you to begin. In Chapter 1, you learned how to save a workbook on disk and how to retrieve it later to continue working on it. At times, however, you may want to save a finished workbook and then clear it from the document window to begin a new workbook. You could exit Excel and then start again to get a new workbook, but a more efficient way to start a new workbook is to use the **File**, **N**ew command or use the New button on the Standard toolbar.

If you have another workbook open, Excel keeps the other workbook open in RAM and gives your new workbook a temporary title—Book1, Book2, Book3, and so on, depending on how many new workbooks have already been opened when you issue the **File**, **N**ew command.

Starting a New Workbook

To start a new workbook using the **File**, **N**ew command, make sure that Excel is running. Then follow these steps:

❶ Click the **F**ile menu and choose **N**ew to display the New dialog box.

❷ Click OK and maximize the document window, if necessary. Your screen should now look like Figure 2.1. Notice that the new workbook is named Book2.

Note

You can also open a new workbook by clicking the New button on the Standard toolbar. You can open an existing workbook by clicking the Open button on the Standard toolbar.

Figure 2.1
A new, blank worksheet.

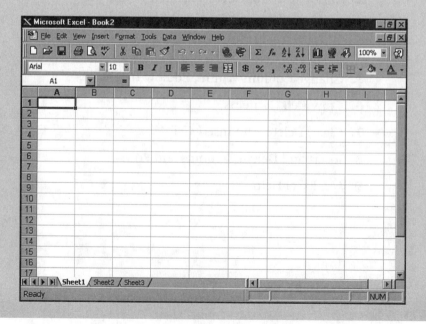

3 In the blank worksheet, enter the data shown in Figure 2.2.

Figure 2.2
The Book2
worksheet.

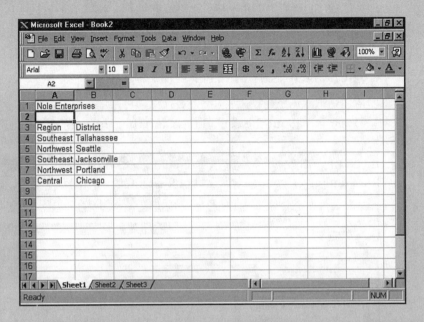

**AutoComplete
feature**
If the first few
characters you
type in a cell
match an exist-
ing entry in that
column, Micro-
soft Excel fills in
the remaining
characters for
you. Excel com-
pletes only those
entries that con-
tain a combina-
tion of text and
numbers; entries
that contain
only numbers,
dates, or times
are not com-
pleted by Excel.

> **Note**
>
> Excel's *AutoComplete feature* automatically fills in the remaining characters for you when you type the first few characters in a cell that match an existing entry in that column.

4 Save the workbook with the name **Nole-1** and leave it open for the next tutorial.

Objective 2: Annotate a Worksheet with Cell Comments

Cell comment
An explanatory note
or comment added
to the worksheet. It
can be displayed,
edited, and printed.

One of the easiest and most efficient ways to document a worksheet is with *cell comments*. For those users of previous versions of Excel, cell comments have replaced cell notes. Cell comments are directly related to a cell. If a cell comment has been assigned to a cell, Excel places a red indicator in the upper-right corner of the cell. Comments are displayed in special text boxes or are printed when you request. Include in comments any information that helps you or the next person using the worksheet.

In this objective, you learn how to add, edit, hide, display, print, and delete cell comments.

Creating, Editing, and Printing Cell Comments

To create cell comments, make sure that the Nole-1 workbook is open and follow these steps:

❶ Click cell A8 to activate that cell.

❷ Choose **Insert, Comment.**

The Comment text box is displayed (see Figure 2.3), and the status bar displays information about the cell address and the author of the comment.

Figure 2.3
The Comment text box.

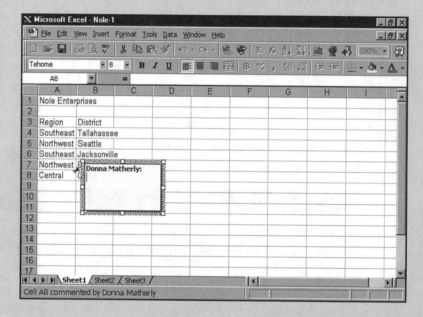

❸ In the Comment text box, type **This region was just created.**

❹ Click anywhere outside the Comment text box to close the Comment text box. Notice the Comment indicator that is displayed in the top-right corner of cell A8 (see Figure 2.4).

Figure 2.4
The Comment indicator.

Comment indicator

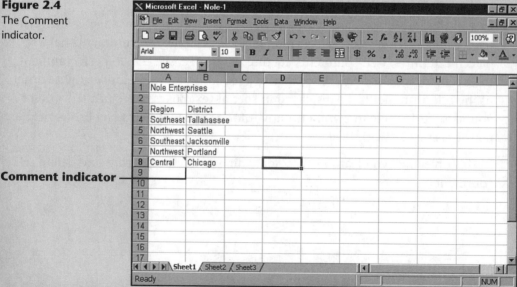

5 Position the cross-shaped pointer over cell A8 and pause briefly. The comment you created in step 3 is displayed, as shown in Figure 2.5.

Figure 2.5
The Comment text box.

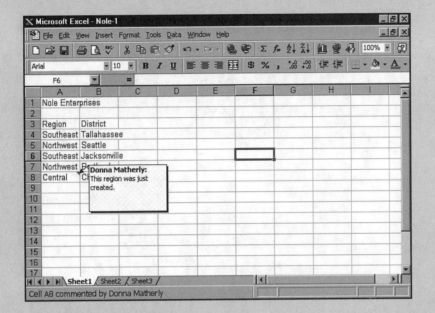

6 Click cell B3 and choose **I**nsert, Co**m**ment. In the Comment text box, enter the comment **Each region will have more districts by the end of 1997.**

Notice the Comment indicator that is displayed in the top-right corner of the cell after you close the Comment box.

7 Edit the comment in cell A8, by selecting A8 and choosing **I**nsert, **E**dit Comment. The Comment text box displays the current comment and the insertion point is positioned at the end of the comment.

8 Delete the period at the end of the comment and type **in July 1997.**

9 Click anywhere outside the Comment text box to close it.

You can print the worksheet with comments displayed at the end of the worksheet.

10 Choose **F**ile, Page Set**u**p; then click the Sheet tab in the Page Setup dialog box.

11 In the Co**m**ments drop-down list box, click At end of sheet, then click **P**rint to print the worksheet and comments.

12 Save your changes to Nole-1 and leave it open for the next tutorial.

Comments can be hidden or displayed in a worksheet. Both shortcut menus and menu bar options can be used to perform these activities.

Hiding, Displaying, and Clearing Comments and their Indicators

To hide, display, and clear comment indicators in the Nole-1 workbook, follow these steps:

❶ Choose **T**ools, **O**ptions. In the Options dialog box, click the View tab. The View tab is displayed (see Figure 2.6).

Figure 2.6
The View tab in the Options dialog box.

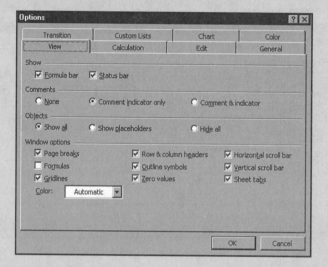

❷ In the Comments section, click **N**one to hide the comment indicators and then click OK. Notice that the comment indicators are now hidden from view.

❸ Choose **T**ools, **O**ptions and then click the View tab to display the View tab of the Options dialog box again.

❹ In the Comments section, click the Co**m**ment & indicator option button to display comments and indicators of all comments on a worksheet. Click OK.

The comment indicators and comments are displayed, regardless of the mouse position (see Figure 2.7).

❺ To print the worksheet with comments as displayed on the worksheet, choose, **F**ile, Page Set**u**p to display the Page Setup dialog box; then click the Sheet tab.

❻ In the Co**m**ments drop-down list box, click As displayed on sheet, then click the **P**rint button to print the worksheet and comments.

❼ Choose **T**ools, **O**ptions and then click the View tab in the Options dialog box.

❽ In the Comments section, click the Comment **i**ndicator only option button; then click OK.

Now comments display only when you rest the pointer over cells that contain them.

Figure 2.7
Comment indicators and comments in cells A8 and B3.

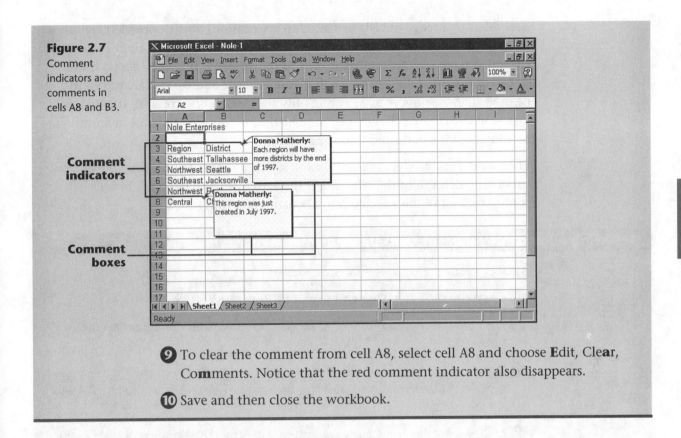

Comment indicators

Comment boxes

9 To clear the comment from cell A8, select cell A8 and choose **E**dit, Cle**a**r, Co**m**ments. Notice that the red comment indicator also disappears.

10 Save and then close the workbook.

Objective 3: Work with Ranges

Range
One or more blocks of cells that can be formatted, moved, copied, or referred to as a unit.

Frequently you will need to perform actions on a block of cells in your worksheet. A group of selected cells is called a *range*. While building a worksheet, you save time by applying a command to a group of cells instead of to individual cells. For example, if you want to format the cell contents of several cells, select all of the cells; then apply the F**o**rmat command. Any command or action you can apply to one cell, you can usually apply to a range of cells. Excel format commands are commonly applied to a range (see Figure 2.8).

Figure 2.8
A selected range.

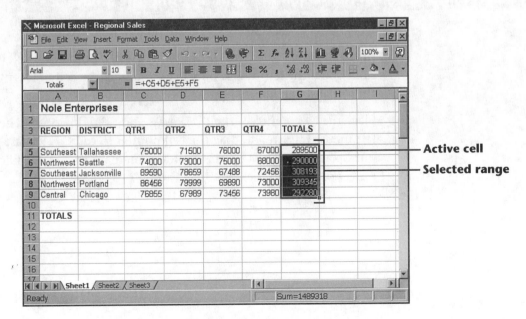

Active cell

Selected range

Excel refers to a range of cells by the address (location) of the upper-left cell in the block, followed by a colon and then the address of the lower-right cell in the block. If you are selecting only the cells in one row, the first cell address is the left cell in the row followed by a colon and then the address of the last cell in the row. Likewise, if you are selecting only the cells in one column, the first cell address in the range is the top cell in the column, followed by a colon and then the address of the bottom cell in the column.

When a range is selected, the cells in the selected range are surrounded by a gray border. The first cell of the selection is the active cell and has a white background; the rest of the selected range is dark (refer to Figure 2.8).

Selecting a Range of Adjacent Cells by Using the Mouse

To select a range of cells, follow these steps:

1 Open the file Chap0201 and save it as **Regional Sales**.

2 Place the cell pointer on cell A5; then press and hold down the left mouse button.

3 Drag the cell pointer to cell A9 and release the mouse button. The thick cell border and darkened cells indicate that the range of cells in the block A5 to A9 are selected.

4 To deselect the range, click any cell outside the range (for example, cell B9).

Leave this workbook open for the next tutorial.

A range is usually one solid rectangular block of adjacent cells in the worksheet. You can also define as one range several blocks of cells in separate parts of the worksheet. These multiple non-adjoining ranges can be very useful, as you learn later in this chapter. This is covered again in Chapter 6, "Creating Charts and Maps," where you chart data.

Selecting a Range of Non-adjoining Cells by Using the Mouse

To select a range of cells in two separate blocks, follow these steps:

1 In the Regional Sales workbook, place the cell pointer on cell C3; press and hold down the left mouse button as you drag the cell pointer to cell G3; then release the mouse button.

2 Place the cell pointer on cell C7; press and hold down Ctrl. Then press the left mouse button and drag the cell pointer to cell G7. Release the mouse button and Ctrl. The thick cell borders and darkened cells indicate that the ranges of cells in blocks C3 to G3 and C7 to G7 are selected (see Figure 2.9).

Figure 2.9
Two selected
non-adjoining
ranges.

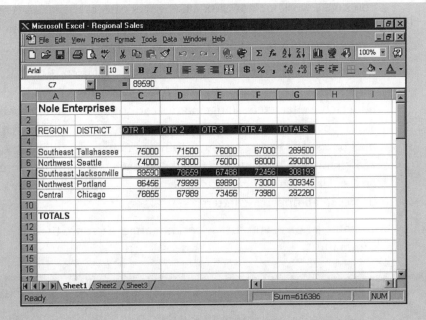

2

❸ To deselect the range, click any cell outside the selected ranges (for example, cell A1).

Leave this workbook open for the next tutorial.

A range can be any size. You can also select a range by using the keyboard. Hold down ⬆Shift and use the arrow keys to select the cells.

After selecting a range, you can use the tools on the Formatting toolbar to apply formats such as boldface, italics, and currency to a cell. (Refer to Objective 3 in Chapter 1 for information about using the toolbars.)

Formatting a Range

To select a range and make the contents of the cells in the range boldface, follow these steps:

❶ In the Regional Sales workbook, select cells A3 through G3.

B

❷ Click the Bold button on the Formatting toolbar. The text in cells A3 through G3 is displayed in boldface.

❸ Click a cell outside the range to deselect the range.

❹ Save your work and keep the workbook open for the next tutorial.

Understanding Range Names

Assigning a meaningful name to a range of cells is useful when you are building a formula. You can use this name in formulas and in dialog boxes. All *range names* defined for a workbook are listed in the Name box at the left end of the formula bar. Named ranges can make calculations easier to create and understand. This section teaches you to use a name to refer to a range of cells. When

Range name
A meaningful name you give to a cell or range of cells.

you save a workbook on disk, all the worksheet range names are also saved on disk; they are available whenever you open the file. You do not need to rename a range every time you open your workbook.

Range names must start with a letter or an underscore, but after the initial character, remaining characters in the name can be letters, numbers, periods, and underscore characters. Range names cannot be the same as cell references, such as A8. Spaces are not allowed in range names. Underscore characters and periods may be used as word separators in range names. A range name can contain up to 255 characters, but only the first 15 characters can display in most scrolling list boxes. Although you can use either upper- or lowercase letters, Excel displays the names in all uppercase letters.

To name a range, you first select the range; then use the **Insert**, **Name**, **Define** command.

Naming a Range

To name the range of cells from G5 to G9 in the Regional Sales workbook, follow these steps:

1 Select cells G5 to G9.

2 Choose **Insert**, **Name**; then choose **Define**.

The Define Name dialog box opens (see Figure 2.10). Excel sometimes suggests an appropriate name in the Names in workbook text box.

Figure 2.10
The Define Name dialog box.

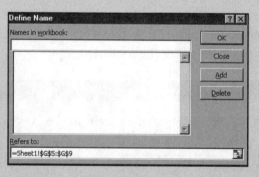

3 In the Names in **w**orkbook text box, type **TOTALS**.

4 Choose OK to close the dialog box.

5 Click cell G5 and notice that the Name box displays the name of the cell, G5.

6 Select the cell range G5:G9 and notice that the Name box displays the range name.

7 Save the workbook and leave it open for the next tutorial.

In Chapter 4, you learn to use the TOTALS range name in a function.

Understanding Natural Language Formulas

A new feature of Excel 97 is natural language formulas. Instead of using cell addresses or a range name in a formula, you can build a formula that refers to the row and column labels. You can use these labels in formulas and in dialog boxes. To avoid typing labels in formulas, you can define label ranges before you start creating formulas. First, select the range you want to use in a row or column. Next, choose the **I**nsert, **N**ame, **L**abel command.

Along with using named ranges, using natural language formulas can make calculations easier to create and understand. This section teaches you to create a natural language label name to refer to a cell. When you save a workbook on disk, all the label ranges are also saved on disk; they are available whenever you open the file.

Defining Label Ranges

To define labels, follow these steps:

1 Select cell C5 in the Regional Sales workbook.

2 Choose **I**nsert, **N**ame; then choose **L**abel to display the Label Ranges dialog box (see Figure 2.11). Notice that C5 is displayed in the Add label range text box.

Figure 2.11
The Label
Ranges dia-
log box.

Selected cell

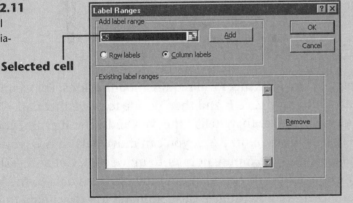

3 Click the **A**dd button to add another label range.

4 In the Add label range text box, enter **F5**.

5 Click OK to close the dialog box.

6 In cell B11, enter the formula: **=Tallahassee QTR 1 - Tallahassee QTR 4** and then press ⏎Enter.

Instead of entering =C5-F5, you entered English language words to initiate the formula. Figure 2.12 shows the result of your calculation.

(continues)

Figure 2.12
The results of using the label ranges in the formula.

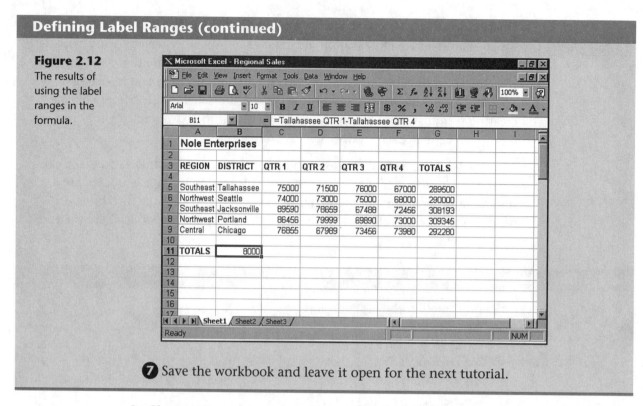

7 Save the workbook and leave it open for the next tutorial.

In Chapter 4, you learn to use these natural language labels in several ways as you work with formulas and functions.

Objective 4: Move Cell Contents

Drag-and-drop
A mouse procedure enabling you to move or copy data.

Clipboard
In Windows, a temporary storage area for data you cut or copy.

At some point, almost any worksheet will require modifications. For example, you may insert data into several cells and then decide to place that data elsewhere in the worksheet. Rather than delete the data and enter it again, you can move the data to a new location. In Excel, you can move data in two ways. One method, *drag-and-drop*, uses the mouse pointer to move data. Cut and paste, the other method, uses the **E**dit, **Cut** command to move selected data to the Windows *Clipboard* and then uses the **E**dit, **P**aste command to extract data from the Clipboard and place that data in a new location. If you make a mistake while editing your worksheet, choose the **E**dit, **U**ndo command before continuing.

Moving Cell Contents Using Drag-and-Drop
The drag-and-drop method enables you move or copy data using the mouse. First, you select the data you want to move. Then you drag it to the new location and drop it there by releasing the mouse button.

Paste area
The new location in the worksheet where selected data will be moved or copied.

If the *paste area* (the new location for the data) is located in an area of the worksheet not visible on-screen, drag the selection to the edge of the window. Excel starts scrolling through the worksheet. Release the mouse button when the gray outline is in the correct location. The selected data drops into the new location.

Using Drag-and-Drop

To use the drag-and-drop method to move the data from column F to column H in the Regional Sales workbook, follow these steps:

1 Select the range G3:G9.

2 Place the mouse pointer on the right edge of the highlighted data. The mouse pointer changes to an arrow.

3 Hold down the left mouse button and drag to column H.

As you drag, a gray outline of the selection moves with the pointer. A border equal in size to the selection outlines the cell or area where the selection (the paste area) will appear (see Figure 2.13).

Figure 2.13
The outline where the selection will appear.

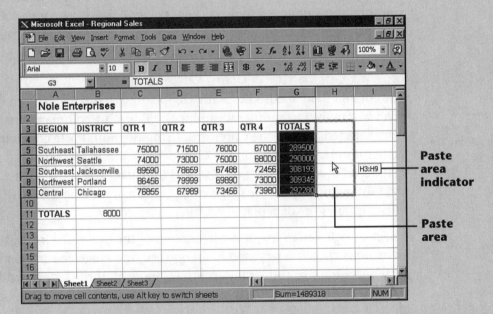

4 Release the mouse button to drop the selected data into the new location.

5 Save your changes to the workbook and leave it open for the next tutorial.

Understanding the Clipboard

Excel and all other Windows applications use the Clipboard for moving and copying data. The Clipboard is an area of computer memory that stores information temporarily so that you can move or copy it. Because the Clipboard is in RAM memory (volatile), information placed on the Clipboard is lost when you turn off the computer. Basic facts about the Clipboard are as follows:

- You can place only one item on the Clipboard at a time

- You can place text or graphics on the Clipboard

- The **E**dit, **C**opy and **E**dit, Cu**t** commands (and the Cut and Copy buttons on the Standard toolbar) place information on the Clipboard

- The **E**dit, **P**aste command (and the Paste button on the Standard toolbar) extracts information from the Clipboard

With the Clipboard, you can copy worksheet cells, formulas, and charts to locations within the same worksheet, to other worksheets, and to other applications. The Clipboard helps you build worksheets, ensure accuracy, and share information.

After you cut or copy information to the Clipboard, you can place that information in another location on the same worksheet, on another worksheet, or in another Windows application that supports the Clipboard. The **Edit**, **P**aste command extracts information that is on the Clipboard and places it into the selected location. Information you have copied to the Clipboard stays on the Clipboard until you use the Cut or Copy command again, or until you turn off your computer.

Although you can access the Clipboard to see what is on it, this is something you should seldom need to do because you will have just cut or copied the selection into the Clipboard. For more information on how to access the Clipboard, refer to your Windows documentation or online Help in Excel.

Moving Cell Contents Using Cut and Paste

Marquee
Moving dashes outlining the area cut or copied to the Clipboard.

The cut and paste method uses the Clipboard to temporarily store information you want moved to another location. The **Edit**, **Cut** command enables you to place selected data on the Clipboard. Using the **Edit**, **P**aste command, you can paste information placed on the Clipboard to another location. To place information on the Clipboard, you first select the data you want moved. Then open the **Edit** menu and choose Cu**t**. A *marquee*, small moving dashes (the marching ants), outlines the data placed on the Clipboard.

Select a single cell in the upper-left corner of the paste area instead of the whole paste range. If you select more than one cell, the range you select must be exactly the same size as the range on the Clipboard. If the ranges are different sizes, a dialog box is displayed. Choose OK, or press ↵Enter, to close the dialog box.

Using Cut and Paste to Move Data

Follow these steps, using the cut and paste method to move the data in the range H3:H9 back to its original location in column G of the Regional Sales workbook:

❶ Select the range H3:H9, if it isn't already selected.

❷ Choose **Edit**, **Cut**. A marquee is displayed around the data.

❸ Click cell G3, the first cell in which you want the data to appear and press ↵Enter. The selected data disappears from column H and appears in cells G3 through G9.

Alternatively, you can use the Edit, Paste command.

❹ Click outside the selected cells to deselect them.

❺ Save your work and leave the workbook open for the next tutorial.

> **Note**
>
> You can also cut and paste selections by using the Cut and Paste buttons on the Standard toolbar.

Objective 5: Change Column Width and Row Height

Best Fit
A command that automatically adjusts the column width or row height to the widest cell in the column.

One of the most frequently used worksheet commands adjusts the width of a column. Text is often cut off because the column is not wide enough to display the entire contents of the cell. If a cell cannot display an entire number or date, the cell fills with ######### (pound signs), or the number is displayed in scientific notation. After you widen the column sufficiently, the number or date is displayed in the cell. You can adjust the column width by using the mouse or the keyboard. Three methods useful for changing column width include dragging the column heading border, using the *Best Fit* feature, and using the Format, **C**olumn, **W**idth command. Most people like to experiment with different column widths to see which looks best. If, however, you know exactly how wide you want a column, you can use the **C**olumn command in the F**o**rmat menu. You can select multiple columns by dragging over the column headings with the mouse.

Changing the Column Width by Dragging the Column Border

To increase the width of column B in the Regional Sales workbook, follow these steps:

1 Position the mouse pointer on the right border of the column B heading. When positioned properly, the mouse pointer changes to a black double-headed horizontal arrow with a vertical bar in the middle.

2 Hold down the left mouse button and drag to the right to increase the column width to 12.00. Notice that a Width indicator is displayed in the area above the column heading. Use this indicator to determine how far to drag to the right.

3 Save your work and leave the workbook open for the next tutorial.

Using the Best Fit Column Width Command

The Best Fit column width command enables you to adjust the column width automatically to the widest cell in the column. To access the Best Fit command using the mouse, you position the mouse pointer on the right border of the column heading. When positioned properly, the mouse pointer changes to a black double-headed horizontal arrow with a vertical bar in the middle. Double-click with the left mouse button. The column adjusts to the widest cell contents in the column.

Adjusting the Column Width Using the Best Fit Command

To change the width of column A in the Regional Sales workbook, follow these steps:

1 Place the mouse pointer on the border between column headings A and B. When positioned properly, the mouse pointer changes into a black double-headed vertical arrow with a horizontal bar in the middle.

2 Double-click the left mouse button. Notice that the width of column A becomes wide enough to accommodate the longest entry—Nole Enterprises.

3 Save your work and leave the workbook open for the next tutorial.

Using the Format, Columns Command to Change Column Width

A third method for changing cell width is to use the Format, Columns, Width command. When using this command, you are prompted to enter the exact column width you desire.

Adjusting the Column Width by Using the Format Columns Command

To set the width of column A in the Regional Sales workbook to exactly 15, follow these steps:

1 Select column A by clicking the column A heading.

2 Choose Format, Column, Width to display the Column Width dialog box (see Figure 2.14).

Figure 2.14
The Column Width dialog box.

3 In the Column width text box, type **15**.

4 Click OK, or press ⏎Enter. The width of column A is set to exactly 15.

5 Click anywhere on the worksheet to deselect the cells.

6 Save your work and keep the workbook open for the next tutorial.

Adjusting Row Height

Adjusting the height of a row is similar to adjusting the width of a column. You can adjust the row height using the mouse or the keyboard. Two methods useful for changing row height include dragging the row heading border, and using the Format, Row, Height command. You select multiple rows by dragging over the row heading numbers.

Increasing Row Height by Dragging the Row Border

To increase the height of row 3 in the Regional Sales workbook, follow these steps:

1 Place the mouse pointer on the border between the row 3 heading (at the left end of row 3) and the row 4 heading. When positioned properly, the mouse pointer changes into a black double-headed vertical arrow with a horizontal bar in the middle.

2 Hold down the left mouse button and drag the arrow down to increase the row height to 18. Notice that a Height indicator appears in the area just above the row 3 heading.

3 Save your changes and leave the workbook open for the next tutorial.

Using the Format, Rows Command to Change Row Height

Another method for changing cell height is to use the **F**ormat, **R**ow, **H**eight command. When using this command, you are prompted to enter the exact row height you desire.

Adjusting the Row Height by Using the Format Rows Command

To adjust the row height of row 3 in the Regional Sales workbook, follow these steps:

1 Select row 3 by clicking the row 3 heading.

2 Choose **F**ormat, **R**ow, **H**eight to display the Row Height dialog box (see Figure 2.15).

Figure 2.15
The Row Height dialog box.

3 In the **R**ow height text box, type **20** and click OK. The height of row 3 is set to exactly 20.

4 Save your work and leave the workbook open for the next tutorial.

Objective 6: Copy Cell Contents

You can copy cell contents using one of three methods: drag-and-drop, AutoFill, or copy and paste. With the drag-and-drop method, you use the mouse pointer to copy cell contents. With the AutoFill method, you use the mouse pointer and fill handle to copy cell contents to cells adjoining the data you want to copy. With the copy and paste method, you use the Clipboard to store contents you want to copy to another location.

Copying with Drag-and-Drop

To use the drag-and-drop method to copy the data in column A to column H in the Regional Sales workbook, follow these steps:

1 Select the data in cells A3 through A9.

2 Position the mouse pointer on the right border (but not the lower-right corner) of the selected data. The mouse pointer should change to an arrow.

3 Hold down the left mouse button and press Ctrl. A plus sign is displayed next to the mouse pointer. The status line displays the prompt Drag to copy cell contents.

4 Drag the data in cells A3 through A9 to column H where you want to place the copied data. A border outlines the area where the copied data will appear.

5 Release the mouse button first; then release Ctrl to drop the copied data into the outlined area. The copied data is displayed in column H.

6 Use the **Edit**, **U**ndo Drag-and-Drop command to undo the AutoFill procedure.

7 Save the workbook and leave it open for the next tutorial.

If you have problems... If the paste area is located in an area of the worksheet not visible on-screen, drag the selection to the edge of the window. Excel will start scrolling through the worksheet. Release the mouse button first and then release Ctrl to drop the copied data into the outlined area.

Fill handle
The black square at the lower-right corner of a selected cell or range.

Copying Cell Contents Using AutoFill

AutoFill is a method that enables you to copy cell contents to adjacent cells. You use the *fill handle*, the black square in the lower-right corner of a selected cell or range (see Figure 2.16). When you use AutoFill to copy data from one location to an adjacent cell or range of cells, a border outlines the area in which the copied data will appear.

Copying with AutoFill

To use AutoFill to copy the data in cells H3 through H11 to column I in the Regional Sales workbook, follow these steps:

1 Select the data in cells G3 through G9.

2 Position the mouse pointer on the fill handle at the lower-right corner of the selected border (see Figure 2.16). The mouse pointer changes to a black cross.

Figure 2.16
A selected range
with fill handle.

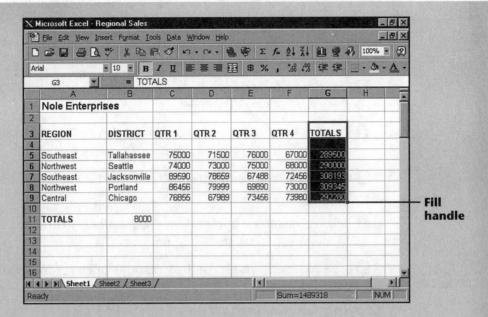

**Fill
handle**

2

❸ Drag the fill handle to the right to copy the selected data to the adjacent
cells in column H.

❹ Release the mouse button. The data is now displayed in column H.

**If you have
problems...**   If the selected cells already contain data, that data is replaced with the contents of the active cell. If you inadvertently replace existing data, open the
Edit menu, and choose the **U**ndo AutoFill command immediately after you
perform the fill to reverse the action.

---

❺ Use the **E**dit, **U**ndo AutoFill command to undo the AutoFill procedure.

❻ Save your work and leave the workbook open for the next tutorial.

Filling a Range with a Data Series

In addition to copying a selected single row or column, AutoFill also enables you
to create a series of numbers based on data you have already entered into the
worksheet. For example, when you enter the numbers 5 and 10 into consecutive
cells within a single row or column, Excel can determine that this series consists
of increments of 5. Using AutoFill, you can extend this series to 15, 20, 25, 30,
and so on, by selecting the range you want to fill and dragging the fill handle.
The selected cells in a column determine the increments of the series. Excel assumes that if you select a series, you want the series extended rather than the
numbers copied.

When you release the mouse button, the selected cells fill with numbers in the
series.

Filling a Range with a Data Series

To fill cells A13 through I13 in the Regional Sales workbook with a data series, follow these steps:

1 Enter the number **1** in cell A14, and the number **3** in cell B14. Then select these two cells by dragging over them with the mouse.

2 Position the mouse pointer on the fill handle located in the lower-right corner of cell B14. The mouse pointer changes to a black cross.

3 Click the left mouse button and drag the fill handle to the right until you reach cell I14.

4 Release the mouse button. Row 14 should fill with a data series with values 1 (column A) through 17 (column I).

5 Save your work and leave the workbook open for the next tutorial.

Copying Cell Contents Using Copy and Paste

Copying cell contents is similar to moving cell contents; however, you use the **E**dit, **C**opy command. You can use the **E**dit, **P**aste command to paste the same information repeatedly. The **E**dit, **P**aste command is available as long as the marquee outlines the copied data. When you paste the copied data by pressing ⏎Enter, the marquee that outlines the copied data disappears, and the **E**dit, **P**aste command appears dimmed, indicating that the command is no longer available. The marquee also disappears if you press ⏎Enter without choosing the command or if you begin to enter data into a cell.

Copying Cells Using Copy and Paste

To copy the number series in row 14 to row 15 in the Regional Sales workbook using the copy and paste method, follow these steps:

1 Select the range A14 through I14, if it isn't already selected.

2 Choose **E**dit, **C**opy. A marquee outlines the data copied to the Clipboard.

3 Select the range A15 to I15 and press ⏎Enter (or choose **E**dit, **P**aste). A copy of the selected data is displayed in the new location, and the original data remains in the original location.

A shortcut is to click only the first cell (A15) of the new location and then press ⏎Enter to paste the information to the new location.

4 To remove the marquee, press ⏎Enter or Esc.

If you have problems... If you inadvertently paste over a formula or other important cell contents, use the **E**dit, **U**ndo Paste command *immediately* after pasting to reverse the procedure.

---

5 Save your work and leave the workbook open for the next tutorial.

Copying Formulas to Multiple Cells

The capability to enter a formula and copy that formula down the rows in a column or across columns can save considerable time. For example, if you need to total rows 5 through 8 of column C and display the result in cell C11, you enter the formula =C5+C6+C7+C8+C9 into cell C11. If you also need to calculate the totals for rows 5 through 9 of columns D, E, F, and G, you can copy the formula in cell C11 to cells D11, E11, F11, and G11. Excel adjusts the formula when it is copied so that the formula totals the proper columns. For example, when the formula in cell C11 is copied to cell E11, the formula is =E5+E6+E7+E8+E9. The cell addresses in the formula are adjusted relative to their new location.

If you copy numbers or text in a worksheet, they will not change when they are copied unless you are copying a series of numbers. In most cases, you will want formulas to change when they are copied. Only if you use absolute cell references (discussed in the next topic, "Understanding Absolute, Relative, and Mixed Cell References") will formulas and functions remain the same when they are copied. The formulas and functions change in a very logical and useful way that will become clear when you look at some examples. First, you need to understand some general guidelines for copying cells in a worksheet.

If you copy the contents of a single cell, you can select multiple cells as a location for the copy. Then you can paste the copied data from the single cell into several cells. If you copy more than a single cell, the paste area you select must be equal to the area of the copied data. To avoid the problem of unequal copy and paste areas, select a single cell for pasting. When you select a single cell for pasting, the **E**dit, **P**aste command automatically pastes the data into an area equal to the copied area. When you select a single cell for pasting, however, you may inadvertently paste over existing data. If you do paste over existing data, you can use the **E**dit, **U**ndo Paste command immediately after pasting to reverse the action.

In Excel, you can easily copy a formula from a single cell to multiple cells. In many worksheets, data is organized in a consistent format with formulas built to calculate the data. You may, for example, have several rows of data with a formula in the last row that adds the numbers in each row. In Figure 2.17, the formula bar displays the formula in cell C11 that adds the values of cells C5 through C9. The corresponding formulas in cells D11, E11, F11, and G11 should be the same as the formula in cell C11 except that the column labels should be different. In this kind of situation, copying the formula from C11 is more efficient than retyping the formula in cells D11, E11, F11, and G11.

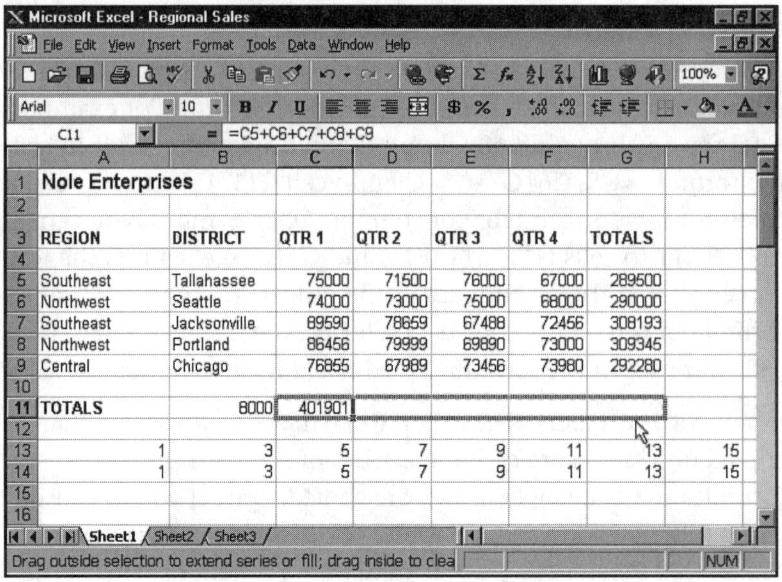

Figure 2.17

Copying a formula.

Although summing a range of numbers is not too difficult, some formulas are very long and complicated. Suppose that you need to enter a long, complex formula repeatedly. Rather than entering the formula manually each time, you can use the **E**dit, **C**opy command to copy a formula to other cells and save a considerable amount of time.

Understanding Absolute, Relative, and Mixed Cell References

You have learned to copy a formula to other cells. When you paste a formula or function, Excel takes the cell address in the copied formula and changes the cell address relative to the location of the pasted formula. If, for example, the formula in cell C11 displays =C5+C6+C7+C8+C9 and this formula is copied and pasted to cells D11 through G11, the formula in cell D11 displays =D5+D6+D7+D8+D9; cell E11 displays =E5+E6+E7+E8+E9; and so on. The copied formula adjusts to the location in which it is pasted.

Relative cell reference

A cell reference that adjusts to its new location when copied or moved.

Cell references that adjust to a pasted location are referred to as *relative cell references*. As you enter formulas, Excel assumes that you want cell addresses to contain relative references.

Absolute cell reference

A cell reference that remains the same when copied or moved.

In some cases, however, you will not want relative cell references. For example, you may have a formula that refers to a single value in another cell, and regardless of where the formula is pasted, you want to refer to that value in that particular cell. If you want a cell reference to remain the same wherever you paste the copied formula, change the cell address from a relative reference to an *absolute cell reference*.

An absolute cell address is indicated by a dollar sign ($) preceding the column letter and a dollar sign ($) preceding the row number of the cell address. For example, $C$5 is an absolute cell reference. To make a cell reference (a cell address) absolute, enter a dollar sign ($) to the left of the column letter and a dollar sign ($) to the left of the row number of the cell address in the formula bar. When in edit mode, you can use F4 to add the dollar signs rapidly to the cell reference.

If the formula in cell C11 displays +$C$5+$C$6+$C$7+$C$8+$C$9 and this formula is copied to other cells, regardless of where the formula is pasted, the formula always refers to the values in cells C5 through C9. In Figure 2.18, the formula copied to cell D11 contains an absolute cell reference that always refers to the values in column C.

Figure 2.18
The results of a formula containing an absolute cell reference.

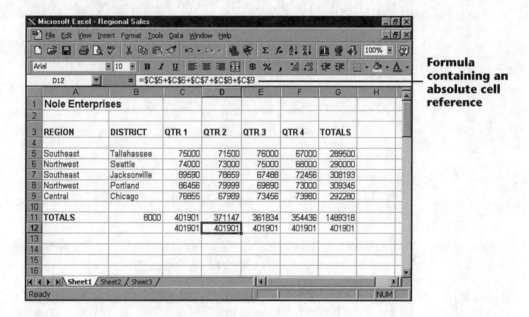

Formula containing an absolute cell reference

Mixed cell reference
A single cell address that contains a relative and an absolute reference.

In most cases, you will want a formula to contain either relative or absolute cell references. Sometimes, however, you will want the column reference of a cell address to remain the same (absolute reference) and the row reference to adjust to the relative position of the formula; or you will want the column to adjust and the row to remain the same. A *mixed cell reference* enables you to have this flexibility.

To mix cell references, place a dollar sign ($) in front of one address component and not the other. If you want the column reference to remain the same regardless of where the formula is copied, for example, place a dollar sign ($) in front of the column letter. If you want the row number to adjust depending on the row in which the copied formula is pasted, do not place a dollar sign in front of the row number of the cell address. The formula =$C11-D11, for example, is a mixed cell address. The column C reference is absolute; the row reference is relative.

Table 2.1 shows the types of cell references.

Table 2.1 Types of Cell References

Cell Reference	Description
A1	In this relative cell reference, the formula adjusts to the relative location when copied or moved.
$A$1	In this absolute cell reference, the formula refers to this cell always, regardless of where the formula is copied or moved.
A$1	In this cell reference, the formula always refers to row 1. The column adjusts to the relative location when copied or moved.
$A1	In this mixed cell reference, the formula always refers to column A. The row adjusts to the relative location when copied or moved.

Copying Formulas with Relative Cell Addresses

To copy a formula with relativecell addresses in the Regional Sales worksheet, follow these steps:

1 In cell C11, enter the formula **=C5+C6+C7+C8+C9** and press (⏎Enter).

2 Click cell C11 again and choose **E**dit, **C**opy. A marquee is displayed around cell C11.

3 Select the range of cells D11:G11. This is the range that you want to contain the formula.

4 Open the **E**dit menu and choose **P**aste. To turn off the marquee around cell C10, press (⏎Enter) or (Esc).

Note that the formula in cell C11, not the result, was copied and adjusted so that each column total is correct (see Figure 2.19).

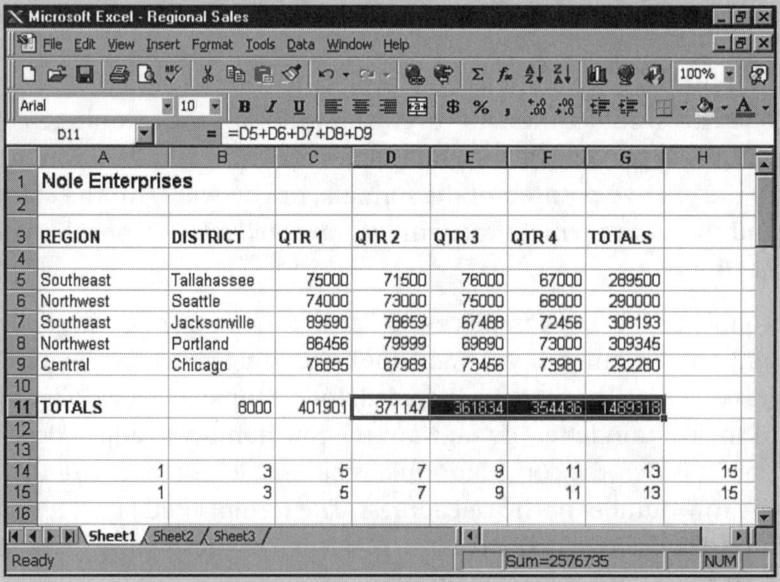

Figure 2.19
The formula in cell C11 copied to the range D11:G11.

5 Save your changes to the worksheet and leave it open for the next tutorial.

Although copying formulas with relative cell addresses is usually desired, frequently formulas need to be copied using absolute cell references. In the following tutorial, you use absolute cell references while copying formulas.

Copying Formulas with Absolute Cell Addresses

To copy a formula with an absolute cell addresses in the Regional Sales worksheet, follow these steps:

1 In cell C12, type the formula **=$C$5+$C$6+$C$7+$C$8+$C$9** and press ↵Enter.

2 Use the same copy and paste technique you used in the preceding tutorial to copy the formula in cell C12 to the range D12:G12.

The results are displayed in the range D12:G12 (see Figure 2.20).

Figure 2.20
The results of the copied formula.

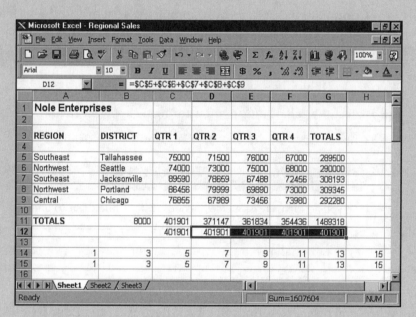

Notice how the formulas in D12 through G12 are identical to the formula in C12. This is because of absolute cell referencing.

3 Save your changes to the worksheet and leave it open for the next tutorial.

Objective 7: Clear, Delete, and Insert Cells

Excel provides the **E**dit, Cle**a**r command for deleting cell contents and the **E**dit, **D**elete command for deleting the cells themselves. Although the two commands sound as if they perform similar functions, they do not. You use the **E**dit, **C**lear command to clear the contents of a cell, including formatting, formulas, and notes. When you clear a cell, the cell contents are removed, but the cell remains in the worksheet. You use the **E**dit, **D**elete command to actually remove the cell from the worksheet. The **E**dit, **D**elete command prompts you to move the surrounding cells to fill the space occupied by the deleted cell.

The two commands are often confused because ⒟ on the keyboard is assigned to the **E**dit, Cle**a**r command. When you press ⒟, the content of the selected range is cleared, but the cells remain.

Clearing Cell Contents

The **E**dit, Cle**a**r command deletes the contents of the selected cell(s) and leaves the cell(s) in the worksheet. When you choose the **E**dit, Cle**a**r command, you use the Clear submenu to select what you want deleted from the cell(s). The Clear submenu provides the following four options:

All	Clears everything from the selected cells including formatting, formulas, and cell notes.
Formats	Removes formatting only from the selected cells.
Contents	Clears formulas from the selected cells.
Co**m**ments	Clears only comments attached to the selected range.

Clearing a Cell or Range

To clear a cell or range, use the Regional Sales worksheet, and follow these steps:

❶ Select the cell or range you want to clear. Select the range A14:I14.

❷ Choose **E**dit, Cle**a**r, **A**ll. The cell contents are deleted.

Note

If you accidentally delete cells, choose **E**dit, **U**ndo Clear to undo the deletion.

❸ Save your changes to the worksheet and leave it open for the next tutorial.

Deleting Cells

When you delete cells from the worksheet using the **E**dit, **D**elete command, Excel removes the cells and prompts you to move surrounding cells to fill the space of the deleted cells. The Delete dialog box is displayed when you select **E**dit, **D**elete.

You can use the Delete dialog box to select how you want the surrounding cells to fill the space of the deleted cells. The Delete dialog box provides the following four options:

Shift cells **l**eft	Shifts surrounding cells to the left
Shift cells **u**p	Shifts surrounding cells up
Entire **r**ow	Shifts the entire row up
Entire **c**olumn	Shifts the entire column to the left

Deleting a Cell or Range

To delete a cell or range, use the Regional Sales worksheet, and follow these steps:

1 Select the cell or range you want to delete. Select the range A15:I15.

2 Choose **E**dit, **D**elete. The Delete dialog box is displayed (see Figure 2.21).

Figure 2.21
The Delete
dialog box.

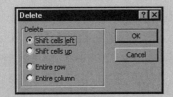

3 Choose the option in the dialog box that represents the direction you want to move the surrounding cells. In this case, click the Shift cells **u**p option button.

4 Choose OK, or press ⏎Enter.

Based on the option selected, surrounding cells shift to fill the deleted space.

> ### Note
>
> If you do not want the surrounding cells to fill the deleted cells, choose **E**dit, Cle**a**r.

5 Save your changes to the worksheet and leave it open for the next tutorial.

Inserting Cells

Inserting cells into a worksheet is the reverse of deleting cells. The **I**nsert, C**e**lls command prompts you to move surrounding cells to make space on the worksheet for the new cells and then inserts the blank cells.

Inserting a Cell or Range

To insert a cell or range in the Regional Sales worksheet, follow these steps:

1 Select the cell or range in which you want blank cells to appear. Select cell C5.

2 Open the **I**nsert menu, and choose the C**e**lls command. The Insert dialog box is displayed (see Figure 2.22).

(continues)

Inserting a Cell or Range (continued)

Figure 2.22
The Insert
dialog box.

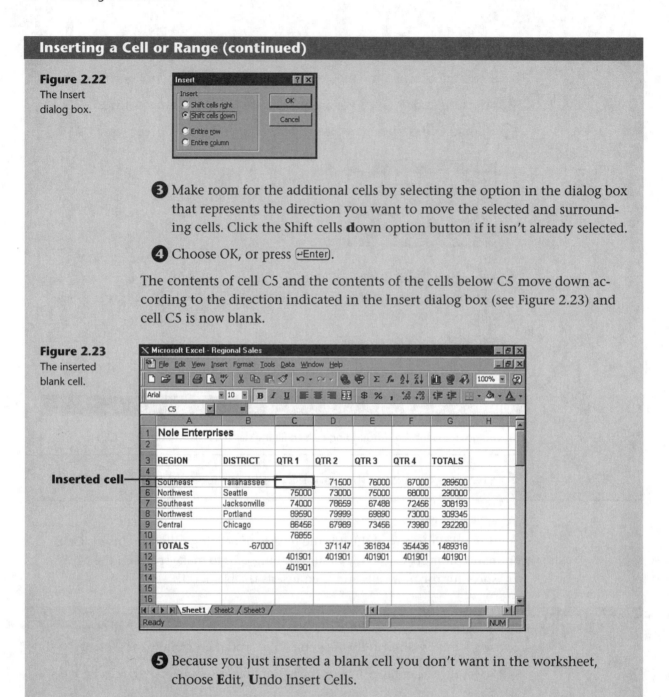

3 Make room for the additional cells by selecting the option in the dialog box that represents the direction you want to move the selected and surrounding cells. Click the Shift cells **d**own option button if it isn't already selected.

4 Choose OK, or press ⏎Enter.

The contents of cell C5 and the contents of the cells below C5 move down according to the direction indicated in the Insert dialog box (see Figure 2.23) and cell C5 is now blank.

Figure 2.23
The inserted
blank cell.

Inserted cell

5 Because you just inserted a blank cell you don't want in the worksheet, choose **E**dit, **U**ndo Insert Cells.

Keep the worksheet open for the next tutorial.

Objective 8: Insert and Delete Columns and Rows

You have learned to modify worksheets by inserting and deleting cells. Sometimes you will want to insert and delete columns and rows. If you want to create additional space in the middle of a worksheet, you can insert a column or row that runs, respectively, through the entire length or width of the worksheet. If you have a column or row that is no longer necessary, you can delete the entire column or row rather than delete the cells.

Inserting a Row

To insert a row in the Regional Sales worksheet, follow these steps:

1 Select row 10 by clicking the row heading 10, at the left of your worksheet.

2 Choose **I**nsert, **R**ows to insert a blank row above the selected row.

An empty row 10 is inserted, and the original rows 10 and higher are renumbered and moved down one row in the worksheet.

3 Click a cell outside the selected row to deselect the row.

4 Save your changes and keep the worksheet open for the next tutorial.

When you insert a column, you do not insert a column heading, so the worksheet looks as if no new column has been added to the worksheet. In the following tutorial, you insert a column in a worksheet.

Inserting a Column

To insert a column in the Regional Sales worksheet, follow these steps:

1 Select column G by clicking the G column heading at the top of your worksheet.

2 Choose **I**nsert, **C**olumns to insert a blank column to the left of the selected column.

An empty column G is inserted, and the original column G and other columns are renamed and moved one column to the right (see Figure 2.24).

Figure 2.24
The inserted blank column.

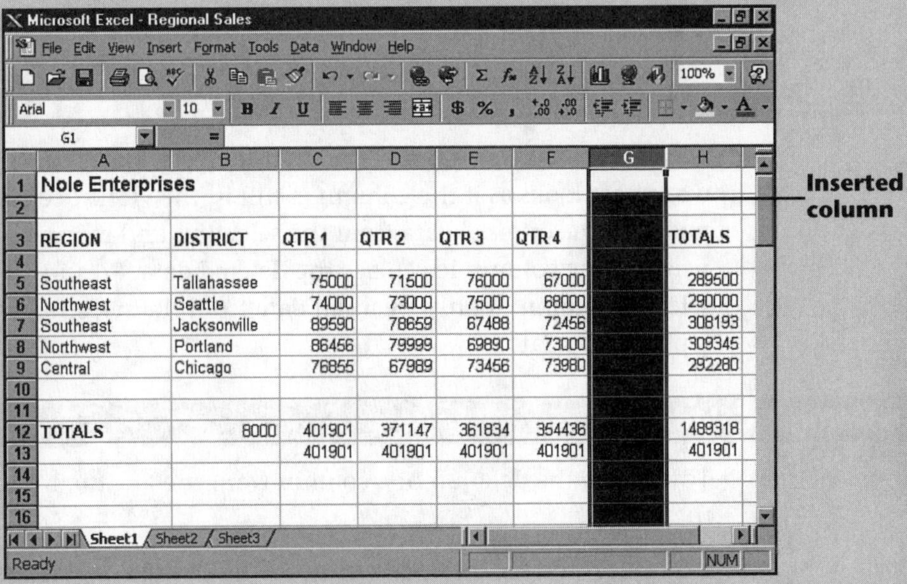

Inserted column

3 Click a cell outside the selected column to deselect it.

(continues)

Inserting a Column (continued)

When you delete a row or column, you do not delete the row or column heading, so the worksheet looks as if the row or column is still in the worksheet. The Delete command pulls out the original data from the selection and moves in the data from the neighboring row or column to replace the deleted data. Pressing Del does not delete the selected row or column; it clears all data from the selection without moving in replacement data.

❹ Save your changes to the worksheet and leave it open for the next tutorial.

When you delete a row, you do not delete the row heading, so the worksheet looks as if the row is still in the worksheet. The Delete command pulls out the original data from the selection and moves in the data from the neighboring row to replace the deleted data. Pressing Del does not delete the selected row; it only clears all data from the selection without moving in replacement data.

Deleting a Row

To practice the deletion of a row from the Regional Sales worksheet, follow these steps:

❶ Select the row you want to delete by clicking its heading; click the row 10 heading.

❷ Choose **E**dit, **D**elete.

The original row 10 data is removed from the worksheet and is replaced by the data in the original row 11. All the other data is moved up one row.

❸ Click a cell outside the selected row to deselect the row.

❹ Save your changes to the worksheet and leave it open for the next tutorial.

When you delete a column, you do not delete the column heading, so the worksheet looks as if the column is still in the worksheet. The Delete command pulls out the original data from the selection and moves in the data from the neighboring column to replace the deleted data. Pressing Del does not delete the selected column; it only clears all data from the selection without moving in replacement data.

Deleting a Column

To practice the deletion of a column from the Regional Sales worksheet, follow these steps:

❶ Select the column you want to delete by clicking its heading; click the column G heading.

❷ Choose **E**dit, **D**elete.

The original column G data is removed from the worksheet and is replaced by the data in the original column H. All the other data is moved to the left one column.

❸ Click a cell outside the selected column to deselect it.

❹ Save your changes to the worksheet and leave it open for the next tutorial.

The **I**nsert menu commands and the **E**dit, **D**elete command are extremely useful; however, these commands can cause problems if you are not careful. Remember that when you are inserting or deleting a column or row, the entire length or width of the worksheet is affected by the change. You may have formulas or data in cells in another section of the worksheet that you cannot see; these cells may be affected by an insertion or deletion. If a formula refers to a cell that is deleted, the cell containing the formula displays the #REF! error value. To undo a deletion, choose **E**dit, **U**ndo Delete immediately after making the deletion. This command reverses the action.

The **I**nsert menu commands are a little more adaptable than the **E**dit, **D**elete command. Formulas adjust to cell address changes when you insert a column or row; however, the command can disorganize areas of the worksheet. Always double-check your worksheet to verify worksheet results when using the **I**nsert menu commands or the **E**dit, **D**elete command.

In the previous tutorials, you inserted and deleted one row and column at a time. To insert or delete multiple adjacent rows or columns, you simply select the multiple row or column headings and then issue the **I**nsert or **D**elete command.

Objective 9: Use Excel Help

Excel provides assistance in a variety of ways. Helpful information is displayed in the status bar at the bottom of the screen. This is especially useful when you want to see the results of a menu action without making the choice. The status bar also displays information about a toolbar button when you place the mouse pointer on that button.

ScreenTips, the small labels that appear next to a toolbar button when you move the pointer to the button, provide a description of the button's action. More extensive help on toolbar buttons is available by using the What's This? feature. This feature is activated when you press ⬆Shift+F1. When you do this, a question mark attaches itself to the mouse pointer. When you click a button in a toolbar, the button won't perform an action; instead, an explanation of the button is displayed.

Another useful feature is Excel's Office Assistant. To display the Office Assistant, click the Office Assistant button located at the right edge of the Standard toolbar or press F1. When you click the button, the Office Assistant displays a list of relevant Help topics. If the list of topics does not include the information you want, you can type a question and the Assistant provides a list of Help topics from which you can choose. To turn off the Office Assistant, click the Close button in the top-right corner of the Office Wizard box. Excel's Help has more information on using the Office Assistant, including how to change the Office Assistant's personality.

The **H**elp menu also provides a variety of help options. You learn about these in the following tutorial.

Using Help

Excel comes with a complete online Help system designed to assist users with commands and other topics.

You access the Help system by selecting an option from the **H**elp menu. The first menu choice, Microsoft Excel **H**elp, displays the Office Assistant (see Figure 2.25). When you use the Office Assistant to provide help, you type your question and the Office Assistant tries to provide an answer.

Figure 2.25
The Microsoft Excel 97 Office Assistant.

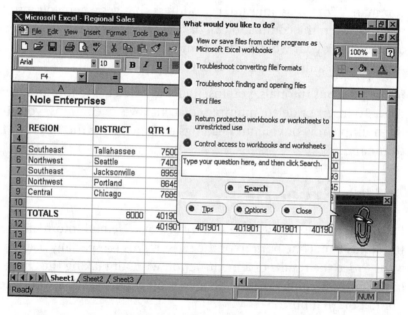

The second menu choice, **C**ontents and Index, displays the Helps Topics dialog box. This dialog box's tabs provide three different methods (Contents, Index, and Find) that you can use to ask Excel for help. The Contents tab is like the table of contents in a book; it provides an overview of the major categories of help available. The Index tab is like the index in the back of a book; it provides an alphabetical list of detailed help available. The Find tab lets you type a word with which you need help and then lists any related Help topics.

The third menu choice, What's **T**his?, as described earlier, provides extensive help on toolbar buttons. When you select this option, a question mark attaches itself to the mouse pointer. When you click a button on a toolbar, the button won't perform an action; instead, an explanation of the button will be displayed.

In the following tutorial, you practice using the various Help options available.

Using the Office Assistant

To use the Office Assistant, follow these steps:

1 To display the Office Assistant, choose **H**elp, Microsoft Excel **H**elp.

Remember that you can also access the Office Assistant by pressing F1 or by clicking the Office Assistant button on the Standard toolbar. The Office Assistant is displayed (refer to Figure 2.25).

2 In the text box, type **How do I save a worksheet?**

3 Click the **S**earch button.

4 Click the Save a workbook option button.

The Save a workbook Help box is displayed (see Figure 2.26). This Help box displays five Help subtopics at the bottom of the informational file. Use the vertical scroll bar to display the subtopic help issues for more information on saving a worksheet. To obtain help on a topic, click the topic.

Figure 2.26
The Save a workbook Help box.

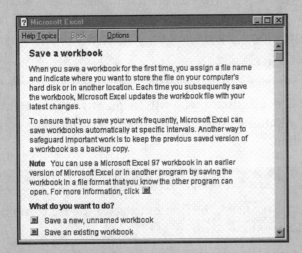

5 Click the Save a new, unnamed workbook topic, located at the bottom of the Save a workbook text. Notice that the mouse pointer changes to a hand.

The Help information under this subtopic is displayed in the Help window (see Figure 2.27).

(continues)

Using the Office Assistant (continued)

Figure 2.27
The Save a new, unnamed workbook Help Window.

⑥ Print the help topic by clicking **O**ptions, **P**rint Topic. In the Print dialog box that is displayed, click OK.

The Help information is printed.

Clicking the **B**ack button (when it is enabled) returns you to the previous Help window (the Save a workbook Help window in this example).

Clicking the **O**ptions button displays the Options menu. The two most useful choices in this menu are **P**rint Topic (which gives you a hard copy of the Help topic information) and **K**eep Help on Top. Keep Help on Top means that the Help topic window will stay open (float) above your worksheet so you can read the Help topic instructions as you work on your worksheet.

⑦ Leave the Office Assistant open for the next tutorial.

In addition to the Office Assistant, you will frequently use the Help Contents feature to aid you in finding information. In the next tutorial, you gain practice using this Help option.

Using Help Contents

To search for a Help topic using the Contents tab of the Help Topics: Microsoft Excel dialog box, follow these steps:

❶ Make sure that the Contents tab of the Help Topics: Microsoft Excel dialog box is displayed on your screen.

❷ Click Getting Help topic and click the **O**pen button.

❸ Click Ways to get assistance while you work; then click the **D**isplay button. You can also double-click a topic to display it.

The Ways to get assistance while you work Help screen is displayed (see Figure 2.28). In this, and in similar Excel Help screens (windows), you click a label (like Office Assistant or ScreenTips) and a yellow note box that contains an explanation appears. After you read the explanation, you can click anywhere on the screen to close it.

Figure 2.28
The Ways to get assistance while you work Help screen.

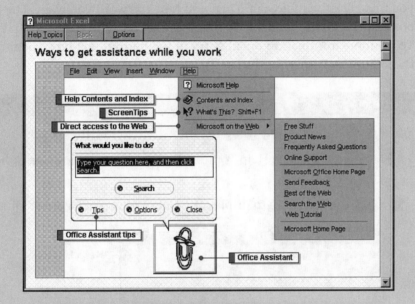

❹ Click the Office Assistant label; a yellow note box is displayed (see Figure 2.29). Read the information in the note box, then click the note box to close it.

Figure 2.29
The note box associated with the Office Assistant label.

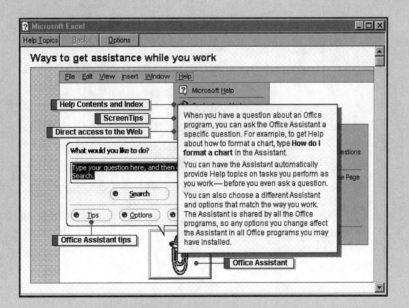

(continues)

Using Help Contents (continued)

5 Click the labels one at a time. After you have read an explanation in a note box, close it by clicking anywhere on-screen.

6 Click the Help **T**opics button to return to the Help Topics: Microsoft Excel dialog box.

When you want to use the Help Index in the Microsoft Excel tabbed dialog box, you first click the Index tab. Then you type the word you want. The bottom text box displays all the available Help topics that relate to the word that you typed. To see more information on an entry in the bottom text box, click the entry and then click the **D**isplay button.

Using the Help Index

To search for a Help topic using the Index tab, follow these steps:

1 Make sure that the Help Topics: Microsoft Excel dialog box is displayed on your screen.

2 Click the Index tab to display the Help Index (see Figure 2.30).

Figure 2.30
The Index tab of the Help Topics: Microsoft Excel dialog box.

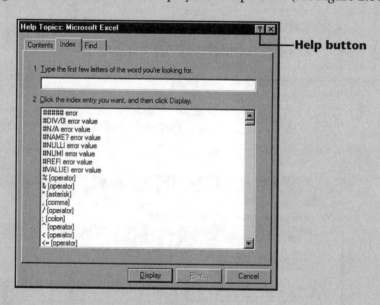

Help button

3 Type **Help** in the first text box.

4 Click overview in the bottom text box list.

5 Click the **D**isplay button to display the Basic worksheet formatting help screen (see Figure 2.31).

Figure 2.31
The Basic worksheet formatting help screen.

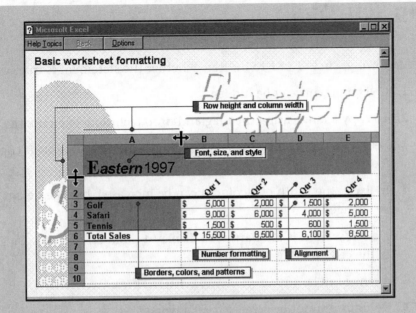

2

6 Click and read the information on the five different topics (the labeled topics).

7 Click the Help **T**opics button to return to the Help Topics: Microsoft Excel dialog box.

8 Close the Help Topics dialog box.

You will find that Help is available in most of Excel's dialog boxes. This help, which is specific to the particular dialog box, is accessed by clicking the dialog box's Help button—the button with the question mark in the upper-right corner. When you click the Help button, a question mark appears next to the mouse pointer. When you click an item or part of the dialog box, helpful information about that item is displayed.

Chapter Summary

This chapter has covered many important worksheet features that are necessary for setting up ranges and moving or copying data. You have also learned step-by-step procedures for inserting and deleting cells, rows, and columns. Additionally, you have learned to adjust column width and row height. Finally, vital information for using Excel Help has been provided.

Checking Your Skills

True/False

For each of the following, circle *T* or *F* to indicate whether the statement is true or false.

T   F   **1.** Cell comments can be hidden.

T   F   **2.** To copy a range using the drag-and-drop technique, you use the mouse and `◆Shift`.

T   F   **3.** Relative cell references remain unchanged when a formula is copied to a new location.

T   F   **4.** In Excel, the width of a column can be increased, but the height of a row cannot be changed.

T   F   **5.** If a cell's width is too narrow to display a number, Excel displays question marks in the cell.

T   F   **6.** A range can be any size.

T   F   **7.** Columns cannot be deleted from a worksheet.

T   F   **8.** Rows cannot be inserted into a worksheet.

T   F   **9.** The **Edit, Cut** command enables you to place selected data on the Clipboard.

T   F   **10.** The **Edit, Paste** command places the contents of the Clipboard in your worksheet.

Multiple Choice

In the blank provided, write the letter of the correct answer for each of the following.

1. When placed on the AutoFill fill handle, the mouse pointer becomes a _____.

    a. double-headed arrow

    b. white cross

    c. black cross

    d. dark rectangle

2. Which of the following characters is used to make a cell address absolute in a formula?

    a. *

    b. $

    c. #

    d. none of the above

3. To automatically adjust the column width to the widest cell contents in the column, place the mouse pointer on the right border of the column heading, and _____.

    a. click

    b. double-click

    c. press `Ctrl`

    d. press `↵Enter`

4. When you paste data into a cell, any data already in the cell is _____ the data you paste.

    a. replaced by

    b. added to

    c. subtracted from

    d. none of the above

5. The moving dashes around a cell that appear when **E**dit, **C**opy is selected are called the _____.

   a. AutoFill

   b. clipping

   c. highlight

   d. marquee

6. Which of the following is a relative cell address?

   a. $D$5

   b. %D5

   c. A0

   d. none of the above

7. To adjust the height of a row, place the mouse pointer on the _____ border of the row heading.

   a. top

   b. bottom

   c. left

   d. right

8. If you delete a cell that is used in a formula, the cell containing the formula displays _____.

   a. ?

   b. ###

   c. #REF!

   d. none of the above

9. The command that enables you to insert blank cells into a worksheet is _____.

   a. **E**dit, **I**nsert

   b. **O**ptions, **I**nsert

   c. both a and b

   d. none of the above

10. If a number is too large to be displayed in a cell, a series of _____ is displayed in the cell.

    a. Error!

    b. ?

    c. *

    d. #

2

Fill in the Blank

In the blank provided, write the correct answer for each of the following statements.

1. The _____ command from the _____ menu will undo an editing change in a worksheet.

2. A(n) _____ is a group of selected cells in the worksheet.

3. The _____ is a temporary storage area containing data you can place in a worksheet using the **E**dit, **P**aste command.

4. When you use the Copy and Paste method to copy the contents of more than a single cell, the _____ area you select must be only one cell or must be the same size as the area of the copied data.

5. The **E**dit, _____ command removes cells from the worksheet and prompts you to move the surrounding cells.

6. A(n) _____ outlines the area you cut or copy to the Clipboard.

7. To clear the contents of the active cell, you press the _____ key.

8. A(n) _____ cell reference is adjusted when a formula is copied to a new location in the worksheet.

9. Label ranges are used in _____ formulas.

10. The _____ commands in the **E**dit menu enable you to copy the contents of the active cell to adjacent cells without using the Clipboard.

Applying Your Skills

Review Exercises

Exercise 1: Modifying Worksheet Columns and Rows

In this exercise, you modify column widths and row heights, insert columns, and boldface column headings.

1. Start Excel, open the Chap0202 workbook and save it as **Best Fit**.

2. Set the width of column A to 20. Use the Best Fit feature to adjust the width of columns B, C, D, and E. Delete row 1.

3. Make the row that contains the heading titles (row 3) twice as high as the other rows.

4. Select the heading titles as a range and make them bold.

5. Insert a new column at Column E. The information currently in Column E will shift to Column F.

6. Set the width of column E to 1.

7. Resave the workbook using the **F**ile, **S**ave command. Print two copies of the worksheet—one to keep and one to turn in to the instructor. Then close the workbook.

Exercise 2: Using Excel Help

In this exercise, you use Excel Help to learn more about cell comments.

1. Open the **H**elp menu and choose **C**ontents and Index.

2. Click the Index tab and enter **comments** in the first text box.

3. Select the formatting topic in the Index list and click the **D**isplay button.

4. Print the Help topic for formatting cell comments.

5. Exit Help.

Exercise 3: Inserting, Printing, and Clearing Cell Comments

In this exercise, you use insert, print, and clear cell comments commands.

1. Open the Chap0203 workbook and save it as **Comments**.

2. In cell E6, enter the comment **This will be a struggle initially but it is doable.**

3. Print the worksheet with the comment(s) displayed at the end of the worksheet.

4. Print two copies of the worksheet (one to keep and one to turn in to your instructor) with comment(s) as displayed on the worksheet.

5. Clear any and all comments from the worksheet.

6. Save and close the worksheet.

Exercise 4: Assigning Range Names and Using Natural Language Formulas

In this exercise, you create a range name and label ranges to be used when creating formulas in future chapters.

1. Open Chap0204 and save it as **Names**.

2. Create label names for each month, January through June, using the **Insert**, **Name**, **Label** command. The label names will consist of the names of each of the months. These labels will be used in natural language formulas in future chapters.

3. Create a range name for the range B9 through G9. Name the range **Totals1**. This range name will be used in future chapters.

4. Print two copies of the worksheet—one to keep and one to turn in to your instructor.

5. Save and close the worksheet.

Exercise 5: Using AutoFill

In this exercise, you use AutoFill to create a worksheet.

1. Open Chap0205 and save it as **Autofill**.

2. Use AutoFill to fill in the remaining workdays (Wednesday through Friday) in row 3.

3. Cells A4 through A25 should contain the hours in the working day from 7:30 a.m. to 12:30 p.m. in half-hour increments. Use AutoFill to fill in the remaining times.

5. Print two copies of the worksheet—one to keep and one to turn in to the instructor.

6. Save and close the file.

Continuing Projects

Project 1: Building a Payroll Worksheet

Cape Enterprises' real estate business is growing and needs to keep better records on their district offices. Management has requested that each district office submit monthly sales records. In this project, you modify the Mexico Beach monthly sales record by:

- boldfacing the column headings
- changing the column width of column A to 15
- changing the column width of columns B through E using the Best Fit feature
- creating a range name for Sales using the range B6:B11
- creating a range name for Percent using the range E6:E11
- inserting a row at row 4

Open Chap0206 and save it as **Real Estate 2**. After making the changes, print two copies (one to keep and one to turn in to your instructor), save and then close the worksheet.

Project 2: Building an Employee Worksheet

Kipper Industries' employee worksheet needs to be modified. In this project you modify the employee worksheet by:

- boldfacing the column headings
- changing the column widths of column A through D using the Best Fit feature
- inserting a column at column B and changing its width to 1
- inserting the comment **As of January, 1997** in cell A3

Open Chap0207 and save it as **Employee 2**. After making the changes, print two copies of the worksheet (one to keep and one to turn in to your instructor) with the comment displayed at the bottom of the worksheet. Save and then close the worksheet.

Project 3: Building the Motor Pool Records Worksheet

Coastal Sales' Motor Pool Records worksheet needs to be modified. In this project, you modify the worksheet by:

- boldfacing the column headings
- changing the column width of all columns using the Best Fit feature
- inserting a row at row 3
- inserting the comment **Used for local trips only** *in cell A10*
- ~~in cell A10,~~ inserting a column at column G with a width of 1

Open Chap0208 and save it as **Vehicle Mileage 2**. After making the changes, print two copies of the worksheet (one to keep and one to turn in to your instructor) with the comment as displayed on the worksheet. Save and then close the worksheet.

Chapter 3

Formatting Worksheets

In Chapter 2, you learned to build a simple worksheet. In this chapter, you learn to make changes to the appearance of your worksheet. The appearance and layout of a worksheet can increase its usefulness and effectiveness. This chapter shows you how to improve the appearance of your worksheet by formatting it. When you format a part of a worksheet, you change the appearance of that element. For example, you can format the text or numbers in a cell to appear in boldface, italic, and color, and in a larger size type. Additional formatting is available for numbers so that they can be displayed as currency (with dollar signs), as percentages (with percent signs), or as dates.

This chapter focuses on formatting numbers and text, aligning cell contents (including centering text over multiple columns and making text read vertically or horizontally), using automatic range formats, changing fonts, and enhancing cells with borders and patterns. This chapter also covers the Formatting toolbar and concludes with a topic vital to the professional appearance of your worksheet—spell checking.

If you need to leave your computer before you complete your work in this chapter, be sure to save your work and close the file you have been using. You can then reopen the file with the saved changes when you want to continue this chapter.

Objectives

By the time you have finished this chapter, you will have learned to

1. Apply Formats to Numbers
2. Change Fonts, Font Sizes, and Font Styles
3. Align Cell Contents
4. Format Cells with Borders and Color
5. Use Conditional Formats
6. Check Spelling in the Worksheet

Objective 1: Apply Formats to Numbers

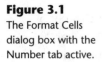

Predefined formats
Standardized formats that come with Excel.

Because numbers are the most common items on a worksheet, Excel offers a variety of *predefined formats* for numbers. You may want a number to appear with two decimal places in some cells and with no decimals in other cells on the same worksheet. You may also want to display negative numbers in red or in parentheses. Often you may want to display currency symbols or the percent sign without having to type the symbol every time you enter a number.

While you are entering numbers, you do not need to be concerned with the way they look. After you have completed your entries, you can apply formatting to numbers and change the way they look on-screen or in print. Remember, formatting affects only the way a number is displayed or printed. Formatting does not change the value of the number stored in a cell and used in calculations.

Excel offers you two different techniques for formatting numbers. You can use the Format menu or the Formatting toolbar. The most commonly used formatting can be done using the toolbar. The complete selection of formatting capabilities, however, is available only through the Format menu.

Understanding the Format Cells Dialog Box

When you use the Format, Cells command, the Format Cells dialog box is displayed (see Figure 3.1). This dialog box with six tabs is really six dialog boxes in one; the commands all relate to changing some characteristic of the selected cell(s). A tabbed dialog box is like a card index. You click a tab to move that tab to the front of the dialog box so that you can use it to format the cell or the contents of the cell.

Figure 3.1
The Format Cells dialog box with the Number tab active.

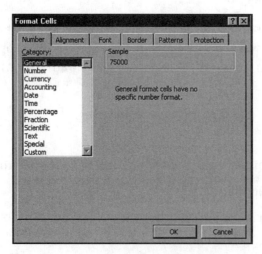

The **C**ategory list shows the types of formats. The General format is the default format for numbers. Depending on the category selected, a variety of information, such as options for number of decimal places, options for date format, and so on, displays to the right of the **C**ategory list. A sample of the selected category is always displayed on the top-right side of the dialog box.

Formatting Numbers Using the Format Menu

To format the number in cell B5 using the Format menu, follow these steps:

❶ Open Chap0301 and save it as **Formatting**.

You need to increase the width of columns A through G to better see the data. You can see the width of a column displayed when you click and hold on the border between column headings.

❷ Select columns A through G by dragging over the column headings.

❸ Choose Format, **C**olumn, **W**idth to display the Column Width dialog box.

❹ In the Column Width text box, enter **12** (see Figure 3.2).

Figure 3.2
The Column Width dialog box.

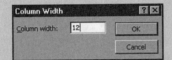

❺ Click OK.

❻ Select cell C5.

❼ Choose Format, C**e**lls to display the Format Cells dialog box.

❽ Click the Number tab, if necessary. The Number tab displays a list of predefined number formats.

❾ Choose Number from the **C**ategory list box. Notice that the value in cell C5 is displayed in the Sample area (see Figure 3.3).

Figure 3.3
The Number tab of the Format Cells dialog box with the Number format chosen.

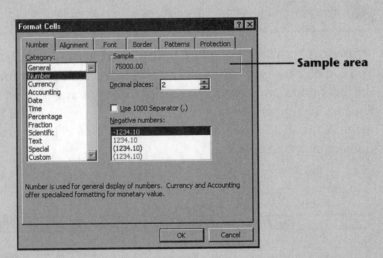

Sample area

❿ Click OK. The number in cell C5 formats to a number with two decimal places (see Figure 3.4).

(continues)

3

Formatting Numbers Using the Format Menu (continued)

Figure 3.4
Cell C5 with the
new format.

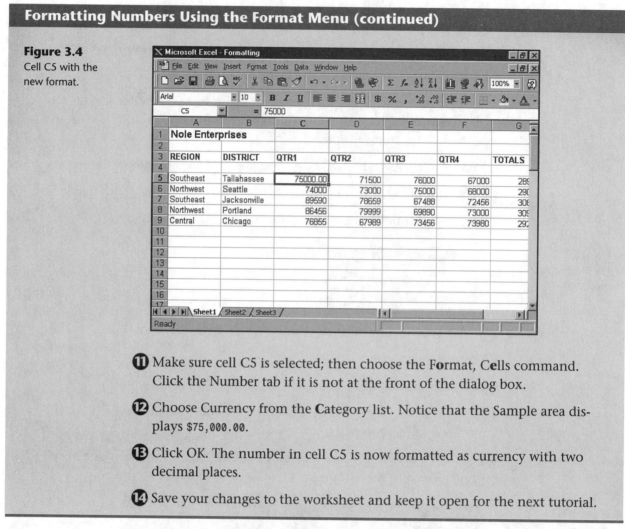

⑪ Make sure cell C5 is selected; then choose the Format, Cells command. Click the Number tab if it is not at the front of the dialog box.

⑫ Choose Currency from the Category list. Notice that the Sample area displays $75,000.00.

⑬ Click OK. The number in cell C5 is now formatted as currency with two decimal places.

⑭ Save your changes to the worksheet and keep it open for the next tutorial.

Applying Number Formats Using the Formatting Toolbar

You can quickly apply commonly used predefined number formats, such as Currency, Comma, and Percent, with the buttons on the Formatting toolbar (see Figure 3.5). Your choice of formats, however, is more limited than in the Format menu. You can also use the Increase or Decrease Decimal buttons to change the number of decimal places.

Figure 3.5
The number
formatting buttons
on the Formatting
toolbar.

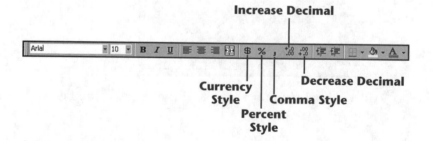

Increase Decimal

Currency Style

Percent Style

Comma Style

Decrease Decimal

Style
A combination of formatting characteristics (such as alignment, borders, font, and number formatting).

Each of the five formatting buttons applies a specific *style*. This default style, set by Excel when it is installed, is usually the one you want to use, but you can change the style associated with a formatting button in the Style dialog box (see Figure 3.6). Press [F1] for an explanation of how to change styles. You can name and save your own style combinations so that you can apply them more efficiently.

Figure 3.6
The Style dialog box.

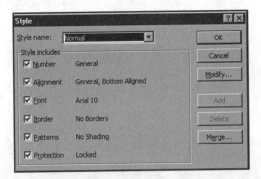

Formatting Numbers Using the Formatting Toolbar

To use the Formatting toolbar to apply a number format to a range of cells in the Formatting workbook, follow these steps:

1 Select the range C5:G9.

> **Note**
>
> The notation C5:G9 means the range of cells from C5 through G9.

2 Click the Comma Style button on the Formatting toolbar.

The numbers in the selected range are displayed with a comma and two decimal places.

3 Click the Increase Decimal button once.

Notice that the numbers in the selected cells now have three decimal places.

4 Click the Decrease Decimal button three times.

Notice the effect on the numbers in the selected cells.

5 Notice the effect on the numbers in the selected cells when you click the Percent Style button; then click the Currency Style button. The actual value in the cell does not change—just the way the number is displayed.

6 Click anywhere outside the selected cells to deselect the range. Your worksheet should now look like Figure 3.7.

(continues)

Formatting Numbers Using the Formatting Toolbar (continued)

Figure 3.7
The worksheet with the new formats applied.

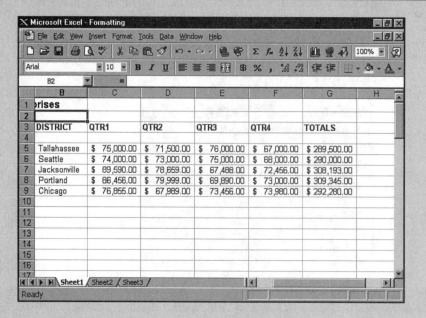

DISTRICT	QTR1	QTR2	QTR3	QTR4	TOTALS
Tallahassee	$ 75,000.00	$ 71,500.00	$ 76,000.00	$ 67,000.00	$ 289,500.00
Seattle	$ 74,000.00	$ 73,000.00	$ 75,000.00	$ 68,000.00	$ 290,000.00
Jacksonville	$ 89,590.00	$ 78,659.00	$ 67,488.00	$ 72,456.00	$ 308,193.00
Portland	$ 86,456.00	$ 79,999.00	$ 69,890.00	$ 73,000.00	$ 309,345.00
Chicago	$ 76,855.00	$ 67,989.00	$ 73,456.00	$ 73,980.00	$ 292,280.00

7 Save your changes to the worksheet and keep it open for the next tutorial.

Changing Date and Time Formats

If you enter 1–1–97 into a cell, Excel assumes that you are entering a date. The cell, therefore, displays the number in a date format. (The default date format is 1/1/97.) If you enter 9:45, Excel assumes that you are referring to a time and displays a time format. To change to another date or time format, you can use the Format, Cells command. The procedure for changing a date or time format is the same as changing a number format. The date and time formats are separate categories of number formats. When you select the Date category in the Category list of the Format Cells dialog box, the date format types are displayed.

Changing a Date Format

To enter and change the date format in the Formatting workbook, follow these steps:

1 In cell A11, enter the date **9–15–97**, and press ↵Enter. The date is displayed in the default format.

2 Click cell A11 and then choose Format, Cells to display the Format Cells dialog box.

3 Because Excel recognizes that the number in cell A11 is a date, the format types for the Date category are displayed in the Type list box.

4 Click the fifth format type, 4–Mar–97. Notice how the date is displayed in the Sample area.

5 Click OK. The date in cell A11 should now be displayed as 15–Sep–97.

6 Save your changes and keep the worksheet open for the next tutorial.

Objective 2: Change Fonts, Font Sizes, and Font Styles

Excel 97 enables you to use as many as 256 different *fonts* (typefaces) on a worksheet. You can also change the size (measured in *points*), change the color, italicize, underline, and boldface a font. Excel offers two ways for you to change a font or to change the appearance of a font. You can use buttons on the Formatting toolbar, or you can use the Font tab of the Format Cells dialog box.

The Formatting toolbar in Excel 97 contains buttons that represent commonly used formatting commands (see Figure 3.8).

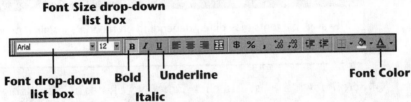

Figure 3.8
The Formatting toolbar.

Font
One complete collection of letters, punctuation marks, numbers, and special characters with a consistent and identifiable typeface, weight (roman or bold), posture (upright or italic), and type size.

Point Size
One point equals 1/72 inch. In Excel, font size and row height are measured in points. The larger the point size, the larger the font size.

Several buttons on the Formatting toolbar are useful for changing font styles. Use the Font box in the Formatting toolbar to change the font of selected cells in a worksheet. To see a list of the available fonts, click the Font box drop-down list arrow.

If you want to increase or decrease the size of the font in a cell, you can use the Font Size box on the left side of the Formatting toolbar. You can change a font, font size, a font style, or a font color by selecting a cell, a range, or the entire worksheet. To select the entire worksheet, click in the area where the column and row headings intersect (in the upper-left corner of the worksheet above row 1 and to the left of column A).

You can apply formatting and color to text or numbers by using the Font tab of the Format Cells dialog box. You can, however, accomplish many of these tasks much faster using the Formatting toolbar. When you click any one of the buttons shown in Figure 3.8, the button looks as if it has been pressed in. If you select a cell that has already been formatted in bold, italic, or underline, the corresponding button appears pressed in to indicate this fact. If you decide that you do not want the formatting, select the cell, and click the appropriate button to change the formatting. The formatting of the text or number in the cell is turned off, and the button returns to its normal state.

Changing the Font and Color Using the Formatting Toolbar

To change the font and font color used in the column headings of the Formatting workbook, follow these steps:

1 Select the range A3:G3.

2 Click the Font box drop-down list arrow at the far left of the Formatting toolbar (see Figure 3.9).

(continues)

Changing the Font and Color Using the Formatting Toolbar (continued)

Figure 3.9
The Font box drop-down list.

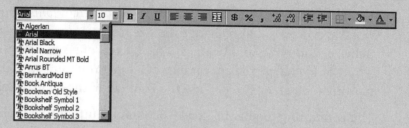

> **Note**
>
> The available fonts may differ, depending on the fonts installed on your computer, which is based on your printer and its capabilities.

3 Scroll down the list and click Times New Roman, if available. (If Times New Roman is not available, click Courier New.) The font used in the headings changes to the selected font.

4 Click the Font box drop-down list arrow to display the list of fonts again.

5 Click the Arial font to return to the default font.

6 Click the Font Color button drop-down list arrow at the right end of the Formatting toolbar. On the palette that is displayed, click the red color (third row) to change the font color to red.

7 Click anywhere outside the selected range to see the font color.

8 Save your changes and keep the worksheet open for the next tutorial.

In addition to using the Formatting Toolbar to change the font and font color, you can also use the Formatting toolbar to change font size. The next tutorial shows you how to perform this activity.

Changing the Font Size Using the Formatting Toolbar

To change the font size of the headings in the Formatting workbook, follow these steps:

1 Select the range of cells A3:G3.

2 Click the Font Size drop-down list arrow. A list of font sizes (in points) is displayed; the greater the number, the bigger the font size.

3 Click 18. Notice that the font size of the headings is increased to 18 points.

4 Click the Font Size drop-down button and click 10 to change the font back to the default size.

5 Save your changes and keep the workbook open for the next tutorial.

You can also use the Formatting toolbar to change font styles, such as bold, italic, and underlining.

Changing the Font Style Using the Formatting Toolbar

To apply boldface, italic, and underlining to the Formatting workbook, follow these steps:

1 Select cell H1.

2 Type your name and click the Enter button (the green check mark) on the formula bar to enter the entry in cell H1 (see Figure 3.10).

Enter button

Figure 3.10
The Enter button (green check mark) for accepting an entry.

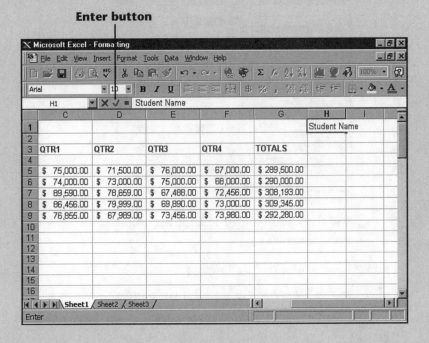

3 Click the Bold button on the Formatting toolbar. Note the effect on the contents of cell H1.

4 Click the Italic button and then click the Underline button.

5 Click cell H3 to deselect cell H1. (You can click any cell other than the selected cell.) You can clearly see the formatting of your name in cell H1.

Notice that the Bold, Italic, and Underline buttons "pop out" because cell H3 is unformatted.

6 Select cell H1 and click the Italic button. Note the effect on the letters in your name.

7 Save your changes and keep the worksheet open for the next tutorial.

You can use the Format, Cells command to control fonts, size, and styles. In the Font tab of the Format Cells dialog box, you can select a font, choose a size for the selected font, and apply a style. The list of fonts available depends on the type of printer you are using.

Changing the Font, Font Size, Font Style, and Font Color Using Menu Commands

To change the font, font size, font style, and font color in a range of cells using the Font tab of the Format Cells dialog box, follow these steps:

1 In the Formatting workbook, select the range A5:A9.

2 Choose Format, Cells to display the Format Cells dialog box.

3 Click the Font tab (see Figure 3.11).

Figure 3.11
The Format Cells dialog box with the Font tab active.

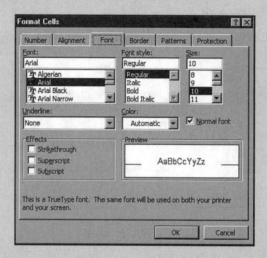

4 Use the scroll bar in the Font list box to scroll down to Times New Roman (or Courier New).

5 Click Times New Roman (or Courier New).

6 In the Size area, click 10 if it isn't already selected.

7 In the Font style area, click Bold Italic.

8 Click the Color drop-down list arrow to display a palette of colors.

9 Click the Dark Blue square in the top row of the palette (third from the right).

> **Note**
>
> The Preview area of the dialog box shows how the font will look.

10 Click OK.

11 Click cell A1 to deselect the range of cells and note the formatting in cells A5:A9.

12 Select the range A3:G3.

13 Again, choose Format, Cells to display the Format Cells dialog box.

14 Click the **C**olor drop-down list arrow and select the Dark Red color in the second row of the color palette.

15 Click OK.

16 Click cell A1 to deselect the range of cells so that you can see the formatting in cells A3:G3.

> **Note**
>
> If you have a color printer, you can print your worksheet in color; otherwise, you will print in black and white.

17 Save your changes and keep the worksheet open for the next tutorial.

3

Objective 3: Align Cell Contents

Sometimes you may want to change the alignment of numbers or text within a cell. You can format numbers and text so that they are left-aligned, right-aligned, or centered in a cell. You can also format long text entries to wrap within a cell, or you can center text across a range of columns. To wrap text within a cell causes a long string of text to appear on multiple lines within a cell. The height of the cell increases as you type so that it can contain the lines of text. You can align a cell entry so that is it is centered across a series of selected cells. You can also align text so that it is vertical in a cell (first letter of the text at the top of the cell, last letter at the bottom of the cell).

Unless you change the alignment, Excel left-aligns text and right-aligns numbers in a cell. This default alignment is called the General alignment. You can apply alignment formatting, such as left, center, and right, to selected cells by using the alignment buttons in the middle of the Formatting toolbar (see Figure 3.12). The Format Cells dialog box also enables you to wrap text, choose horizontal or vertical alignment, and choose orientation options for vertical text. The steps for aligning data and text using both the Formatting toolbar and the Format Cells dialog box are outlined in the text and tutorials that follow.

Figure 3.12
The alignment buttons on the Formatting toolbar.

Align Left   **Merge and Center**
          Center   **Align Right**

Using the Formatting Toolbar

To use the Formatting toolbar to align text in the Formatting workbook, follow these steps:

❶ Select the range A3:G3.

❷ Click the Align Right button on the Formatting toolbar to apply alignment formatting to the selection. Notice how the text in the selection moves to the right in each cell.

❸ Click the Center button to align the text in the center of each cell.

❹ Click the Align Left button to left align the text in each cell.

❺ Select cells A11 and B11.

❻ Click the Merge and Center button. Notice how the date is centered across the selected cells and the vertical grids in cells A11:B11 are no longer displayed.

❼ Save your changes and keep the workbook open for the next tutorial.

You can also use the Format Cells dialog box to align text in a selected cell or cells.

Using the Alignment Tab of the Format Cells Dialog Box

As indicated earlier, the Alignment tab of the Format Cells dialog box offers a number of alignment options (see Figure 3.13).

Figure 3.13
The Format Cells dialog box with the Alignment tab active.

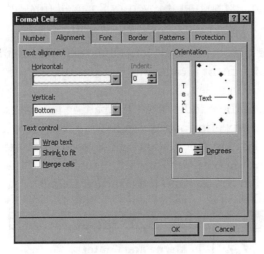

Horizontal options include General, Left (Indent), Center, Right, Fill, Justify, and Center Across Selection. General, the default Horizontal alignment, aligns text to the left and numbers to the right. Left (Indent), Center, and Right, respectively, left-align, center, and right-align text or numbers. The Fill option repeats the contents of the selected cell until the cell is full. Justify, which can be used only with two or more lines of wrapped text, aligns wrapped text within a cell on both the left and the right. Center Across Selection aligns cell contents in the center of a selected group of cells.

Vertical options include Top, Center, Bottom, and Justify. Bottom is the default Vertical alignment. Select Top to align the entry with the top of the cell. Use Center to center the entry between the top and bottom edges of the cell. Justify is used to align cell contents to both edges.

The **W**rap text check box makes wide text entries wrap into multiple lines within the cell. The Shrin**k** to fit check box automatically shrinks the size of the text so that it fits in one cell. The **M**erge cells check box enables you to select a range of cells and merge them into one cell.

In the following tutorials, you align text using various alignment options.

Right-Aligning Text Using the Alignment Tab of the Format Cells Dialog Box

To right-align selected text in the Formatting workbook, follow these steps:

❶ Select the range A5:A9.

❷ Choose F**o**rmat, C**e**lls to display the Format Cells dialog box.

❸ Click the Alignment tab.

❹ Click the **H**orizontal drop-down arrow and select Right.

❺ Choose OK, or press `↵Enter`. The text right-aligns.

❻ Save your changes and keep the worksheet open for the next tutorial.

In the following tutorial, you indent text in a range using the Alignment tab of the Format Cells dialog box.

Indenting Text Using the Alignment Tab of the Format Cells Dialog Box

To indent selected text in the Formatting workbook, follow these steps:

1 Select the range A5:A9.

2 Choose Format, Cells to display the Format Cells dialog box.

3 Click the Alignment tab, if necessary, and then click the **H**orizontal drop-down arrow and select Left (Indent).

4 Click the **I**ndent scroll box up arrow and select 1.

5 Choose OK, or press ⏎Enter. The text in cells A5 through A9 indents from the left column edge by 1 character.

You can also select the cells whose contents you want to indent and click the Increase Indent button on the Formatting toolbar. Each click increases the indent by one point.

6 Save your changes and keep the worksheet open for the next tutorial.

In the following tutorial, you center text using the Alignment tab of the Format Cells dialog box.

Centering Text Using the Alignment Tab of the Format Cells Dialog Box

To center selected text in the Formatting workbook, follow these steps:

1 Select the range A5:A9, if it isn't already selected.

2 Choose Format, Cells to display the Format Cells dialog box.

3 Click the Alignment tab, if necessary. Click the **H**orizontal drop-down arrow and select Center.

4 Choose OK, or press ⏎Enter. The text centers within the width of the column.

5 Save your changes and keep the worksheet open for the next tutorial.

If you have used a word processing program, you are familiar with word wrap. This option in Excel enables you to display a long line of text on multiple lines inside a cell.

Wrapping Text Using the Alignment Tab of the Format Cells Dialog Box

To wrap a string of text within a cell in the Formatting workbook, follow these steps:

1 Select cell A12, and type the following text:

This is an example of formatted text in Excel.

2 Press ⏎Enter to enter the text into the cell. Notice that the text extends across other cells.

3 Click cell A12 again.

4 Choose For**m**at, C**e**lls to display the Format Cells dialog box. Click the Alignment tab if it is not in front.

5 Click the **W**rap text check box so that a check mark appears in it.

6 Choose OK, or press ⏎Enter. Row 12 increases in height, allowing all the text to be displayed in cell A12 (see Figure 3.14).

Figure 3.14
The result of wrapping text in cell A12.

Wrapped text ⎯

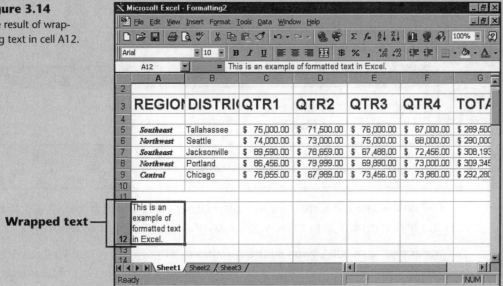

7 Save your changes to the worksheet and leave it open for the next tutorial.

Sometimes, you may want to center a title across several cells in a worksheet. You can easily accomplish this task by using Excel's text-centering capability.

You can center text from one cell horizontally over a selected range of columns by using the Center **A**cross Selection option button on the Alignment tab of the Format Cells dialog box. The text from the left-most cell in the selection is centered across all selected blank cells to the right. (Selected cells defining the range of columns must be blank.)

Centering Text Across Multiple Columns Using the Format Cells Dialog Box

To center text in cell A1 of the Formatting workbook over columns A through G, follow these steps:

1 Select cells A1:G1 (the range of columns you plan to center the text across).

2 Choose F**o**rmat, C**e**lls to display the Format Cells dialog box.

3 Click the Alignment tab, if necessary.

4 Click the **H**orizontal drop-down arrow and select Center Across Selection.

5 Choose OK, or press ⏎Enter. The text centers across the width of seven columns.

> ### Caution
> Remember, the text to be aligned must be in the left-most column and the columns to the right must be blank.

6 Save your changes and keep the worksheet open for the next tutorial.

Excel 97 enables you to format text to align either vertically or horizontally. When aligning text vertically, you usually need to increase the height of the row.

To format text vertically, you use the Alignment tab of the Format Cells dialog box. In the Orientation section, you click the box next to the Orientation gauge.

Aligning Text Vertically

To format text in the Formatting workbook to be displayed vertically, follow these steps:

1 Select cell G3.

2 Choose the F**o**rmat, C**e**lls command; then click the Alignment tab.

3 Click the **V**ertical drop-down arrow and select Center.

4 In the Orientation section, click the text box (see Figure 3.15).

Figure 3.15
The Alignment tab
of the Format Cells
dialog box.

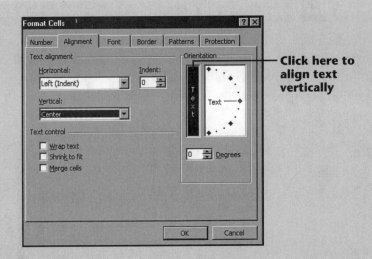

**Click here to
align text
vertically**

5 Choose OK, or press (⏎Enter). Your screen should now look like Figure 3.16.

Figure 3.16
The text in cell G3 is
now vertically
aligned.

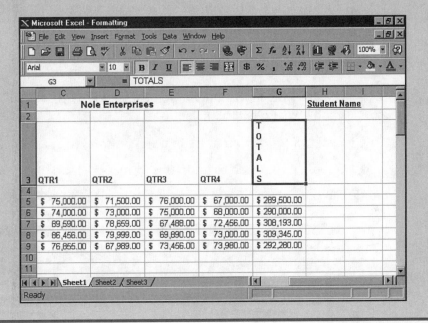

To adjust the column width or row height for vertical text, follow the steps for
the Best Fit feature covered in Chapter 2, "Building a Worksheet." You can also
use the **R**ow or **C**olumn command in the F**o**rmat menu.

Rotating Text Using the Degrees Scroll Box and the Orientation Gauge

Two methods are available for rotating text in the Formatting workbook. You can either type in the degree of rotation in the **D**egrees scroll box, or you can drag the line in the Orientation gauge box to achieve the desired degree of rotation. Follow these steps:

1 Select cell G3.

2 Choose F**o**rmat, C**e**lls to display the Format Cells dialog box; then click the Alignment tab, if necessary.

3 Click the **H**orizontal drop-down arrow and select Right.

4 In the Orientation section, click the **D**egrees scroll box down arrow to select –45.

5 Click OK. The text is now displayed at a –45 degree angle.

You can also drag the line in the Orientation gauge box to select a specific angle for the cell entry.

6 Select cell A1, then choose F**o**rmat, C**e**lls to display the Format Cells dialog box; then click the Alignment tab, if necessary.

7 Drag the line in the Orientation gauge box to 20. Notice that the **D**egrees scroll box also reads 20.

8 Click OK to see your entry in cell A1 displayed at a 20-degree angle.

9 Choose **E**dit, **U**ndo to undo this format orientation.

10 Choose OK, or press ⏎Enter. Your screen should now look like Figure 3.17

Figure 3.17
The text in cell G3 is now rotated at a –45 degree angle.

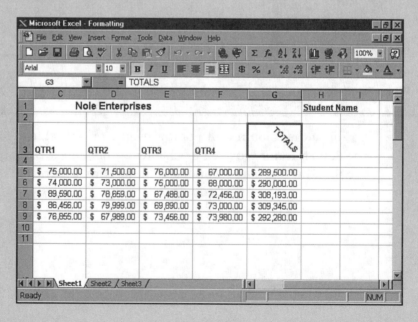

11 Save your changes and keep the worksheet open for the next tutorial.

Objective 4: Format Cells with Borders and Color

So far, most of this chapter has focused on formatting numbers or text (the contents of cells). This objective deals specifically with applying formats to cells themselves. Formatting cells includes adding a border around a cell or range of cells, filling a cell with a color or pattern, and using a combination of predefined formats (automatic formatting) to format a range or a whole worksheet.

To place borders around a cell or to place a single or double underline below a series of cells, you use the Border tab of the Format Cells dialog box or the Border button on the Formatting toolbar (see Figure 3.18).

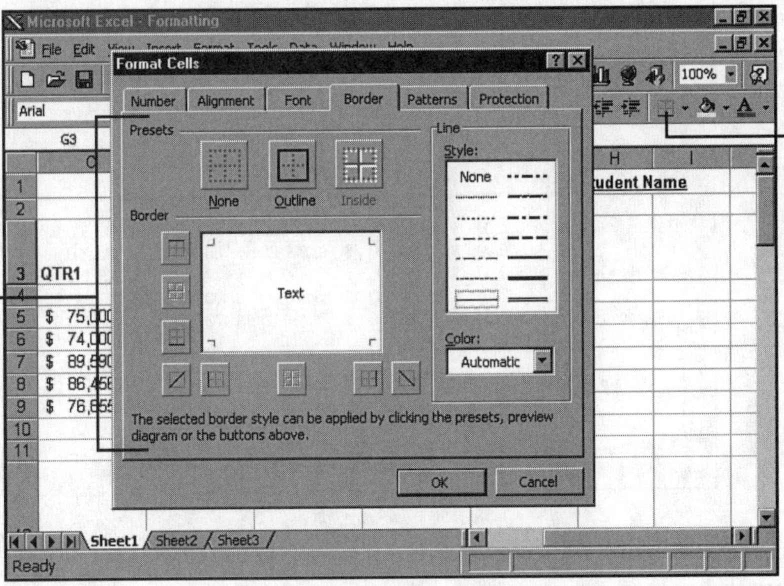

Figure 3.18
The Border tab of the Format Cells dialog box and the Borders button on the Formatting toolbar.

Border tab of the Format Cells dialog box

Borders button

Three Presets options are available, **N**one, **O**utline, and **I**nside. The **N**one option removes any existing borders in the selected cell(s). The **O**utline option applies an outline around the selected cell(s). The **I**nside option inserts a border separating each cell in a selected range of cells. The icons around the Text box in the Border section actually represent creating borders for the left, right, top, bottom, right diagonal, and left diagonal of a cell or group of cells. Not only can you select where the border will appear, Excel provides 13 different line styles from which you can choose and a wide range of border colors.

Applying a Border Using the Format Cells Dialog Box

To use the Format Cells dialog box to apply a bottom border to selected cells of the Formatting workbook, follow these steps:

1 Select the range A3:G3.

2 Choose F**o**rmat, C**e**lls to display the Format Cells dialog box; then click the Border tab (refer to Figure 3.18).

3 In the **S**tyle list box of the Line section, select the thickest black line.

(continues)

Applying a Border Using the Format Cells Dialog Box (continued)

4 In the Border section, click the third icon from the top (the bottom line icon) to add a thick border to the bottom of the cells.

5 Click OK.

6 Click cell A1 to deselect cells A3:G3 so that you can see the effect of the cell formatting you applied (see Figure 3.19).

Figure 3.19
The cells A3:G3 are now formatted with a bottom border.

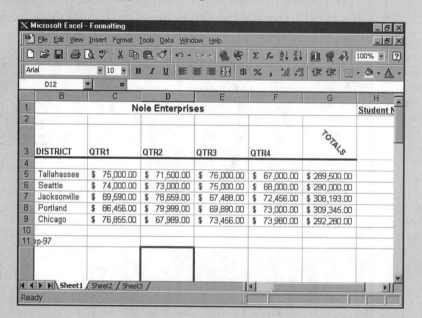

7 Save your changes and leave the worksheet open for the next tutorial.

You can apply frequently used borders, such as an outline around a selected cell or range, by using the Borders button on the Formatting toolbar. The Borders button always applies either Excel's default border (a bottom border) or the most recent border you selected from the palette of borders. As you click selections from the palette, the Borders button changes to show which kind of border it will apply.

Using the Borders Button

To use the Borders button to place a border around the range A5:A9 in the Formatting workbook, follow these steps:

1 Select cells A5:A9.

2 Click the down arrow next to the Borders button on the Formatting toolbar. A palette of borders is displayed (see Figure 3.20).

Figure 3.20
The Borders palette.

❸ Click the square in the lower-right corner of the palette—the square with thick border on all four sides of the selection.

❹ Click cell A1. Notice that the range A5:A9 is now surrounded by a thick border. Because of the location of the range of cells, you won't see the border on all four sides until you perform a Print Preview or print the worksheet. Notice also that the Borders button has changed to show the selected border; now you can simply click the Borders button to apply the thick borders.

❺ Save your work and keep the worksheet open for the next tutorial.

3

Adding Colors and Patterns to Cells

In addition to adding borders to cells, you can enhance a cell with patterns and colors. The Patterns tab of the Format Cells dialog box enables you to choose colors as well as patterns from the **P**attern drop-down list (see Figure 3.21).

Figure 3.21
The Patterns tab of the Format Cells dialog box.

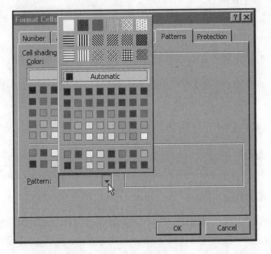

In the Cell shading section of the dialog box is a palette of colors; click the one you want to use in the selected cell(s). The Sample box in the lower-right corner of the dialog box shows you a sample of the formatting. If you click the **P**attern drop-down arrow, you can select from a palette of patterns in black and white or color.

Tip

If you don't like the formatting you have chosen after it has been applied, choose **E**dit, Undo Format Cells before proceeding with another command. If you like the formatting and want to apply the same formatting to another area, select the new area, and choose **E**dit, **R**epeat Format Cells immediately after the formatting has been applied.

Adding Color and a Pattern to a Range of Cells

To apply color and a pattern to a second range in the Formatting workbook, follow these steps:

1 Select cells A3:G3.

2 Choose **F**ormat, **C**ells and click the Patterns tab in the Format Cells dialog box.

3 In the **C**olor palette of the Cell shading section, click the pale blue color in the fifth row (fourth from the right).

4 Click OK.

5 Click outside the selected cells to see the color.

6 Select cells A2:G2.

7 Choose **F**ormat, **C**ells to display the Patterns tab of the Format Cells dialog box again.

8 Click the **P**attern drop-down arrow to display a color and pattern palette.

9 Click the second pattern from the left in the third row (Thin Vertical Stripe) and click OK.

10 Click outside the selection to see the result.

11 Save your changes and keep the worksheet open for the next tutorial.

Using the Format Painter

After you have formatted your worksheet using any of the preceding procedures, the Format Painter offers an easy way to reuse the formats. The Format Painter button on the Standard toolbar enables you to copy any number of cell formats at the same time.

Using the Format Painter

To use the Format Painter button to copy formats in the Formatting workbook, follow these steps:

1 Select the cells containing the column headings, cells A3:G3.

 2 Click the Format Painter button on the Standard toolbar. Notice that a paintbrush icon is added to the mouse pointer.

3 Select the range A10:G10; this is where you want to apply the format. Click outside the selection to see that the selected cells are now formatted the same as the source cells (see Figure 3.22).

Figure 3.22
Cells A10:G10 formatted after using the Format Painter button.

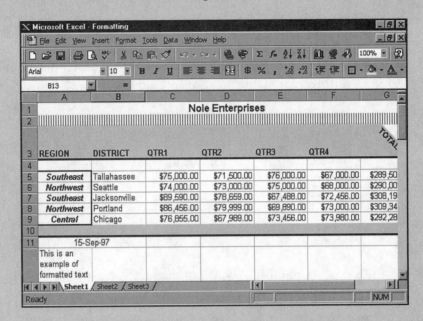

Note

To copy the formatting to more than one item, select the cells containing the formats you want to copy, double-click the Format Painter button, then click each cell to which you want to apply the formats. When you are finished, press Esc or click the Format Painter button to turn off the feature.

4 Save your work and keep the worksheet open for the next tutorial.

If you aren't sure which colors and formats work well together, Excel's AutoFormat feature assists you in making formatting decisions. AutoFormat enables you to select from 16 predefined range formats. These formats are a combination of number formats, cell alignments, column widths, row heights, fonts, borders, and other formatting options. You can apply automatic formatting using the AutoFormat dialog box, which you access by choosing F**o**rmat, **A**utoFormat.

Using Excel's AutoFormat Feature

To format a range in the Formatting workbook using the AutoFormat feature, follow these steps:

1 Select the range A1:G10. Most often, you will apply the formatting to your entire work area.

2 Open the Format menu and choose the **A**utoFormat command. The AutoFormat dialog box is displayed (see Figure 3.23).

Figure 3.23
The selected format displayed in the Sample box of the AutoFormat dialog box.

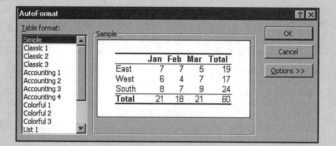

3 Select Accounting 1 from the **T**able format list box. In the Sample box, Excel displays the selected format.

4 Choose OK, or press ↵Enter.

5 Click a cell outside the selected range to see the change.

6 Save your changes and keep the worksheet open for the next tutorial.

Objective 5: Use Conditional Formats

Conditional formats are a new feature in Excel 97. Conditional formats make it easy to format cells depending on whether or not specific conditions in the cell are met. For example, you could format a cell so that it is displayed in red with a border around it if the value in the cell falls below a lower limit and displays the cell in blue if the cell's value exceeds an upper limit.

This feature can be used to apply a different font style, pattern, shading, or border to cells whose values fall outside or within the limits you specify. Several options are available when you choose the Conditional Formatting feature (see Figure 3.24).

Figure 3.24
The Conditional Formatting dialog box.

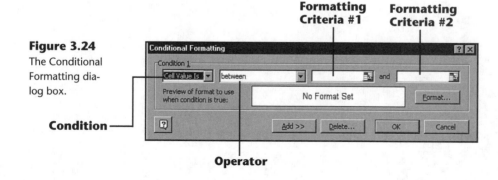

The left-most column enables you to decide if you want to use the values in the selected cells as the formatting criteria (Cell Value Is), or to evaluate data or a condition other than the values in the selected cells (Formula Is). The second column displays the operators available for setting the conditional format. The third column (and fourth column if needed) enables you to enter a value or a formula for the condition you want to format in the selected cell range.

To use the values in the selected cells as the data criteria, click Cell Value Is, select the comparison phrase, then type a value in the appropriate formatting value box.

To evaluate data or a condition other than the values in the selected cells, use a formula as the data criteria. Click Formula Is in the box on the left and then enter the formula in the box on the right. The formula must evaluate to a logical value of TRUE or FALSE. For example, if you selected Formula Is, entered the formula =IF(d3*3>100,1,d3*3) in the formula box, and then added a format when cell D3 had a value greater than 100, the formatting changes would occur.

3

Applying and Adding Conditional Formats to Cells Using Cell Labels as the Formatting Criteria

To apply conditional formats to the Formatting workbook, follow these steps:

❶ Select the range A5:A9.

❷ Choose Format, Conditional Formatting to display the Conditional Formatting dialog box (refer to Figure 3.24). Close the Office Assistant if it appears.

❸ Because you want to use the labels in the selected cells as the formatting criteria, select Cell Value Is in the first drop-down text list, if it isn't already selected.

The alternative option is to select Formula Is, but because the entries in column A are labels, you must use the first option.

❹ In the operators drop-down list box (second box from the left), select equal to.

> ### Note
>
> When the Cell Value Is option is selected, eight conditional operators are available in the second drop-down list box.

❺ In the formatting criteria text box, enter **Southeast**.

❻ Click the Format button to display the Format Cells dialog box.

The Format Cells dialog box enables you to select the format elements you want to apply. With conditional formatting, you can apply only one conditional format to a cell at a time.

(continues)

Applying and Adding Conditional Formats to Cells Using Cell Labels as the Formatting Criteria (continued)

7 Click the Patterns tab and choose bright yellow (fourth row, third from the left) for the cell shading; then click OK.

8 Click the **A**dd button to add another condition to the selected cell range.

> **Note**
>
> Up to three conditions can be specified in one conditional format.

9 Select Cell Value Is in the first drop-down list box.

10 Select equal to in the operators drop-down list box.

11 In the formatting criteria text box, enter **Northwest**.

12 Click the Format button to display the Format Cells dialog box.

13 Click the Patterns tab; choose bright blue (second row, third from the right) for the cell shading and then click OK.

14 Click OK to close the dialog box; then click cell A1 to see the results of the conditional formatting in cells A5:A9.

> **Note**
>
> If only one cell had been selected before you chose the Conditional Formatting command, you must use the Format Painter button for the format to be applied to all cells.

15 Save your changes and keep the worksheet open for the next tutorial.

In the next tutorial, you use cell values, instead of cell labels as the formatting criteria.

Applying and Adding Conditional Formats to Cells Using Cell Values as the Formatting Criteria

To apply conditional formats to the Formatting workbook, follow these steps:

1 Select the range C5:F9.

2 Choose F**o**rmat, Con**d**itional Formatting to display the Conditional Formatting dialog box.

3 Because you want to use the values in the selected cells as the formatting criteria, select Cell Value Is in the first drop-down text box.

4 Select between in the operators drop-down list box.

5 In the first formatting criteria text box, enter **65,000**; enter **70,000** in the second formatting criteria text box.

6 Click the Format button to display the Format Cells dialog box.

7 Click the Patterns tab and choose bright yellow for the cell shading; then click OK.

8 Click the **A**dd button to add another condition.

9 Select Cell Value Is in the first drop-down text list.

10 Select between in the operators drop-down list box.

11 In the first formatting criteria text box, enter **70,001**; enter **75,000** in the second formatting criteria text box.

12 Click the Format button to display the Format Cells dialog box.

13 Click the Patterns tab; choose pale yellow (fifth row, third from the left) for the cell shading and then click OK.

14 Click the **A**dd button to add another condition.

15 Select Cell Value Is in the first drop-down text box.

16 Select between in the operators drop-down list box.

17 In the first formatting criteria text box enter **75,001** and enter **95,000** in the second formatting criteria text box.

18 Click the Format button to display the Format Cells dialog box.

19 Click the Patterns tab; choose light pink (fifth row, first color on the left) for the cell shading and then click OK.

20 Click OK to close the Conditional Formatting dialog box; then click cell A1 to see the results of the conditional formatting in cells C5:C9.

21 Save your changes and keep the worksheet open for the next tutorial.

Changing and Removing Conditional Formats

In the following tutorials you change and remove conditional formats in the Formatting workbook.

Changing Conditional Formats

To change conditional formats in the Formatting workbook, follow these steps:

1 Select cell A5.

Cell A5 has the conditional format you want to change.

2 Choose Format, Conditional Formatting to display the Conditional Formatting dialog box (see Figure 3.25).

(continues)

3

Changing Conditional Formats (continued)

Figure 3.25
The Conditional Formatting dialog box showing two existing conditional formats.

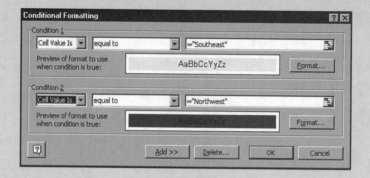

3 In the Condition **1** section, click the F**o**rmat button.

4 Select pale blue (fourth row, fourth from the right) as the new format color; then click OK.

5 Click OK again to return to the worksheet to see the change in color.

> ### Note
>
> The color change affected only the selected cell. To change the color of the other cell meeting the condition (Southeast), you must use the Format Painter button.

6 Select cell A5; then click the Format Painter button on the Standard toolbar.

7 Select cell A7. The selected cell automatically receives the formatting from the source cell (A5).

8 Save your changes and keep the worksheet open for the next tutorial.

In the following tutorial, you remove conditional formats.

Removing Conditional Formats

To remove conditional formats from the Formatting workbook, follow these steps:

1 Select cells A5:A9.

These cells have the conditional format you want to remove.

2 Choose **E**dit, Cle**a**r, **F**ormats. The formats are removed (see Figure 3.26).

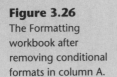

Figure 3.26
The Formatting
workbook after
removing conditional
formats in column A.

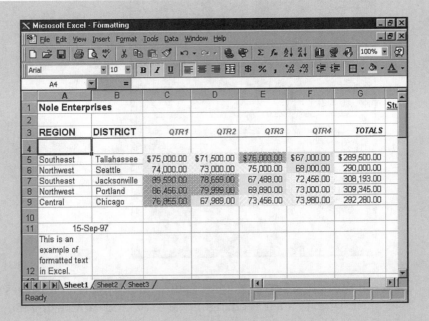

3 Save your changes and keep the worksheet open for the next tutorial.

Objective 6: Check Spelling in the Worksheet

Spell check
A feature enabling
you to check for
misspelled words,
unusual capitaliza-
tion, and repeated
words.

The *spell check* feature in Excel enables you to check for spelling errors and correct errors in worksheets, macro sheets, and charts. Excel provides two ways for
you to perform a spelling check. You can click the Spelling button on the Standard toolbar, or you can choose the **S**pelling command in the **T**ools menu. Excel
displays misspelled words, repeated words in a single cell, and words that do not
display a normal pattern of capitalization. You can spell check the entire
worksheet, a chart, a single word, or a defined range. If you do not select a word
or range of words, Excel checks the spelling for all text in the worksheet, including headers, footers, footnotes, annotations, and hidden text.

In addition to the spell check feature, Excel provides an AutoCorrect feature.
With the AutoCorrect feature, you type a word or abbreviation and Excel auto-
matically replaces it with the text or graphic you have previously specified in the
AutoCorrect dialog box (see Figure 3.27).

Figure 3.27
The AutoCorrect
dialog box.

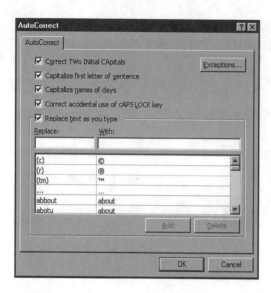

AutoCorrect is also available to automatically correct mistakes that you frequently make such as changing *hte* to *the* and capitalizing more than the first letter in a sentence. AutoCorrect entries can be added during a spelling check and as you enter labels and text into your Excel worksheet.

Caution

Do not use the AutoCorrect feature or the Spell Check feature to add words to the Microsoft dictionary on public-use computers, such as classroom computers. Add words only to your own personal computer system or that of your organization.

Spell Checking Your Worksheet

To use the spell checker on the Formatting workbook, you begin by entering a misspelled word that the spell checker can find. Follow these steps:

1 To enter a misspelled word, make cell G3 the active cell; type **Totl** and press **Enter**.

2 Select cell A1 to begin spell checking from the beginning of the worksheet. Spell checking starts from the point of the active cell and moves forward to the end of the worksheet.

3 Choose **T**ools, **S**pelling. Excel begins checking for misspelled words, repeated words, and unusual capitalization. The Spelling dialog box is displayed if a word appears to be misspelled (see Figure 3.28).

Figure 3.28
The Spelling dialog box.

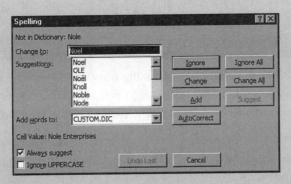

④ When the spell checker questions the word `Nole`, click the **I**gnore button.

Each time a word is displayed in the dialog box, you can choose to ignore the word, ignore all identical words found throughout the worksheet, change the word, change all identical words found throughout the worksheet, include the word as an AutoCorrect selection, or add the word to the dictionary.

To leave a word unchanged, choose the **I**gnore button. To leave the word unchanged throughout the entire worksheet, select I**g**nore All.

To delete a repeated word, choose the **D**elete button. Excel removes the repeated word and the unnecessary spaces between the remaining words.

To add a word to the dictionary, choose the **A**dd button. This choice adds the new word to the list of correctly spelled words in the spelling check dictionary.

To add a word to the AutoCorrect list, choose the A**u**toCorrect button. This choice adds the new word to the list of AutoCorrect words.

To clear the dialog box, choose OK, or press ⎋.

Caution

Make sure that a word is spelled correctly before you add it to the dictionary.

---

❺ If the spell checker questions the spelling of your name in cell H1, click the **I**gnore button.

❻ When the spell checker finds `Totl` misspelled, scroll down the Suggesti**o**ns list box and select Total. `Total` now appears in the Change **t**o text box.

(continues)

Spell Checking Your Worksheet (continued)

> **Note**
>
> To substitute the misspelled word with the word suggested in the Change **t**o text box, choose the **C**hange button. To change all examples of the same word found throughout the entire worksheet, choose the Change All button.
>
> To use a different correction, select a word from the Suggestions list box and choose the **C**hange or Change All button. If Excel cannot suggest an alternative word, the misspelled word appears in the Change **t**o text box. You can ignore the word by choosing the **I**gnore button, or you can type a new word in the Change **t**o text box and then choose the **C**hange button.

7 To replace the misspelled word with *Total*, choose the **C**hange button.

8 When Excel has finished spell checking a worksheet, a message box is displayed indicating that the spell check is complete for the entire worksheet (see Figure 3.29).

Figure 3.29
The message box indicating that the spell check is complete.

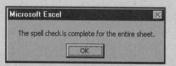

9 Save the worksheet.

10 Print two copies of the worksheet—one to keep and one to turn in to your instructor.

11 Close the workbook.

> **Note**
>
> If a misspelled word is entered in all uppercase letters, Excel does not identify it as misspelled. To be spell checked, a word must be all lowercase or have only the first letter (or first few letters) capitalized.

You can also spell check your worksheet by using the Spelling button on the standard toolbar. First, select the cell where you want the spelling check to start. Next, click the Spelling button to display the Spelling dialog box.

Chapter Summary

This chapter covers the commands and features that enable you to improve the appearance of your worksheets. You have learned about number formats, including date and time formats. You learned how to format using the AutoFormat feature and the Conditional Format feature. You learned to center text over columns, align text vertically and horizontally, change fonts, style, and apply justification. Finally, you learned how to check the spelling in your worksheet.

Chapter 4, "Using Functions," introduces you to Excel Functions. Excel has over 200 built-in functions to assist you in developing formulas. You learn what a function is, what the various types of functions are, and what some of the built-in functions do.

Checking Your Skills

True/False

For each of the following statements, circle *T* or *F* to indicate whether the statement is true or false.

T F **1.** If you want dollar signs or commas to appear in the numbers in your worksheet, you must type them as you enter each number into a cell.

T F **2.** Three different number formats are available in Excel.

T F **3.** If you type 7–10–97 in a cell, Excel performs a subtraction operation.

T F **4.** A button on the Standard toolbar enables you to italicize text in a worksheet.

T F **5.** You can insert a heavy dark line below the contents of a cell by using the **B**order command in the F**o**rmat menu.

T F **6.** An Excel Style is a combination of formatting characteristics.

T F **7.** You can use the Excel spelling checker to check charts and worksheets for misspellings.

T F **8.** The F**o**rmat, **C**enter command enables you to select long text entries and spread the text over a selected area.

T F **9.** The Patterns tab of the Format Cells dialog box enables you to choose foreground and background colors.

T F **10.** The formatting criteria for conditional formats must be numbers (values or formulas).

Multiple Choice

In the blank provided, write the letter of the correct answer for each of the following.

1. The spell checker is accessed from the _____ menu.

   a. Help

   b. Format

   c. Tools

   d. Options

2. Which of the following refers to the range of cells from A5 to E5?

   a. A5-E5

   b. A5:E5

   c. A5>E5

   d. none of the above

3. Which of the following alignments is the Excel default for numbers in cells?

   a. left

   b. center

   c. right

   d. wrap

4. Which of the following *cannot* be formatted using the Formatting toolbar?

   a. fonts

   b. type size

   c. column width

   d. numbers

5. Which of the following alignments is the Excel default for text in cells?

   a. left

   b. center

   c. right

   d. wrap

6. To _____ text within a cell causes a long string of text to appear on multiple lines within a cell.

   a. align

   b. justify

   c. wrap

   d. locate

7. Which of the following formats in the Style dialog box is the Excel default?

   a. Normal

   b. Standard

   c. Currency

   d. none of the above

8. In the spell checker, which of the following buttons replaces a misspelled word in a worksheet?

   a. Add

   b. Change

   c. Replace

   d. Select

9. Which of the following formatting tools is found on the Formatting toolbar?

   a. Bold

   b. Center

   c. Italic

   d. all the above

10. Which of the following can be done to the contents of a cell using the Format, Cells command?

   a. applying double underlining

   b. using a color in a cell

   c. placing an outline around a cell

   d. all the above

Fill in the Blank

In the blank provided, write the correct answer for each of the following statements.

1. To display text vertically, you first choose the _____ command in the Format menu.

2. Use the _____ to copy existing formats to other cells.

3. You can use the _____ button on the Formatting toolbar to center text in a cell.

4. You can change the appearance of text, numbers, or cells in a worksheet by using a(n) _____ command.

5. _____ format is the Excel default for numbers in a cell.

6. _____ alignment is the Excel default for text in a cell.

7. When applying borders, the _____ inserts a border separating each cell in a selected range.

8. You can underline the contents of a cell by using one of the buttons on the _____ toolbar.

9. When using the Conditional Format feature, up to _____ conditions can be specified in one conditional format.

10. Use the _____ menu to access the Spelling feature.

Applying Your Skills

Review Exercises

Exercise 1: Using the AutoFormat Command

In this exercise, you use the AutoFormat feature and the Spell check feature.

1. Open Chap0302 and save it as **Autoformat**.

2. Spell check the worksheet, correcting any misspelled words.

3. Use the AutoFormat command to apply the Classic 2 format to your worksheet.

4. Print two copies of the worksheet—one to keep and one to turn in to your instructor.

5. Save and then close the worksheet.

Exercise 2: Using Format Features

In this exercise, you use several formatting commands.

1. Open the Chap0303 and save it as **Formatting 2**.

2. Use the Font Size button to increase the font size of the heading, 1st Quarter 1997, to 14.

3. Use the Bold button to make the headings boldface; then use the Border command to underline the column headings with a thick, bright blue line.

4. Change the font size of the column headings to 10.

5. Center the column headings over each column.

6. Use the Format, Cells command to format all the numbers as currency with zero decimal places.

7. Use the spell checker to check for misspellings in the worksheet. Are names always identified as possible misspellings?

8. Print two copies of the worksheet—one to keep and one to turn in to your instructor.

9. Save and then close your worksheet.

Exercise 3: Aligning Entries

In this exercise, you practice aligning cells.

1. Open Chap0304 and save it as **Formatting 3**.

2. Use the Font Size button to increase the font size of the title, Cape Sales & Marketing, to 14.

3. Use the Font Size button to increase the font size of the subtitle, Sales & Bonuses First Quarter, 1997, to 12.

4. Use the Center Across Selection option to center the entries in Rows 1 and 2 across columns A through B.

5. Use the Bold button to make the title and the subtitle boldface.

6. Center the column headings, Employee and 1st Quarter Sales, over each column.

7. Change the font size of the column headings to 10 point.

8. Use the Format, Cells command to format all the numbers with zero decimal places.

9. Rotate the column headings at a –45 degree angle.

10. Adjust the height of row 3 to 66 so that the headings display at a –45 degree angle.

11. Use the Wrap text feature to wrap the text in cell A20.

12. Print two copies of the worksheet—one to keep and one to turn in to your instructor.

13. Save and then close the worksheet.

Exercise 4: Creating Conditional Formats

In this exercise, you create conditional formats in column F of a worksheet.

1. Open Chap0305 and save it as **Formatting 4**.

2. Select the range F4:F18.

3. In the Conditional Formatting dialog box for the first condition, enter the following information:

Condition 1	>80,000	Red (in third row)
Condition 2	>70,000	Yellow (in fifth row)
Condition 3	>60,000	Lime green (in fourth row)

4. If necessary, use the Best Fit feature to adjust column widths to display their contents.

5. Print two copies of the worksheet—one to keep and one to turn in to your instructor.

6. Save and close the worksheet.

Exercise 5: Using the Format Painter

In this exercise, you use the Format Painter to copy cell formats.

1. Open Chap0306 and save it as **Formatting 5**.

2. Select cell B4 (Cherry Drink); then choose Format, Cells and click the Patterns tab.

3. In the Cell Shading Color palette, click the red square.

4. Select cell B5 (Lemon Drink); then choose Format, Cells and click the Patterns tab.

5. In the Cell Shading Color palette, click the yellow color.

6. Select cell B6 (Cola Drink); then choose Format, Cells and click the Patterns tab.

7. In the Cell Shading Color palette, click the brown color located in the third row.

8. Select cell B4 (Cherry Drink) and use the Format Painter button to copy the format to every cell in column B that contains the entry Cherry Drink.

9. Select cell B5 (Lemon Drink) and use the Format Painter button to copy the format to every cell in column B that contains the entry Lemon Drink.

10. Select cell B6 (Cola Drink) and use the Format Painter button to copy the format to every cell in column B that contains the entry Cola Drink.

11. Print two copies of the worksheet—one to keep and one to turn in to your instructor.

12. Save and close the worksheet.

Continuing Projects

Project 1: Aligning a Worksheet

Open the Cape Enterprises Client Satisfaction form, Chap0307. Bold the title. Center the title across columns A through F. Align the column headings so that the text is wrapped, centered vertically, and aligned at a 90 degree angle. If necessary, adjust the column width and row height to display the headings.

Place a thick, outline border around the column headings. Insert the current date in cell A2 and format it using the date format 03/04/97. Save the workbook as **Real Estate 3**, and print two copies of the worksheet—one to keep and one to turn in to your instructor.

Project 2: Formatting a Worksheet

Open the financial workbook, Chap0308. Change the font size of the entry in cell A1 to 12 points. Bold the entries in cells A1 and A2. Center the entries in rows 1 and 2 across columns A through F. Italicize the entries in row 4. Place a thick, outline border around the entries in rows 1 and 2. Color the Week 1 entries yellow; color the Week 2 entries green; color the Week 3 entries pink; color the Week 4 entries blue and color the Total entries in column F red. Insert a double-line border at the bottom of the entries in row 9. Save the workbook as **Employee 3**. Print two copies of the worksheet—one to keep and one to turn in to your instructor.

Project 3: Applying Conditional Formats to a Worksheet

Open Chap0309 and save it as **Vehicle Mileage 3**. Change the font of the title in A1 to 12 points. Center the contents of rows 1 and 2 of columns A through F. Insert the current date in cell A3 and format it using the date format March 4, 1997. Create conditional formats for the range B5 through F10 using the following conditions: Condition 1>70=red; condition 2>50=bold; condition 3>30 italic. Print two copies of the worksheet. Resave the workbook.

Chapter 4

Using Functions

Excel provides nearly 200 built-in functions. A function is a predefined formula that performs calculations on the data in your worksheet. Knowledge of these functions empowers you as a worksheet user and helps you work more efficiently.

Using an Excel function in your worksheet is often much easier and more efficient than writing a formula yourself. With a function, you do not have to enter mathematical operators as you do in a formula. As you build a worksheet, you usually find that Excel has functions to save you time and effort. You can use a function by itself in a cell, as part of a formula, or in another function.

When you work with only a few cells, building a mathematical or financial formula by typing the formula and selecting cells may not seem difficult. If you need to total 50 cells, however, typing the correct formula to perform this calculation would take a great deal of time, and one typing error would make the formula incorrect. Using the SUM function makes accurately totaling a column or row easy.

This chapter explains functions, illustrates types of functions, and demonstrates how to enter functions. The types of functions included in Excel range from functions that accomplish relatively simple tasks, such as SUM, AVERAGE, or DATE and TIME functions, to functions that perform complex financial and statistical calculations, such as COS, which returns the cosine of an angle and SLN, which returns the straight-line depreciation of an asset for one period. After completing a few of the tutorials in this chapter, you will find yourself comfortable using functions and excited about the possibilities they offer for creating comprehensive worksheets.

If you need to leave your computer before you complete your work in this chapter, be sure to save your work and close the file you have been using. You can then reopen the file with the saved changes when you want to continue this chapter.

Objectives

By the time you have finished this chapter, you will have learned to

1. Understand Functions

2. Enter Functions into a Worksheet

3. Use the AutoSum Button

4. Use the Conditional Sum Wizard

5. Understand and Use the Paste Function

6. Use the Paste Function for a Variety of Functions

Objective 1: Understand Functions

Function
A predefined formula consisting of a name and one or more arguments.

Argument
The number(s), cell(s), or named range(s) that a function uses in its calculations.

A *function* is a formula, predefined by Excel, consisting of the equal sign (=), the function's name and, inside parentheses, the *argument*. The SUM function, for example, adds the numbers in selected cells. The selected cells make up the argument portion of the function. The argument of a function can be a single cell, a range of cells, a named range, or a number. Some functions require a single argument; others require multiple arguments. Multiple arguments are separated by commas. The formula bar in Figure 4.1 displays a simple SUM function that adds a list of numbers.

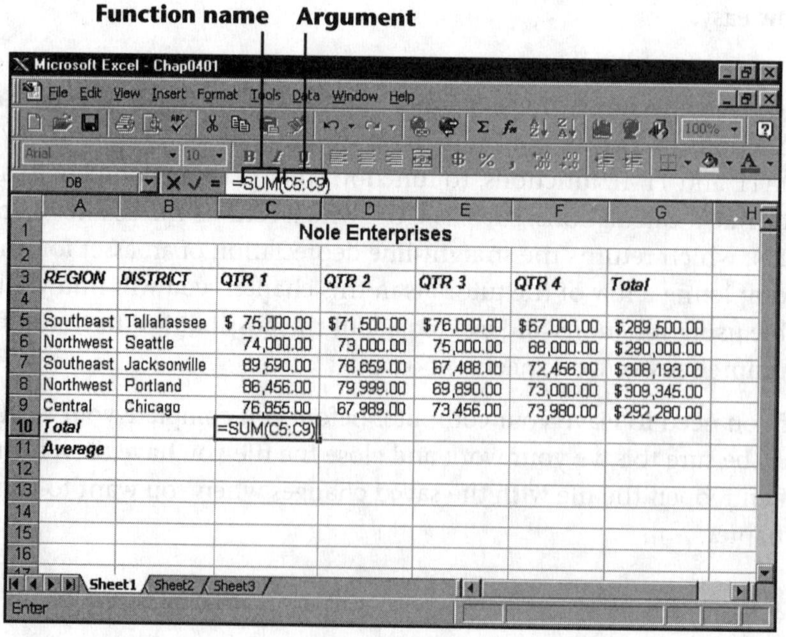

Function name   Argument

Figure 4.1
The SUM function in the formula bar.

The argument in the function is the range of cells C5 through C9. The result of this function is the sum of the values in cells C5 through C9. As with a formula, the result of a function is displayed in the cell that contains the function (cell C10), and the function is displayed in the formula bar when the cell is active.

The function in Figure 4.1 contains one argument. Other functions, however, may contain several arguments.

Objective 2: Enter Functions into a Worksheet

You have two ways to enter a function into an active cell: type the function and argument, or use the Paste function. The SUM function is probably the most frequently used function. A third way (the AutoSum button) is often available when you want to enter the SUM function if the entries to be summed meet certain criteria (as you learn about in Objective 3). In the following sections, you learn all three methods to enter functions.

Entering a Function by Typing

When typing a function, you can enter both a function name and the argument(s). Remember that, as previously mentioned, the argument of a function can refer to a range. If, for example, you are using the SUM function to add a group of numbers, you could select the range you want to sum. When a range is selected, the range appears in parentheses in the formula bar. The cell address of the first cell in the range is followed by a colon and the cell address of the last cell in the range.

4

Using the SUM Function

To use the SUM function to add cell entries, follow these steps:

1 Open Chap0401 and name it **Functions 1**.

2 Select cell C10 and type **=SUM(C5:C9)** (in either upper- or lowercase letters with no spaces in the formula) and press ⏎Enter. Notice that the total sales for QTR 1 is now displayed in cell C10.

3 Select cell C10 again. Notice that the SUM function is displayed in the formula bar.

4 Save your changes and keep the worksheet open for the next tutorial.

The AVERAGE function is another commonly used function. In the next tutorial, you learn how to use the AVERAGE function.

Using the AVERAGE Function

To find the average (the mean) of the sales for the first quarter in the Functions 1 workbook, follow these steps:

1 Make cell C11 the active cell.

2 Type **=AVERAGE(C5:C9)** and press ⏎Enter.

The average sales for QTR 1 is now displayed in cell C11.

3 Save your changes and keep the worksheet open for the next tutorial.

After entering the function and the opening parenthesis, you can indicate to Excel which range of cells to use as the argument by clicking and dragging over the cells; you do not have to type the final parenthesis.

Entering a Function Argument by Clicking and Dragging

To enter a function in the Functions 1 workbook by clicking and dragging, follow these steps:

❶ Select cell D10 and type **=SUM(**.

❷ Place the mouse pointer on cell D5. Press and hold down the left mouse button while you drag the mouse pointer to cell D9. Release the mouse button.

Notice that the range is selected and is now the argument of the function displayed in the formula bar and in cell D10.

❸ Press ⏎Enter to complete the function.

The sales figure for QTR 2 is now displayed in cell D10.

❹ Save your changes and keep the worksheet open for the next tutorial.

If you have problems... When you enter a function, one of the most common errors is leaving out a comma between arguments. Another common mistake is inserting spaces into the function. Do not enter spaces anywhere in a function.

If you need to edit a function, select the formula bar by pressing F2 or clicking the formula bar. When in edit mode, the values in the cell addresses referenced in the function display colored borders. The cell references in the function appear in the same color as the borders. This feature, the Range Finder, is new in Excel 97. Use normal editing procedures to make insertions or deletions. In some cases, if you have an error in your function, a message dialog box is displayed. The message prompts you to correct the error. Choose OK or press ⏎Enter to clear the error message dialog box. The part of the function causing the error is selected in the formula bar, you can then determine what the error is. Check for such mistakes as missing commas, too many commas, or blank spaces in the selected area.

Using Named Ranges in Functions

Using a named range as the argument of a function is especially efficient. This practice also makes a calculation easier to understand if a coworker uses your worksheet or if you are modifying a worksheet that you created months ago. Which of the three following examples is easier to understand?

=G5+G6+G7+G8+G9

=SUM(G5:G9)

=SUM(TOTALS)

Using a Named Range in a Function

In Chapter 2, "Building a Worksheet," you learned how to name a range and created a range named TOTALS. When you saved the workbook, the range name information was saved with the worksheet. After you have named a range in a worksheet, when you save your workbook, you also save the range name. Functions 1 is a workbook similar to the one you worked with in Chapter 2. The range name and labels that you created in Chapter 2 are contained in Functions 1. In the following set of tutorials, you use that named range in a SUM function and an AVERAGE function.

Using a Named Range in a SUM and an AVERAGE Function

The name TOTALS applies to the range G5:G9 in the Functions 1 workbook. To find the sum and average of the totals in column G, follow these steps:

1 Select cell G10.

2 Type **=SUM(TOTALS)** and press ⏎Enter.

The total sales for all regions for all four quarters appears in cell G10.

3 In cell G11 type **=AVERAGE(TOTALS)** and press ⏎Enter.

The average sales for all regions for all four quarters appears in cell G11.

4 Use the Format Painter to format the values in cells G10 and G11 so that they display as the entries in cells G5:G9.

5 If necessary, use the Best Fit feature to widen column G to display the values.

Your worksheet should appear similar to Figure 4.2.

Figure 4.2
The Functions 1 workbook after using named ranges in the Total column.

	Microsoft Excel - Functions 1						
	File Edit View Insert Format Tools Data Window Help						
	Arial ▾ 10 ▾ **B** *I* U ≡ ≡ ≡ ⊞ $ % , ⁀.⁀⁀ ⁀⁀ ⊞ ▾ ⌀ ▾ **A** ▾						
	G11 = =AVERAGE(Totals)						
	A	B	C	D	E	F	G
1	Nole Enterprises						
2							
3	*REGION*	*DISTRICT*	*QTR 1*	*QTR 2*	*QTR 3*	*QTR 4*	*Total*
4							
5	Southeast	Tallahassee	$ 75,000.00	$ 71,500.00	$76,000.00	$67,000.00	$ 289,500.00
6	Northwest	Seattle	74,000.00	73,000.00	75,000.00	68,000.00	$ 290,000.00
7	Southeast	Jacksonville	89,590.00	78,659.00	67,488.00	72,456.00	$ 308,193.00
8	Northwest	Portland	86,456.00	79,999.00	69,890.00	73,000.00	$ 309,345.00
9	Central	Chicago	76,855.00	67,989.00	73,456.00	73,980.00	$ 292,280.00
10	*Total*		$401,901.00	$371,147.00			$1,489,318.00
11	*Average*		$ 80,380.20				$ 297,863.60
12							
13							
14							
15							
16							
	Sheet1 / Sheet2 / Sheet3 /						
	Ready						

6 Save your changes and keep the worksheet open for the next tutorial.

The Standard toolbar and the formula bar contain a number of elements that relate to functions and named ranges (see Figure 4.3 and Table 4.1)

Figure 4.3
Standard toolbar and formula bar buttons that relate to functions.

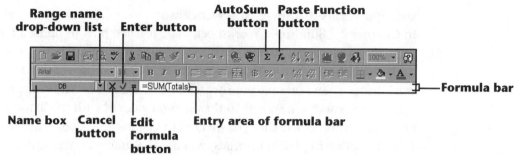

Range name drop-down list • Enter button • AutoSum button • Paste Function button • Formula bar

Name box • Cancel button • Edit Formula button • Entry area of formula bar

=SUM(Totals)

Table 4.1 Standard Toolbar and Formula Bar Elements for Creating Functions	
Name	**Description**
Standard Toolbar	
AutoSum	Enables you to total a range, places the SUM function in a cell or cells.
Paste Function	Guides you through the process of creating any function.
Formula Bar	
Name box	Shows cell reference or name of active cell.
Range Name drop-down list	Displays a list of named cells or ranges.
Cancel button	Click to cancel the function.
Enter button	Click to enter the function into the cell.
Edit formula button	Click to display the Formula Palette.
Entry area	Displays formula function as you create or edit it.

Objective 3: Use the AutoSum Button

AutoSum button
Clicking this button is an efficient way to total rows or columns in your worksheet.

Although you can enter a formula or SUM function to total a column or a row of your worksheet, clicking the *AutoSum button* is usually more efficient. AutoSum attempts to generate the SUM function based on the data you have entered into your worksheet. You can use the AutoSum button efficiently only when the cell containing the total is at the bottom of a column of numbers or at the end of a row of numbers. Using AutoSum is almost always faster than writing a formula.

Using the AutoSum Button

To use the AutoSum button to total a column of numbers in the Functions 1 workbook, follow these steps:

❶ Select cell E10.

Σ

❷ Click the AutoSum button.

=SUM(E5:E9) is displayed in the formula bar and the range of cells immediately above cell E10 is enclosed in a marquee (see Figure 4.4).

Figure 4.4
AutoSum produces
this function.

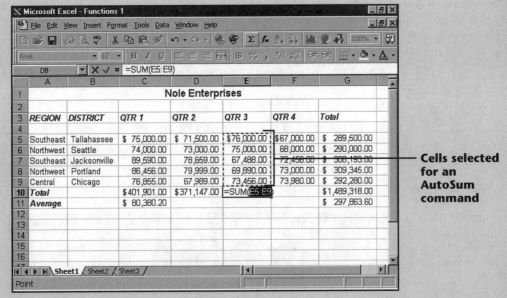

Cells selected
for an
AutoSum
command

❸ Press ⏎Enter to indicate that you want this calculation entered into cell E10.

The total of the numbers is displayed in cell E10 ($361,834.00).

❹ Delete the SUM functions in cells C10, D10, and E10 to prepare for the
next tutorial. Keep the worksheet open.

If your worksheet has a blank row at the foot of each column and you select a
range of columns and then click the AutoSum button, a SUM function for each
column is placed in the empty cell at the bottom of each column.

Using the AutoSum Button on a Range of Columns

To automatically enter SUM functions for the values in columns C, D, E, and F
of the Functions 1 worksheet, follow these steps:

❶ Select the range C5:F9.

❷ Click the AutoSum button to display totals in cells C10:F10.

❸ If necessary, use the Best Fit feature to widen columns to display the values.

❹ Verify that Excel has placed the appropriate SUM functions in cells C10,
D10, E10, and F10.

❺ Delete the entries from cells G5:G11 and the SUM functions in cells C10,
D10, E10, and F10 to prepare for the next tutorial. Keep the worksheet
open.

You can also use the AutoSum button to sum one or more rows. You need a
blank column at the end of the rows, and you need to include the blank column
in the selection. In the next tutorial, you use AutoSum to enter sum formulas for
rows and columns at the same time.

Using the AutoSum Button to Sum Rows and Columns

To automatically create SUM functions for the rows and columns of a selection in the Functions 1 workbook, follow these steps:

1 Select the range of cells C5:G10.

2 Click the AutoSum button.

Your screen should now look like Figure 4.5. Note that the correct SUM functions for both the columns and the rows have been entered in the proper positions. AutoSum gives you one way to "work smarter—not harder" in Excel.

Figure 4.5
The worksheet with the functions to sum the rows and columns.

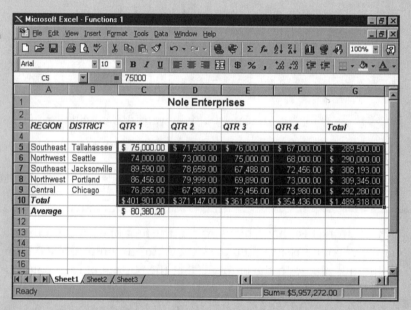

3 Save your changes and keep the worksheet open for the next tutorial.

Objective 4: Use the Conditional Sum Wizard

A new feature in Excel 97 is the Conditional Sum Wizard. The Conditional Sum Wizard enables you to sum only the data in a list that meets specified criteria. You can specify more than one condition to fine-tune a summary report.

Using the Conditional Sum Wizard

To use the Conditional Sum Wizard to total a column of numbers in the Functions 1 workbook, follow these steps:

1 Clear all functions from row 10.

2 Select the range A3:F9.

3 Choose **T**ools, **W**izard, **C**onditional Sum to display the Step 1 Conditional Sum Wizard dialog box (see Figure 4.6).

Figure 4.6
Step 1 of the
Conditional Sum
Wizard.

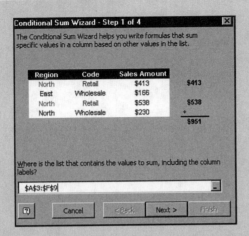

④ Click the Next button to display Step 2 of the Conditional Sum Wizard
dialog box (see Figure 4.7).

Figure 4.7
Step 2 of the
Conditional Sum
Wizard.

4

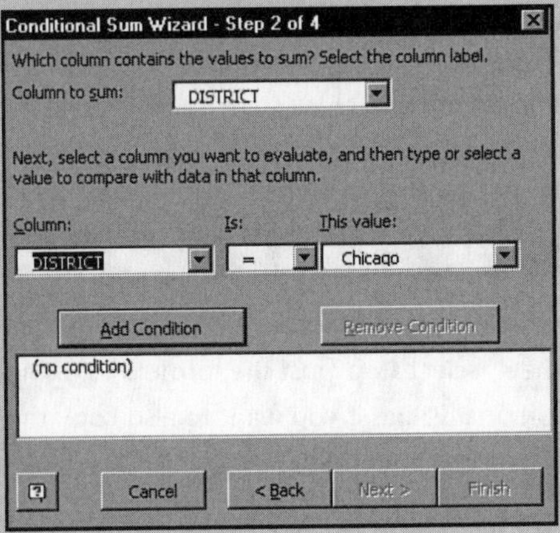

⑤ Click the Column to **s**um drop-down arrow and select Qtr 1 from the list.

⑥ In the **C**olumn drop-down list, select REGION.

⑦ In the **I**s drop-down list, select =, if it is not already selected; = is the default
setting.

⑧ In the **T**his value drop-down list, select Southeast.

⑨ Click the **A**dd Condition button (see Figure 4.8).

(continues)

Using the Conditional Sum Wizard (continued)

Figure 4.8

The condition REGION=Southeast added to the Step 2 Conditional Sum Wizard dialog box.

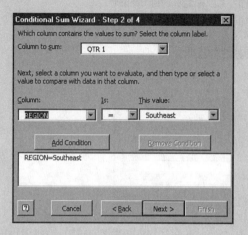

⓾ Click the Next button to display the Step 3 Conditional Sum Wizard dialog box.

⓫ Select **C**opy just the formula to a single cell option button, if it isn't already selected; then click Next to display the Step 4 Conditional Sum Wizard dialog box.

> **Note**
>
> If you want to copy only the sum formula resulting from the parameters you specified in the worksheet, select **C**opy just the formula to a single cell. Select **C**opy the formula and conditional values if you want to also copy the current parameters to the worksheet, so you can change the parameters.

⓬ Enter **C10** in the **T**ype or select a cell and then click the Finish button.

The conditional sum formula is copied into the specified cell (C10). If you make changes in the list, the results of the conditional sum automatically update, like any other formula.

⓭ Use the Format Painter to format the value in cell C10 so that it appears similar to cell C5.

Your screen should now look like Figure 4.9.

Figure 4.9
The worksheet with a conditional sum function in cell C10.

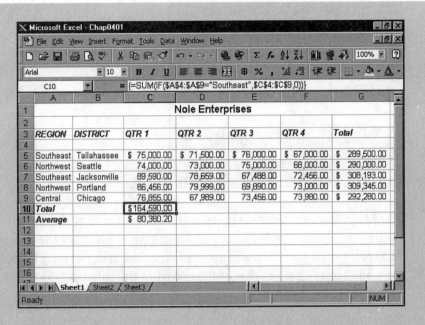

⑭ Save your changes and keep the worksheet open for the next tutorial.

4

Objective 5: Understand and Use the Paste Function

Paste Function
A sequence of dialog boxes that aid in the entry of functions in your worksheet.

So far in this chapter, you have entered functions by typing them or using the AutoSum button for the SUM function. Now you learn how to enter functions by using the *Paste Function*. The Paste Function consists of two dialog boxes that help you build your function. This tool is probably the fastest and most accurate way of entering functions—especially the functions with multiple arguments or function names that are hard to remember.

Formula Palette
Used to edit functions in formulas or to create formulas in functions.

You can access the Paste Function by selecting the **F**unction command from the **I**nsert menu or by clicking the Paste Function button on the Standard toolbar (refer to Figure 4.3). The Paste Function is designed to help you quickly find and select the appropriate function from the list of functions in Excel. Another role of the Paste Function is to guide you through the steps of entering a function and to supply the correct arguments for the function using the *Formula Palette*.

The Paste Function has two dialog boxes. In the first dialog box, the Function **c**ategory list shows the function categories (see Figure 4.10), discussed later in this chapter. The Function **c**ategory list also includes the categories Most Recently Used and All.

Figure 4.10

The first Paste Function dialog box.

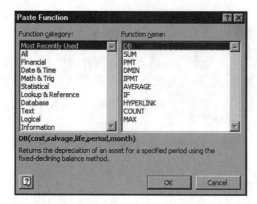

The Most Recently Used category is the collection of your recently used functions. The All category provides an alphabetical list of all the functions available in Excel. When you click a function name, the area near the bottom of the dialog box displays a short description of what the function does and a list of its arguments.

The contents of the second Paste Function dialog box change according to the function you select in the first dialog box. Figure 4.11 shows the second dialog box as it appears when you select the PMT function in the first dialog box.

Figure 4.11

The second Paste Function dialog box.

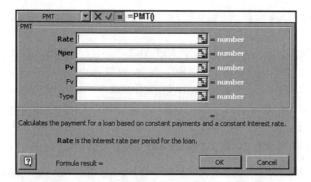

For functions with multiple argument values, the argument values you must enter (required arguments) appear in boldface type in the dialog box. The optional argument values are in normal type. In Figure 4.11, Rate (periodic interest rate), Nper (term), and Pv (present value) are the argument values you must supply; Fv (future value) and Type are optional argument values.

> **Caution**
>
> Make sure that the selected cell does not currently contain a function. Otherwise, the Formula Palette dialog box will display.

Building a SUM Function Using the Paste Function

To enter a SUM function in the Functions 1 workbook using the Paste Function, follow these steps:

1 Click cell C12 to select it.

2 Click the Paste Function button to display the first Paste Function dialog box (refer to Figure 4.10).

> ### Caution
>
> You can't use the AutoSum button in this situation because it attempts to include in the sum any numbers in cells C10 through C11, and these cells do not contain relevant sales figures (they display totals calculated using other Excel procedures). Remember, you can use the AutoSum button efficiently only when the cell containing the total is at the bottom of a column of numbers or at the end of a row of numbers.

3 The SUM function is in the Math & Trig category; click Math & Trig in the Function category list.

4 In the Function name list, scroll down the list and select SUM.

Your screen should now look like Figure 4.12.

Figure 4.12
The first Paste Function dialog box with the SUM function selected.

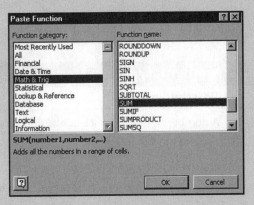

5 Click OK to display the second Paste Function dialog box.

6 In the Number1 argument edit box, type **C5:C9**.

You must enter values or cell references for each required argument before the function will work properly. Note that 401901, the sum of the values currently in that range, is displayed at the bottom of the dialog box to the right of Formula result = (see Figure 4.13).

(continues)

Building a SUM Function Using the Paste Function (continued)

Figure 4.13
The second
Paste Function
dialog box with
the SUM
function
selected.

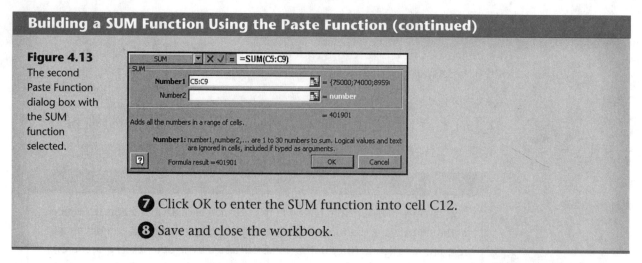

7 Click OK to enter the SUM function into cell C12.

8 Save and close the workbook.

Now that you see how the Paste Function works, in the next objective you use it to enter some new functions.

Objective 6: Using the Paste Function for a Variety of Functions

This section provides a brief description of some of the most commonly used worksheet functions, lists the arguments for each function, and provides tutorials.

Table 4.2 lists the types of arguments and their descriptions.

Table 4.2 Function Argument Types	
Argument Type	**Description**
Value	A number or cell reference containing a value.
Logical	Result is TRUE or FALSE.
Num	A number or numeric formula.
Text	Nonnumeric data; text must be enclosed in quotation marks.
Array	A range of values treated as a single group.
Serial number	A date and time.
Reference	A cell or range address.

Excel has nearly 200 built-in functions. Most of these functions are grouped (for easy access) into one of the following categories:

Database

Date & Time

DDE & External

Engineering

Financial

Information

Logical

Lookup & Reference

Math & Trigonometry

Statistical

Text

A complete listing of all the functions and a short explanation of each function is available under the Worksheet Functions topic in Excel's Help. If you need more information on the function, click the function's name in the list. You are then given an explanation of the function and examples of its use.

Understanding Database Functions

The database functions are a group of functions that refer to areas of a worksheet that are organized as a database. Most of the functions provide summary statistics, such as averages, counts, sums, and standard deviations on Excel databases. In Chapter 7, "Managing Data," you learn about Excel databases.

Understanding Date and Time Functions

Serial number
A date expressed as a number. Days are numbered from the beginning of the twentieth century.

To keep track of the date and time, Excel counts the number of days that have passed since the beginning of the 20th century. Excel uses a date *serial number* that starts with January 1, 1900, as day 1. All days from this date forward are numbered sequentially. For example, 1/25/1900 has the date serial number 25, and so on. If you use a date function to find the serial number for July 4, 1997, the serial number returned is 35615 (the number of days that have passed since January 1, 1900). Excel includes date functions for converting the day, month, year, and time to serial numbers and functions to convert a serial number to the actual date or time.

> **Caution**
>
> In order for the NOW function to show the correct date and time, your computer must have the time and date set properly.

The date and time cell formats discussed in Chapter 3, "Formatting Worksheets," are designed to be used with the date and time functions so that you have complete control over the appearance of dates and times in your worksheet. When a date function is used in a cell, the cell's format is automatically changed from General, the default, to a date format. To see the actual serial number of a date, you use the DATE function in a cell and then change the format of the cell back to General.

The functions TODAY and NOW enable you to use the current date or the current date and time, respectively. The NOW function is useful for documents that must always include the current date and time. Some of the date and time functions are listed in Table 4.3.

Table 4.3   Some Commonly Used Date and Time Functions

Function	Description
DATE(year,month,day)	Returns specified date.
DATEVALUE(date_text)	Returns date text as a serial number.
DAY(serial_number)	Returns day, as an integer from 1 to 31, corresponding to serial number.
DAYS360(start_date,end_date)	Returns number of days between two dates.
HOUR(serial_number)	Returns hour, as an integer from 0 to 23, corresponding to serial number.
NETWORKDAYS	Returns the number of (start_date,end_date,holidays) whole working days between start_date and end_date; working days exclude weekends and any dates identified in holidays.
NOW( )	Returns serial number of current date and time.
TIME(hour,minute,second)	Returns serial number of time specified by hour, minute, and second.
TODAY( )	Returns serial number of current date.
YEAR(serial_number)	Returns year corresponding to serial number.

Note

For a complete listing of Excel functions, see Help.

Entering a Date Function into a Cell

To enter a date function into a cell, follow these steps:

❶ Click the New button on the Standard toolbar to start a new workbook.

❷ With cell A1 selected, click the Paste Function button to display the first Paste Function dialog box.

❸ In the Function category list, click Date & Time.

❹ In the Function name list, click NOW.

❺ Click OK to display the second Paste Function dialog box (see Figure 4.14). The NOW function has no arguments.

Figure 4.14
The second Paste Function dialog box for the NOW function.

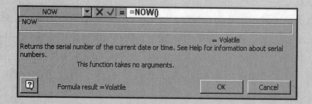

❻ Click OK. The date and time are displayed in cell A1 (see Figure 4.15).

Figure 4.15
The date and time displayed in a worksheet.

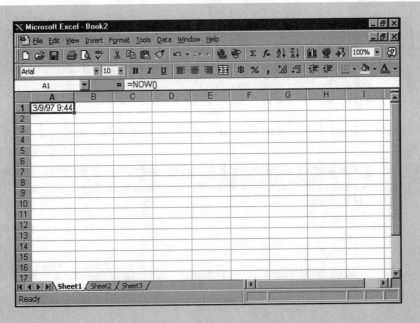

7 Choose Format, Cells. In the Format Cells dialog box, click the Number tab. In the Category list box, select Number to see the serial number of the date and time in the sample box.

8 In the Category list box, select Time. In the Type list box, select 3/4/97 1:30 PM to see the date as it is displayed in Figure 4.15.

> **Note**
>
> The cell won't display AM or PM; only if the cell is selected will the formula bar display AM or PM.

9 Close without saving the workbook.

Understanding Financial Functions

Annuity calculations
Calculations based on a series of even payments over a specified time.

Excel has built-in financial functions to calculate payments on a loan, depreciation, present and future values, internal rate of returns, net present value, and other *annuity calculations*. An annuity function performs a calculation based on a series of even payments over a specified time. You don't have to understand higher finance to use these functions—you just fill in the blanks. The factors involved in solving most annuity problems are PV (present value) or FV (future value), NPER (number of periods), PMT (payment each period), and RATE (periodic interest rate). These factors are all available as functions in Excel.

The arguments for the PMT function are Nper, Rate, Pv, Fv, and Type; Type and Fv (future value) are optional arguments. The periodic interest rate is the annual interest rate divided by 12; the interest rate must be in months because the payments are in months. The present value is the amount of the loan. Because this payment is an outflow of cash, the result always appears in the cell as a negative number.

Table 4.4 summarizes some of Excel's financial functions.

Table 4.4 Some Commonly Used Financial Functions	
Function	**Description**
ACCRINT(issue,first_interest, settlement,coupon,par, frequency,basis)	Accrued interest for a security that pays periodic interest.
ACCRINTM(issue,settlement,rate, par,basis)	Accrued interest for a security that pays interest at maturity.
CUMPRINC(rate,nper,pv, start_period,end_period,type)	Cumulative principal paid on a loan between start_period, and end_period.
DISC(settlement,maturity,pr, redemption,basis)	Discount rate for a security.
EFFECT(nominal_rate,nper)	Effective annual interest rate.
FV(rate,nper,pmt,pv,type)	Future value of an investment.
FVSCHEDULE(principal,schedule)	Future value of an initial principal after applying a series of compound interest rates.
IRR(values,guess)	Internal rate of return for list of values.
NPV(rate,value1,value2,...)	Net present value for list of values.
PV(rate,nper,pmt,fv,type)	Present value of an investment.
SLN(cost,salvage,life)	Straight-line method of depreciation.

Entering a Financial Function into a Cell

To use the PMT function to calculate the monthly payments on a $15,000 loan at 9 percent for 3 years, follow these steps:

1 Click the New button on the Standard toolbar to start a new workbook.

2 Change the width of column A to 15.

3 With cell A1 selected, click the Paste Function button to display the first Paste Function dialog box (refer to Figure 4.10).

4 In the Function **c**ategory list box, click Financial.

5 In the Function **n**ame list box, click PMT.

6 Click OK to display the second Paste Function dialog box (refer to Figure 4.11).

7 In the Rate argument edit box, type **0.09/12** (to convert annual to monthly interest rate) and press ⌨Tab⌨ to move to the next argument edit box. Do not press ⌨Enter⌨.

8 In the Nper argument edit box, type **36** (the number of payment periods) and press ⌨Tab⌨ to move to the next argument edit box.

9 In the Pv argument edit box, type **15000** (the amount of the loan).

The second Paste Function dialog box should now look like Figure 4.16.

Figure 4.16
The PMT required arguments filled in.

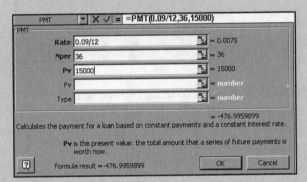

10 Click OK. The monthly payment of $477.00 should appear in red in cell A1. Because this is money being paid out, Excel recognizes it as a negative number. Excel displays negative numbers in red and/or in parentheses.

11 Close without saving the workbook.

Understanding Information Functions

You can use Excel's information functions to analyze cells, columns, rows, and ranges. These parts of a worksheet may need to be analyzed before you perform a calculation, function, or macro.

The IS functions enable you to test the type of entry in a cell or range; the functions return a logical value of TRUE or FALSE. If a cell meets the condition of the function, the value of the cell is TRUE. If the cell does not meet the function condition, the value is FALSE. For example, if you want to determine whether a cell is blank, you can use the ISBLANK function. If the cell is blank, the value is TRUE; otherwise, the value of the cell is FALSE. The IS functions are generally used with IF functions to establish the contents of a cell or range. In Figure 4.17, the two functions are combined to establish whether cell D10 contains text. The IF and ISTEXT functions are entered as a combined function in cell A1.

Figure 4.17
The IF and ISTEXT functions used together in cell A1.

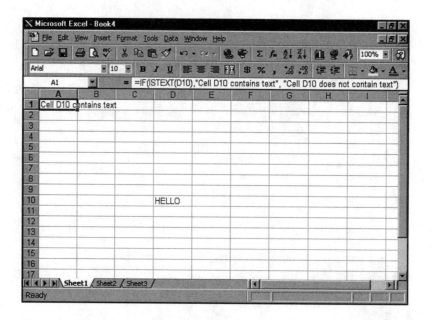

The IF function includes arguments to define value_if_true and value_if_false. The value_if_true argument is defined as the message Cell D10 contains text. The value_if_false argument is defined as the message Cell D10 does not contain text. If the result of the function in cell A1 is true, cell A1 displays the message Cell D10 contains text. If the result of the function in cell A1 is false, cell A1 displays the message Cell D10 does not contain text. You must enter text arguments in quotation marks.

Understanding Logical Functions

Excel's logical functions are used frequently for testing conditions and making decisions. The IF function enables you to set conditions. You can combine the IF function with other logical functions, such as AND and OR, to test for multiple conditions. Logical functions are listed and described in Table 4.5.

Table 4.5   Logical Functions

Function	Description
AND(logical1,logical2,...)	Returns TRUE if every argument is TRUE.
IF(logical_test,value_if_true, value_if_false)	Returns value_if_true if test is TRUE; returns value_if_false if logical value is FALSE.
NOT(logical)	Reverses TRUE and FALSE logicals.
OR(logical1,logical2,...)	Returns true if any argument is TRUE.

Using the IF Function

To use the IF function to see whether the numbers in two cells are equal, follow these steps:

1 Click the New button on the Standard toolbar to start a new workbook.

2 Enter **5** in cell A1 and **10** in cell B1.

3 In cell D1, enter the following IF function:

=IF(A1=B1,"THE NUMBERS ARE EQUAL","THE NUMBERS ARE NOT EQUAL"); then press ⏎Enter.

This function displays the message THE NUMBERS ARE NOT EQUAL in cell D1 because the numbers in cells A1 and B1 are not equal. If the numbers were equal, the function would displays the message THE NUMBERS ARE EQUAL in cell D1.

4 Enter the number **5** in cell B1 and press ⏎Enter, and note the result (THE NUMBERS ARE EQUAL).

5 Edit the IF function in cell D1 so the function is now **=IF(A1=B1, A1–B1,A1*B1)**. 0 displays in cell D1.

6 Enter the number **6** in cell A1; note that 30 displays in cell D1.

7 Close without saving the workbook.

4

Understanding Lookup and Reference Functions

Array
A rectangular range of values or formulas treated as one group.

Lookup functions are used to retrieve a value or cell reference from a table or an *array* in a worksheet. Examples of lookup functions include LOOKUP, MATCH, and various INDEX functions. Table 4.6 lists some of the lookup functions.

Table 4.6   Lookup and Reference Functions

Function	Description
HLOOKUP(lookup_value,table_array, row_index_num)	Searches across the top row of range until value is met.
LOOKUP(lookup_value,array)	Value in array selected by lookup value.
VLOOKUP(lookup_value,table_array, col_index_num)	Searches down the first column of range until value is found.

Using the Lookup and Reference Worksheet Functions

When you need to find values in lists or tables or when you need to find the reference of a cell, you can use the lookup and reference worksheet functions. There are two Lookup functions: VLOOKUP, which searches for a value in the leftmost column of a table and then returns a value in the same row from a column you specify in the table; and HLOOKUP, which searches for a value in the top row of a table or an array of values and then returns a value in the same column from a row you specify in the table or array. Both LOOKUP functions are useful for teachers and professors when developing gradebooks using Excel.

Using the HLOOKUP Function

To use the HLOOKUP function to determine letter grades; follow these steps:

1 Open Chap0402 and save it as **Grades**.

2 Select cell B3 and click the Paste Function button to display the first Paste Function dialog box.

3 In the Function **c**ategory list box, click Lookup & Reference.

4 In the Function **n**ame list box, click HLOOKUP, and then click OK.

5 In the Lookup_value edit box, type **C3** (the location of the first cell to be evaluated) and press [Tab⇆] to move to the next argument edit box.

6 In the Table_array edit box, type **$A$15:$K$16** and press [Tab⇆] to move to the next argument edit box. In the Row_index_num argument edit box, type **2**.

The range $A$15:$K$16 represents the range of grades and their numeric percentage as displayed in the worksheet. The Row_index num argument entry of 2 indicates that the second row in the range $A$15:$K$16 contains the results to be inserted in C3 (the location of the first cell to be evaluated).

7 Click OK.

The course grade of A- is displayed in cell B3.

8 Copy the function to cells B4:B13. *Hint*: Select cell B3, then click the Copy button on the Standard toolbar. Select the range B4:B13, then click the Paste button.

The worksheet should now look like Figure 4.18.

Figure 4.18
The results of the copied function.

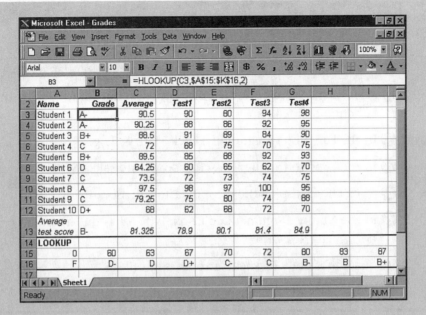

9 Print two copies of the worksheet—one to keep and one to turn in to your instructor. Save and then close the worksheet.

Understanding Math and Trig Functions

Excel's built-in mathematical functions enable you to perform standard arithmetic operations. Other mathematical functions enable you to round and truncate numbers. These types of mathematical functions are the basis for using mathematical functions in building a worksheet.

Excel also includes several trigonometric functions, used primarily to build complex scientific and engineering formulas, and matrix functions, used primarily for solving complex problems that involve several unknown variables in an array, a rectangular range of values or formulas treated as a single group.

You can use three mathematical functions to round a number to certain specifications. The INT function rounds a number down to the nearest integer. The TRUNC function shortens a number to its next lower integer, and the ROUND function rounds a number up or down. Some of the commonly used built-in mathematical functions are listed in Table 4.7.

Table 4.7 Commonly Used Math and Trig Functions

Function	Description
ABS(number)	Absolute value of number.
INT(number)	Number rounded down to the nearest integer.
RAND( )	Random number between 0 and 1.
ROUND(number,num_digits)	Rounds number to specified number of digits.
SQRT(number)	Square root of number.
SUM(number1,*number2*,...)	Total of arguments.
TRUNC(number,num_digits)	Changes number to an integer by truncating the decimal portion.

Entering a Math and Trig Function in a Cell

To determine the square root of a number, follow these steps:

1 Click the New button on the Standard toolbar to open a new workbook.

2 Select cell A5 and click the Paste Function button to display the first Paste Function dialog box.

3 In the Function **c**ategory list, click Math & Trig.

4 In the Function **n**ame list, scroll down and select SQRT.

5 Click OK to display the second Paste Function dialog box.

6 In the Number argument edit box, type **68** as the argument of the function; then click OK.

The square root of 68 (8.246211) appears in cell A5.

7 Close the workbook without saving it.

Understanding Statistical Functions

Excel includes a comprehensive set of statistical functions. These functions enable you to find the average, minimum, maximum, standard deviation, or variance of a group of values in your worksheet. Many commonly used statistical tests, such as the T-test, Chi-Squared, and F-test, are available as functions. Other statistical functions include the TREND, LINEST, LOGEST, and GROWTH functions. You can use these functions to calculate lines and curves that fit data. Table 4.8 lists some of the most commonly used statistical functions built into Excel.

Table 4.8 Statistical Functions

Function	Description
AVERAGE(number1,*number2*,...)	Returns average of defined range.
COUNT(value1,*value2*,...)	Returns total of nonblank cells in range.
MAX(number1,*number2*,...)	Returns largest number in defined range.
MEDIAN(number1,number2,...)	Returns middle value in defined range.
MIN(number1,*number2*,...)	Returns smallest number in defined range.
MODE(number1,*number2*,...)	Returns the most frequently occurring value in a range of data.
STDEV(number1,*number2*,...)	Returns standard deviation for a sample.
VAR(number1,number2,...)	Returns variance for a sample.

Entering a Statistical Function into a Cell

To enter a statistical function into a worksheet, follow these steps:

❶ Open Chap0401.

❷ In cell C10, type **=MAX(C5:C9)** and press ⏎Enter. This function finds the largest value in the range (89,590).

Keep this worksheet open for the next tutorial.

In a small worksheet, the usefulness of functions, such as MAX and MIN, may not be obvious. In a worksheet with hundreds or thousands of entries, these functions are essential.

Understanding Text Functions

Excel includes a number of built-in text functions that help you find or edit text in a cell or range. Several of these functions are listed in Table 4.9.

Table 4.9   Text Functions

Function	Description
LOWER(text)	Changes text to all lowercase.
PROPER(text)	Changes text to lowercase with first character capitalized.
TEXT(value,format_text)	Converts number value to formatted text value.
UPPER(text)	Changes text to all uppercase.
VALUE(text)	Converts text to numbers.

Entering a Text Function into a Cell

To enter a text function into a cell, make sure that the Chap0401 worksheet is open. Follow these steps:

❶ In cell A4, type **=LOWER(A3)** and press ⏎Enter.

Because cell A3 contains REGION, cell A4 contains the same text in lowercase letters.

❷ Close Chap0401 without saving your changes.

Chapter Summary

In this chapter, you have been introduced to functions. You have learned what a function is, what an argument is, and how you use functions to improve accuracy and efficiency in formulas. You have also learned how to use AutoSum and the Function Wizard.

This chapter provides several tables outlining the different types of functions, giving the required and optional arguments, and summarizing what each function does. Excel's Help contains a complete reference for all Excel functions.

Chapter 5, "Managing Workbooks," deals with various aspects of managing worksheets and workbooks. The chapter introduces you to the Excel commands for moving among worksheets in workbooks, moving and copying worksheets, inserting and deleting worksheets in a workbook, setting up the printer, previewing a document before printing, and adjusting margins and columns in Print Preview mode. You learn how to define a print area, define titles to be printed on every page, change the printer orientation, and create headers and footers for a document.

Checking Your Skills

True/False

For each of the following, circle *T* or *F* to indicate whether the statement is true or false.

T F **1.** AutoSum is useful when the cell containing the total is at the bottom of column of numbers or at the end of a row of numbers.

T F **2.** The parameters in a function are the pieces of data a function acts on to produce a result.

T F **3.** A properly entered function begins with =.

T F **4.** If multiple arguments are used in a function, they must be separated by semicolons.

T F **5.** All functions require an argument.

T F **6.** Spaces cannot be included in a function.

T F **7.** Use the Conditional Sum Wizard when you need to sum data that meets specific criteria.

T F **8.** Functions can be entered into a cell only by using the Paste Function.

T F **9.** Functions can be edited in the formula bar.

T F **10.** Excel serial numbers begin with January 1 of the current year.

Multiple Choice

In the blank provided, write the letter of the correct answer for each of the following.

1. Which of the following is *not* a category of functions available in Excel?

    a. Date and Time

    b. Statistical

    c. Financial

    d. Graphics

2. Day number 1 in Excel is _____.

    a. 1/1/1900

    b. today's date

    c. January 1 of the current year

    d. none of the above

3. In Excel, a date expressed as a number is a(n) _____.

    a. argument

    b. parameter

    c. array number

    d. serial number

4. Which of the following can be used as an argument in a function?

    a. a cell

    b. a range

    c. a number

    d. all the above

5. Which function returns the serial number of today's date?

    a. SERIAL

    b. DAY

    c. DATEVALUE

    d. none of the above

6. Which function returns the current date and time?

    a. TIMEVALUE

    b. TODAY

    c. NOW

    d. none of the above

7. Excel stores dates as _____.

    a. functions

    b. text

    c. serial numbers

    d. all the above

8. Which of the following functions converts a number to an integer by cutting off the decimal portion?

    a. INTER

    b. ABS

    c. TRUNC

    d. all the above

9. Which of the following functions returns the serial number of today's date?

    a. DATE

    b. DAY

    c. DATEVALUE

    d. none of the above

10. Which of the following functions could be used to calculate your monthly payment for a new car?

    a. COST

    b. IRR

    c. PMT

    d. RATE

4

Fill in the Blank

In the blank provided, write the correct answer for each of the following statements.

1. A(n) _____ is a predefined formula.

2. In a function, the _____ appears inside parentheses.

3. The _____ function tells you the number of days between two dates.

4. The function that rounds a number to a specified number of digits is the _____ function.

5. A complete explanation of all the functions available in Excel is found in Excel's _____.

6. The _____ number of a date is the number of days from the beginning of this century.

7. The _____ function can be used to calculate the monthly payments on a home loan.

8. The _____ function finds the largest number in a range of numbers.

9. The _____ function returns the most frequently occurring number in a range of numbers.

10. The _____ function returns the average of a range of numbers.

Applying Your Skills

Review Exercises

Exercise 1: Applying SUM, AVERAGE, and DATE & TIME Functions

In this exercise, you use several commonly used Excel functions.

1. Open Chap0403 and save it as **Coastal**.

2. Use the SUM function to calculate total expenses for each month.

3. Use the AutoSum button to calculate totals in column F.

4. Use the AVERAGE function to calculate averages in column G.

5. Format the values in the Average column as numbers with no decimal places.

6. Use the NOW function in cell A15 to display the current date and time in the default format.

7. Print two copies of the worksheet—one to keep and one to turn in to your instructor.

8. Save and close the worksheet.

Exercise 2: Using the Conditional Sum Wizard

In this exercise, you use the Conditional Sum Wizard to calculate totals.

1. Open Chap0404 and save it as **Beverages**.

2. In cells A58, A59, and A60 enter **TOTAL**.

3. In cell B58 enter **Cherry Drink**.

4. In cell B59 enter **Lemon Drink**.

5. In cell B60 enter **Cola Drink**.

6. Use the Format Painter to copy the format for each of the three beverage types displayed in cells B4:B57 to cells B58:B60.

7. Select the range A2:D57; then use the Conditional Sum Wizard to sum the Cherry Drink beverage and insert the value in cell D58. Hint: the column to **s**um is Units Sold, the **C**olumn = Beverage Type, **I**s = equal, and **T**his value = Cherry Drink.

8. Repeat step 7 for the Lemon Drink and the Cola Drink. Insert the Lemon Drink total in cell D59. Insert the Cola Drink total in cell D60.

9. Print two copies of the worksheet—one to keep and one to turn in to your instructor.

10. Save and then close the worksheet.

Exercise 3: Using Statistical Functions

In this exercise, you use several statistical functions to calculate the MIN, MAX, and the AVERAGE.

1. Open Chap0405 and save it as **Cape Sales**.

2. In cell B20 insert the MAX function for the range B4:B18.

3. In cell B21 insert the MIN function for the range B4:B18.

4. In cell B22 insert the AVERAGE function for the range B4:B18.

5. Print two copies of the worksheet—one to keep and one to turn in to your instructor.

6. Save and then close the worksheet.

Exercise 4 Using Logical Functions

In this exercise, you create and copy an IF function statement.

1. Open Chap0406 and save it as **Bonus**.

2. In cell H5 enter the function: **=IF(G5>5000,"Bonus!","No Bonus!")**.

3. Copy the function to cells H6:H32.

4. Print two copies of the worksheet—one to keep and one to turn in to your instructor.

5. Save and then close the worksheet.

Exercise 5: Using Lookup Functions

In this exercise, you create and copy a LOOKUP function.

1. Open Chap0407 and save it as **Evaluation**.

2. In cell F4 enter the function **(=HLOOKUP(E4,$A$21:$D$22,2)**.

3. Copy the function to cells F5:F18. Notice that only one employee will receive a warning.

4. Print two copies of the worksheet—one to keep and one to turn in to your instructor.

5. Save and then close the worksheet.

Continuing Projects

Project 1: Using Statistical Functions in the Cape Enterprises Worksheet

Open the Cape Enterprises Client Information form, Chap0408, and save it as **Real Estate 4**. In cells B35:F38, use AVERAGE, MEDIAN, COUNT, and STANDARD DEVIATION statistical functions to determine the average, median, count, and standard deviation for the data in columns B:F. Print two copies of the worksheet (one to keep and one to turn in to your instructor); then save the worksheet.

Project 2: Inserting SUM, AVERAGE, and IF Functions in the Kipper Industries Sales Worksheet

Open the Kipper Industries Sales worksheet, Chap0409, and save it as **Employee 4**. In cells B11:F12, use SUM and AVERAGE statistical functions to determine the total and average sales for each week in July. In cell G5 enter the function: **=IF(F5>100000,"YES!","NO!")**. Copy the function to cells G6:G9. Print two copies of the worksheet (one to keep and one to turn in to your instructor); then save the worksheet.

Project 3: Applying Math & Trig, Date & Time, and Lookup Functions to the Coastal Sales Worksheet

Open the Coastal Sales worksheet, Chap0410, and save it as **Vehicle Mileage 4**. In column H, insert totals for each vehicle, using the SUM function. In column I, insert averages for each vehicle using the AVERAGE function. In cell J5, insert the function =HLOOKUP(H5,$A$13:$C$14,2). Copy the function to cells J6:J10. Print two copies of the worksheet (one to keep and one to turn in to your instructor); then save the worksheet.

Chapter 5

Managing Workbooks

Organizing and printing the worksheets in Excel workbooks are valuable skills. In the first section of this chapter, you learn how to organize your worksheets: to name, move, copy, insert, and delete a workbook's sheets. Next, you learn how to use Excel's Zoom command to view your worksheet at different degrees of magnification. By zooming out, you reduce the image of your worksheet so that you can see more of it on your screen. By zooming in, you magnify an area of the worksheet so that you can format it more precisely.

Controlling the way your worksheets and charts are printed is also an important skill in Excel. By completing the tutorials in the last sections of this chapter, you learn to print professional-looking worksheets. You learn how to set up a page for printing, preview your printout on-screen, define a print area, use *headers* and *footers*, and choose where the page breaks will occur in a large worksheet.

If you need to leave your computer before you complete your work in this chapter, be sure to save your work and close the file you have been using. You can then reopen the file with the saved changes when you want to continue this chapter.

Header
Repeated text, such as a page number and document title, that appears at the top of each page of the document.

Footer
Repeated text, such as a page number and document title that appears at the bottom of each page of the document.

Objectives

By the time you have finished this chapter, you will have learned to

1. Move among the Worksheets in a Workbook
2. Rename Worksheets
3. Move and Copy Worksheets within Workbooks
4. Insert and Delete Worksheets in a Workbook
5. Use the Zoom Command
6. Set Up the Page for Printing
7. Add Headers and Footers
8. Use Print Preview
9. Insert Manual Page Breaks
10. Print Worksheets

Objective 1: Move among the Worksheets in a Workbook

In Excel, most of your work will involve the use of worksheets. As you have learned, worksheets are contained in workbooks. At the bottom of each worksheet window is a tab that identifies that worksheet. After you have opened a workbook, you can go directly to a worksheet by clicking its tab.

> **Note**
>
> Worksheets are also referred to as sheets. Worksheet tabs are also referred to as sheet tabs or tabs.

In Excel, you can see the tabs for only a few worksheets in your workbook at the bottom of your screen. However, you can scroll a different set of tabs into view. To see the tabs for other sheets, you click the tab scrolling buttons to the left of the sheet tabs (see Figure 5.1). The two outermost tab scroll buttons—the ones with the arrow and the vertical line—scroll to the first or the last tab in the workbook. The two innermost tab scroll buttons—the ones without the line—scroll one tab in the direction of the arrow.

Figure 5.1
The tab scrolling buttons and sheet tabs.

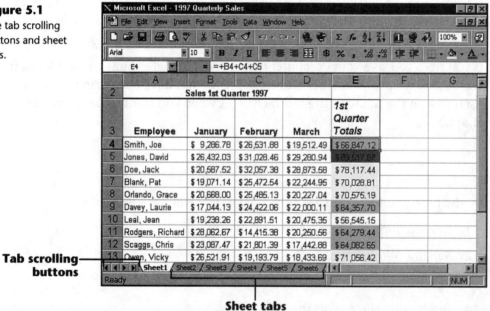

Moving among Worksheets

To move among the worksheets in a workbook, follow these steps:

❶ Open Chap0501 and save it as **1997 Quarterly Sales**.

❷ Place the mouse pointer on the tab labeled Sheet3, and click the left mouse button. Notice that data for February sales is displayed.

❸ Click the tab for Sheet1. Notice that it is just as you left it, displaying summary information for the first quarter.

❹ Click the tab for Sheet3 again. You can see that Sheet1 and Sheet3 are two separate worksheets.

The worksheet tabs and tab scrolling buttons enable you to move quickly among the worksheets in a workbook.

❺ Click the right-arrow tab scrolling button several times. Notice that the sheet tabs change as you scroll to the right. Next, click the right-arrow button with the vertical line to display the last sheet name in the workbook (Sheet11).

❻ Click the left-arrow tab scrolling button several times. Notice that the sheet tabs change as you scroll to the left. Next, click the left-arrow button with the vertical line to display the Sheet1 tab.

❼ Click the Sheet1 tab to display Sheet1—the first worksheet in the workbook.

❽ Save your changes and keep the workbook open for the next tutorial.

Objective 2: Rename Worksheets

A workbook can contain one worksheet (sheet) or as many as 255 worksheets. When you start a new workbook, Excel (by default) provides three blank worksheets named Sheet1, Sheet2, and Sheet3. You can add or delete worksheets in a workbook.

Sheet1, Sheet2, or Sheet3 are not useful worksheet names because you can't tell from the tab name what is in the worksheet. Worksheet names have not been an issue for you so far because you have generally used only the first worksheet in a workbook and you have named the workbook file so that you know what is in the worksheet in the workbook. You will find that grouping and organizing your worksheets and charts into workbooks is helpful—even necessary. Meaningful names on the sheet tabs are invaluable when you want to find information quickly.

You can use blank sheets for one of three different purposes: as worksheets, charts, or Visual Basic modules. You are already familiar with worksheets. You learn about charts in Chapter 6, "Creating Charts and Maps," and about Visual Basic modules (sometimes called macros) in Chapter 8, "Using Excel Macros to Automate Repetitive Tasks."

When you have more than just a few sheets in a workbook, it is helpful to use tab (sheet) names that indicate both the type—worksheet, chart, or macro—and the contents of the sheet. You can change tab names by using the Format menu, a shortcut menu, or by double-clicking the sheet tab. Tab names can be up to 31 characters long, and the tab of the active worksheet is always shown in boldface type.

5

Renaming a Sheet Tab

To change the name of a sheet tab in the 1997 Quarterly Sales workbook so that the tab name describes the sheet's contents, follow these steps:

❶ Click the Sheet1 tab to make this the active worksheet.

❷ Click the Sheet1 tab with the right mouse button to display a shortcut menu of sheet commands (see Figure 5.2).

You can also access the sheet commands from the menu bar, but using the shortcut menu is more efficient. The menu command for renaming a worksheet tab is **F**ormat, **Sh**eet, **R**ename.

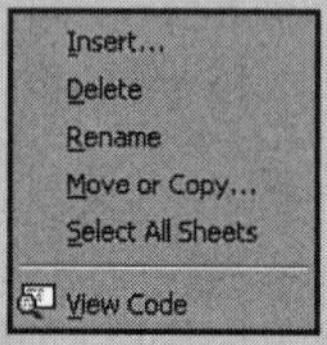

Figure 5.2
The shortcut menu of sheet commands.

Insert...
Delete
Rename
Move or Copy...
Select All Sheets
View Code

Note

In this book, when you should click with the right mouse button, you will be told to right-click; otherwise, click with the left mouse button.

❸ Click (with the left mouse button) the **R**ename command in the shortcut menu.

The Sheet1 tab is highlighted, as shown in Figure 5.3.

Figure 5.3
Ready to enter a new name for the Sheet1 worksheet.

| | | | | | Sheet1 / Sheet2 / Sheet3 / Sheet4 / Sheet5 / Sheet6 / | | | |
Ready

❹ Type **1st Quarter**, then press **↵Enter**. The sheet tab now indicates the contents of the worksheet (see Figure 5.4).

You can use up to 31 characters (including spaces) in a sheet name.

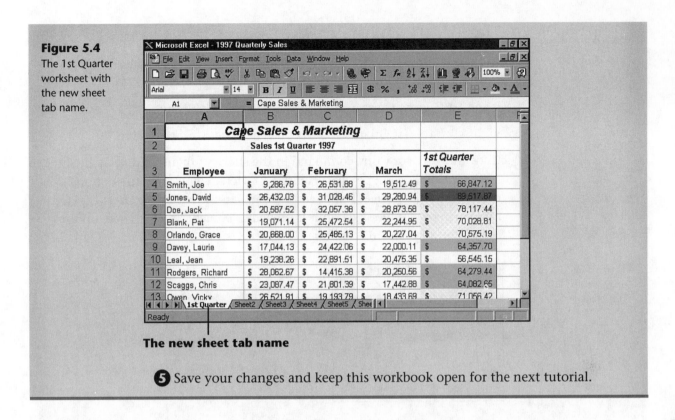

Figure 5.4
The 1st Quarter worksheet with the new sheet tab name.

The new sheet tab name

5 Save your changes and keep this workbook open for the next tutorial.

Objective 3: Move and Copy Worksheets within Workbooks

An Excel workbook is used in much the same way that you use an indexed three-ring notebook or a file folder. You place in the notebook or folder the papers that belong together. For example, in one notebook, you may place all the sheets that contain work done in one fiscal year or in the first quarter of a year. You might also organize your worksheets according to the project, vendor, or funding source.

In your workbooks, just as in your system of notebooks or files, you need to move and copy worksheets and charts (you learn about charts in Chapter 6). Up to this point in learning Excel, you have not created enough worksheets to feel the need to organize them or to move copies of a worksheet from one workbook into another workbook.

The tutorials in this objective show you how to move and copy worksheets. You can move worksheets by using the **E**dit menu, a shortcut menu, or by pressing Ctrl as you drag a sheet tab to copy the worksheet, or by pressing ⬆Shift as you drag a sheet tab to move a worksheet. As you use Excel, you will often encounter situations in which you need the skills you develop by completing the following tutorials.

Moving a Worksheet within a Workbook

To move the 1st Quarter worksheet and place it between Sheet4 and Sheet5 in the same workbook, follow these steps:

1 If the 1st Quarter sheet is not the active sheet, click its tab.

2 Right-click the 1st Quarter tab to open the Sheet shortcut menu.

3 Click the **M**ove or Copy command in the shortcut menu to display the Move or Copy dialog box (see Figure 5.5). Here, you can set the options to control whether a sheet is moved or copied and whether the sheet is placed in a different workbook when it is moved or copied. You use these options in later tutorials in this chapter.

Figure 5.5
The Move or
Copy dialog box.

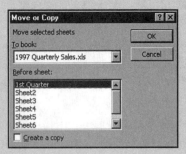

4 Because you want to move the active sheet and place it between Sheet4 and Sheet5, click Sheet5 in the **B**efore sheet list (refer to Figure 5.5).

5 Click OK to move the 1st Quarter worksheet to its new position (see Figure 5.6).

Figure 5.6
The 1st Quarter
worksheet in its
new position.

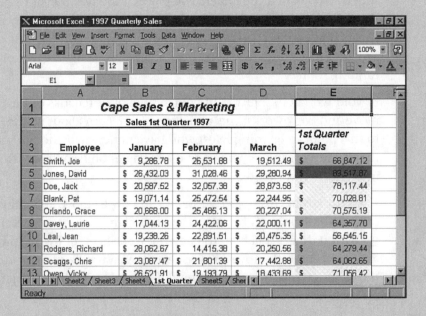

6 Save your changes and keep this workbook open for the next tutorial.

At times, you may want to have more than one copy of a worksheet in a workbook—perhaps to keep a record of figures at different times. You can add a copy of a worksheet to a different location in your workbook by using the Sheet shortcut menu.

Copying a Worksheet within a Workbook

To copy the 1st Quarter worksheet and place the copy between Sheet8 and Sheet9 in the same workbook, follow these steps:

1. If the 1st Quarter sheet is not the active sheet, click its sheet tab.
2. Right-click the 1st Quarter sheet tab to open the Sheet shortcut menu.
3. Click the **M**ove or Copy command in the menu to display the Move or Copy dialog box (refer to Figure 5.5).
4. Click the **C**reate a copy check box in the lower-left corner. You want to copy the active sheet and place the copy between Sheet8 and Sheet9 in the same workbook.
5. Scroll down in the **B**efore sheet list box until Sheet9 appears in the list.
6. Click Sheet9 and click OK.

The 1st Quarter worksheet has been copied to its new position (see Figure 5.7).

The 1st Quarter worksheet now appears twice in the workbook. Notice that Excel automatically names the copy 1st Quarter (2) so that you aren't confused by the duplicate names.

5

Figure 5.7
The 1st Quarter copy in the workbook.

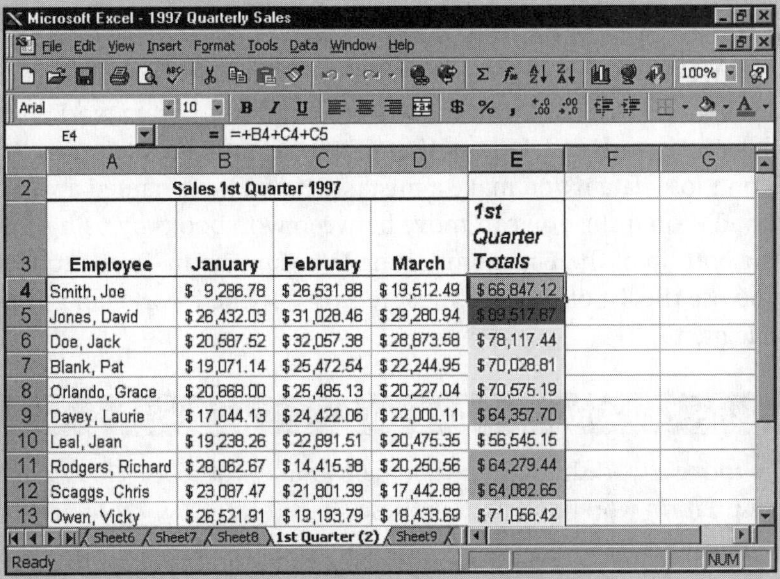

	A	B	C	D	E
2		Sales 1st Quarter 1997			
3	Employee	January	February	March	1st Quarter Totals
4	Smith, Joe	$ 9,286.78	$ 26,531.88	$ 19,512.49	$ 66,847.12
5	Jones, David	$ 26,432.03	$ 31,028.46	$ 29,280.94	$ 89,517.87
6	Doe, Jack	$ 20,587.52	$ 32,057.38	$ 28,873.58	$ 78,117.44
7	Blank, Pat	$ 19,071.14	$ 25,472.54	$ 22,244.95	$ 70,028.81
8	Orlando, Grace	$ 20,668.00	$ 25,485.13	$ 20,227.04	$ 70,575.19
9	Davey, Laurie	$ 17,044.13	$ 24,422.06	$ 22,000.11	$ 64,357.70
10	Leal, Jean	$ 19,238.26	$ 22,891.51	$ 20,475.35	$ 56,545.15
11	Rodgers, Richard	$ 28,062.67	$ 14,415.38	$ 20,250.56	$ 64,279.44
12	Scaggs, Chris	$ 23,087.47	$ 21,801.39	$ 17,442.88	$ 64,082.65
13	Owen, Vicky	$ 26,521.91	$ 19,193.79	$ 18,433.69	$ 71,056.42

7. Save your changes and keep this workbook open for the next tutorial.

Moving and Copying between Two Workbooks

Frequently, you may want to reuse all or part of a worksheet that you have already created rather than create a new one from scratch. You can keep the layout and formulas from the original worksheet but replace the data. By using the Copy command, you can copy within the same workbook, but what if you have already set up a worksheet to keep track of sales during the first quarter of 1997 and want to copy the sheet with all its headings, formats, and calculations into a workbook for 1998?

In the following tutorials, you learn how to move and copy worksheets to different workbooks. To make this move or copy, you must have both the workbook that is the source of the sheet and the workbook that is the destination for the sheet open at the same time. Use the **F**ile, **O**pen command to open a second workbook without closing the first workbook. You also need to move back and forth between the two open workbooks. By default, Excel displays the names of the four most recently used worksheets at the bottom of the **F**ile menu. (You can use the **T**ools, **O**ptions, General tab to display the nine worksheets most recently used.)

Remember, Excel displays only one workbook at a time even though several workbooks are open. To move between them, open the **F**ile menu and click the name of the workbook you want to see on-screen. You can also move to any open workbook, even if it has not been named and saved, by using the list of open workbooks at the bottom of the **W**indow menu. When several workbooks are open, you can tell which workbook is currently displayed because its name is shown in the window's title bar. A workbook does not have to be on-screen if you want to copy or move a worksheet to it; however, it must be open.

Moving a Worksheet to Another Workbook

In the following tutorial, you open a new workbook. Then you move the 1st Quarter (2) sheet to the new workbook. You do not need to create a new workbook if you want to move the worksheet to an existing workbook. You are creating a new workbook here so that you have a workbook to practice with and you won't lose data if you make a mistake. If you have named a workbook (and saved it on disk), you can move between workbooks by using the listed files at the bottom of the **F**ile menu or the **W**indow menu. In the following tutorial, you use the list of the four most recently opened workbooks at the bottom of the **F**ile menu.

To Move a Worksheet to Another Workbook

To move a worksheet from the open source workbook, 1997 Quarterly Sales, to a destination workbook, follow these steps:

 ❶ Click the New button on the Standard toolbar to open a new workbook. Then save the workbook with the name **1998 Quarterly Sales**.

You now have an open destination workbook for the worksheet that you will remove from the 1997 Quarterly Sales workbook.

❷ Switch to the 1997 Quarterly Sales workbook by selecting 1997 Quarterly Sales from the bottom of the **F**ile menu (see Figure 5.8).

Figure 5.8
The list of workbooks in the File menu.

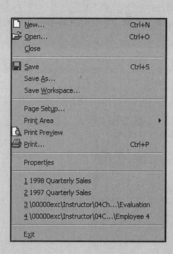

The 1997 Quarterly Sales workbook is now on-screen. The 1998 Quarterly Sales workbook is also open.

❸ Right-click the 1st Quarter (2) tab, and then choose **M**ove or Copy from the shortcut menu.

❹ Click the **T**o book drop-down arrow to display the names of the workbooks you have open and that can be used as destination workbooks (see Figure 5.9).

Figure 5.9
The **T**o book list.

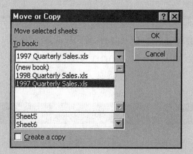

❺ Click 1998 Quarterly Sales.xls.

❻ In the **B**efore sheet list, click Sheet3; then click OK.

Excel displays the worksheet in its new location between Sheet2 and Sheet3 of 1998 Quarterly Sales (see Figure 5.10).

(continues)

To Move a Worksheet to Another Workbook (continued)

Figure 5.10
The worksheet in its new location.

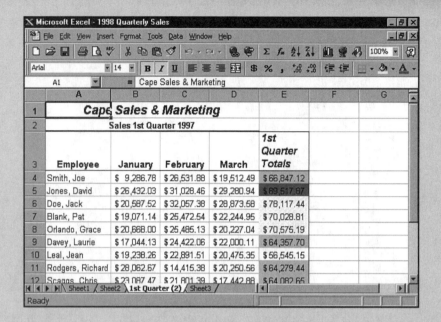

❼ Close the 1998 Quarterly Sales workbook, and save the changes.

❽ Check to make sure that the 1st Quarter (2) worksheet is not in the 1997 Quarterly Sales workbook. (It should not be there because you moved it to the 1998 Quarterly Sales workbook.)

❾ Save your changes to 1997 Quarterly Sales and keep it open for the next tutorial.

In the following tutorial, you copy a sheet from 1997 Quarterly Sales into a new workbook; the copied worksheet will be the only worksheet in the new workbook.

Copying a Worksheet to Another Workbook

To copy a worksheet to another (new and empty) workbook, follow these steps:

❶ Click the Sheet2 tab of the 1997 Quarterly Sales workbook.

❷ Right-click the Sheet2 tab; then choose **M**ove or Copy from the shortcut menu.

❸ Click the **T**o book drop-down arrow to display the names of the destination workbooks you have open and available.

Notice that 1998 Quarterly Sales is not available because it is not open; you closed it in step 8 of the preceding tutorial.

❹ Click (new book) in the **T**o book list.

❺ Click the **C**reate a copy check box so that it has a check mark in it; then choose OK.

The new workbook is displayed as Sheet2 in the new workbook. If you want to keep it, you need to name and save the workbook on your disk.

6 Check to see whether the worksheet Sheet2 is still in the workbook 1997 Quarterly Sales. (Sheet2 should still be in the 1997 Quarterly Sales workbook because you copied, not moved, the worksheet.)

7 Save your changes and keep this workbook open for the next tutorial.

Objective 4: Insert and Delete Worksheets in a Workbook

Just as you sometimes need to insert a blank piece of paper into a three-ring notebook, you sometimes need to insert a blank sheet into an Excel workbook. You also need to remove old or unused sheets from a notebook or file, and you will need to do the same in an Excel workbook. In the following tutorials, you insert a blank sheet into a workbook and delete sheets from a workbook.

Adding a Sheet to a Workbook

To add a new worksheet to the 1997 Quarterly Sales workbook, follow these steps:

1 Right-click the Sheet3 tab.

2 Choose **Insert** from the Sheet shortcut menu to display the Insert dialog box (see Figure 5.11).

Notice that the worksheet icon is already selected by default.

Figure 5.11
The Insert dialog box.

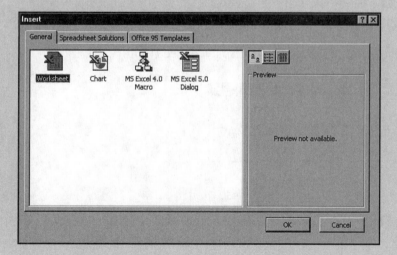

3 You want to insert a new worksheet. Click OK. The new worksheet is inserted into the workbook (see Figure 5.12).

(continues)

Adding a Sheet to a Workbook (continued)

Figure 5.12
A new worksheet
(Sheet1).

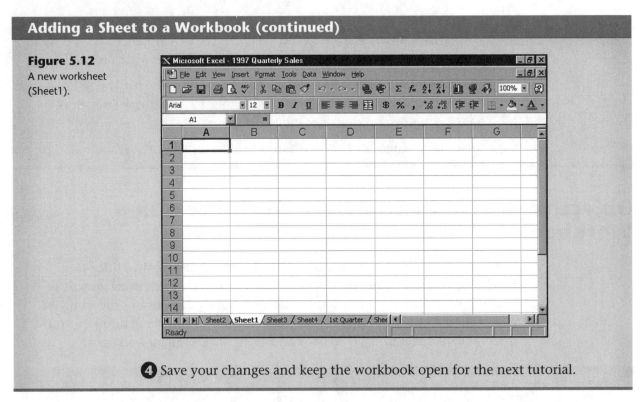

4 Save your changes and keep the workbook open for the next tutorial.

You can also easily delete a sheet from a workbook. In the following tutorial, you learn how to delete a sheet.

Deleting a Worksheet from a Workbook

To delete Sheet1 from the 1997 Quarterly Sales workbook, follow these steps:

1 Right-click the Sheet1 tab.

2 From the shortcut menu, choose **D**elete.

The Delete warning box is displayed (see Figure 5.13).

Figure 5.13
The Delete
warning box.

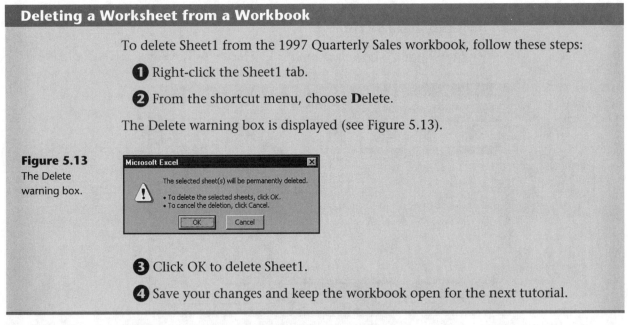

3 Click OK to delete Sheet1.

4 Save your changes and keep the workbook open for the next tutorial.

You can also delete multiple adjacent sheets from your workbook. You delete several sheets in the following tutorial.

Deleting Adjacent Sheets from a Workbook

To delete Sheets 9 through 11 from the 1997 Quarterly Sales workbook, follow these steps:

1 Click the Sheet9 tab. Then press and hold down ⬆Shift and click the Sheet11 tab. Notice that sheet tabs 9 through 11 are selected.

2 Right-click the Sheet11 tab and choose **D**elete.

3 Click OK in the Delete warning box. Sheets 9 through 11 are deleted.

4 Save your changes and keep the workbook open for the next tutorial.

You use a similar technique to delete nonadjacent worksheets from your workbook. This technique is illustrated in the following tutorial.

Deleting Nonadjacent Worksheets from a Workbook

To delete Sheets 5, 7, and 8 from the 1997 Quarterly Sales workbook, follow these steps:

1 Click the Sheet5 tab. Then press and hold down Ctrl, and click the Sheet7 and Sheet8 tabs. Sheet tabs 5, 7, and 8 are selected.

2 Right-click the Sheet8 tab and choose **D**elete.

3 Click OK in the Delete warning box. Sheets 5, 7, and 8 are deleted.

4 Save the workbook and keep it open for the following tutorial.

5

Objective 5: Use the Zoom Command

Excel's **Z**oom command in the **V**iew menu enables you to select varied degrees of magnification or reduction for viewing your worksheet. The Zoom Control Box button at the right side of the Standard toolbar is another way to zoom. The zoom reduction capability is useful when you want to see more of a worksheet on-screen. Magnifying (enlarging) an area of the worksheet enables you to see details and polish your formatting before you print. You can view the worksheet in size increments varying from 10 percent to 400 percent of the normal size. The Zoom command does not affect the way your worksheet prints; the command affects only what you see on your screen. Excel provides five preset Zoom levels.

Using the View Zoom Command to See More of a Worksheet

To use the **View**, **Z**oom command to see more of a worksheet in the 1997 Quarterly Sales workbook, follow these steps:

❶ Select Sheet2.

❷ Open the **V**iew menu and choose the **Z**oom command. The Zoom dialog box is displayed (see Figure 5.14).

Figure 5.14
The Zoom
dialog box.

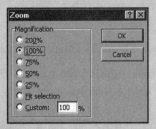

❸ Click the **5**0% option button and choose OK. Notice that you can now see more of the worksheet. The data, however, appears quite small and pound (#) signs appear in a number of cells. Recall that pound signs appear when a cell is not wide enough to accommodate a value.

❹ Return to the standard zoom size by choosing **V**iew, **Z**oom. Click the **1**00% option button and choose OK.

Keep the workbook open for the next tutorial.

You can zoom in on an area of your worksheet so that you can see it in more detail. This feature is useful for those who cannot clearly see the numbers and text displayed in Excel's standard magnification.

Magnifying a Section of a Worksheet

To increase the magnification of a worksheet in the 1997 Quarterly Sales workbook, follow these steps:

❶ Make cell A8 of Sheet 2 the active cell.

❷ Choose **V**iew, **Z**oom to display the Zoom dialog box (refer to Figure 5.14).

❸ Click the 200% option button and choose OK. Recall that pound (#) signs appear when a cell is not wide enough to accommodate a value.

❹ Return to the standard Zoom size by choosing **V**iew, **Z**oom. Click the **1**00% option button and choose OK.

Keep the workbook open for the next tutorial.

You can also zoom by using the Zoom Control Box on the Standard toolbar. Many users find that this method is more convenient than using the menu bar.

Using the Zoom Control Box

To use the Zoom Control Box on the Standard toolbar to decrease the magnification of a worksheet in the 1997 Quarterly Sales workbook, follow these steps:

1 Click the Zoom Control box drop-down arrow to display a list of magnifications.

2 In the list, click 75%. Notice that you can now see more rows and columns in your worksheet.

3 Click the Zoom Control box drop-down arrow again and select 100% to return to the standard view of your worksheet.

Keep the workbook open for the following tutorial.

Objective 6: Set Up the Page for Printing

Sometimes you may want to change certain print settings for a single document only. Excel's **F**ile, Page Set**u**p command enables you to change printer settings that affect only the active document. When you choose the **F**ile, Page Set**u**p command, the Page Setup tabbed dialog box is displayed (see Figure 5.15). You use the options in this tabbed dialog box to control the way a worksheet appears on the page. If a workbook consists of several worksheets, you must set up each worksheet for printing.

Figure 5.15
The Page Setup dialog box with the Page tab selected.

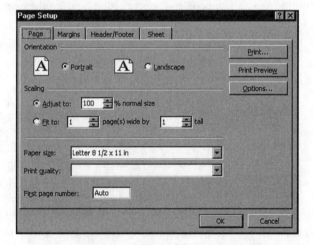

Gridlines
The intersecting horizontal and vertical lines on a worksheet.

The **F**ile, Page Set**u**p command also provides capabilities for adding headers and footers to a document, changing margins, turning on or off worksheet *gridlines*, choosing page order, and positioning worksheet data on the page. The Scaling options function only on printers that are capable of scaling and will not be covered in this text. For more information on the **F**ile, Page Set**u**p command, see *Special Edition Using Microsoft Excel 97*, from Que Corporation.

The Page Setup dialog box contains four tabs: Page, Margins, Header/Footer, and Sheet. To access the options on a tab, click the tab to display its contents. Excel's Help contains detailed information on these options. This book gives an overview of the most frequently used options.

Table 5.2 outlines the options that the **F**ile, Page Set**u**p command provides.

Table 5.2 **Important Page Setup Dialog Box Options**	
Option	**Description**
Page Tab	
Orientation	Po**r**trait prints worksheet columns vertically down the length of the paper. **L**andscape rotates the worksheet and prints it sideways on the page so that more columns can fit on one page. Use **L**andscape when you have few rows but many columns of data in your worksheet and need to fit all the columns on one page.
Paper si**z**e	You can specify paper size, appropriate for letter, legal, executive, or envelope (A4) sizes.
Fi**r**st page number	If pages are numbered in the header or footer, this option controls the starting page number. Generally, you start numbering on the first page and leave this setting at Auto.
Margins Tab	
Left, Right, Top, Bottom	Use these controls to specify the amount of space between the left, right, top, and bottom edges of the paper and the printing area.
Center on Page	Centers the document horizontally between left and right margins or vertically between top and bottom margins.
Header/Footer Tab	
Custom Header button	Displays the Header dialog box, in which you can alter the default header.
Custom Footer button	Displays the Footer dialog box, in which you can alter the default footer.
Sheet Tab	
Page order	Changes the page numbering and printing sequence on your worksheet. **D**own, then Across prints down rows page by page and then returns to the top of the next set of columns and prints down page by page. Acro**s**s, then Down prints and numbers a group of rows across columns to the right until all data is printed page by page and then goes down to the next set of rows and prints across.
Gridlines	Turns worksheet gridlines on or off for printing.
Black & white	If color formats have been used in cells and text boxes, but you have a black and white printer, use this option. The colors are removed when printing to a non-color printer.
Row & co**l**umn headings	Turns row number headings and column letter headings on or off for printing.

The **P**rint and Print Previe**w** buttons are displayed in all the Page Setup tabbed dialog boxes. Clicking the **P**rint button displays the Print dialog box so that you can immediately print your worksheet. The Print Previe**w** button displays (on a Preview screen) your worksheet as it will look when printed. To leave the Preview screen, click the **C**lose button at the top of the screen. You can try the Print Previe**w** button on your own, or you can wait until previewing is covered in detail later in this chapter.

Using the Page Setup Command to Change Print Settings

To change the default print settings in the 1997 Quarterly Sales workbook, follow these steps:

1 Print the 1st Quarter worksheet by choosing **F**ile, **P**rint. The worksheet prints according to the default page setup settings.

2 Choose **F**ile, Page Set**u**p to display the Page Setup tabbed dialog box.

3 Click the Page tab if it is not at the front of the dialog box.

4 Click the **L**andscape option button in the Orientation section so that the rows print down the length of the page.

5 Click the Sheet tab.

6 Click the Row and co**l**umn headings check box. (A check mark displays.)

7 Click the **G**ridlines check box to turn on this setting. (A check mark displays.)

8 Click the **P**rint button. The Print dialog box is displayed.

9 Click OK to print the worksheet with the new page setup settings.

10 Compare the first (default) printout with the second printout to see the effect of the changes.

Keep the workbook open for the following tutorial.

Sometimes you may find that the original (default) page setup settings are better than your altered settings for printing a document. In the following tutorial, you learn how to return to the default page setup settings.

Using the Default Page Setup Settings

To return to the default page setup settings in the 1997 Quarterly Sales workbook, follow these steps:

1 Choose **F**ile, Page Set**u**p to display the Page Setup dialog box. Click the Page tab if it is not at the front of the dialog box.

2 Choose the Po**r**trait option button in the Orientation section so that the data columns print down the page.

3 Click the Sheet tab.

4 Click the Row and co**l**umn headings check box to turn off this setting. (The check mark disappears.)

5 In the Sheet tab, click the **G**ridlines check box. (The check mark disappears.)

6 Click the **P**rint button to display the Print dialog box.

7 Click OK to print the worksheet with the current Page Setup settings.

Keep the workbook open for the following tutorial.

Defining the Print Area

Print area
Section of
worksheet defined
to be printed.

To print only a part of a worksheet, you must define that portion as a *print area*. If you select nonadjoining sections of your worksheet and define the multiple sections as a single print area, Excel prints each nonadjoining area on a separate page. If you do not define a print area, Excel assumes that you want to define the entire worksheet as the print area.

Defining a Print Area

To define a print area in the 1st Quarter worksheet of the 1997 Quarterly Sales workbook, follow these steps:

❶ Choose **F**ile, Page Set**u**p to display the Page Setup dialog box.

❷ Click the Sheet tab if it is not at the front of the dialog box.

❸ Click in the Print **a**rea text box, and type the range to print: **E3:E18**.

❹ Click the **P**rint button to display the Print dialog box. Click OK to print the worksheet. Only the range you defined as the print area prints.

Keep the workbook open for the next tutorial.

You may find that you need to remove a print area that you have set up. In the following tutorial, you learn how to do this.

Removing a Print Area

To remove the print area that you set in the 1997 Quarterly Sales workbook, follow these steps:

❶ Choose **F**ile, Page Set**u**p to display the Page Setup dialog box.

❷ Click the Sheet tab if it is not at the front of the dialog box.

❸ In the Print **a**rea text box, click and drag over E3:E18 to select it and press Del.

❹ Click OK.

❺ Print the worksheet. The entire worksheet will print.

Keep the workbook open for the next tutorial.

Sometimes you may need to print areas of the worksheet that are not adjacent. The next tutorial explains how to do this.

Defining a Print Area Containing Nonadjacent Cell Ranges

To define a print area that consists of two nonadjacent ranges in the 1st Quarter worksheet of the 1997 Quarterly Sales workbook, follow these steps:

❶ Choose **F**ile, Page Set**u**p to display the Page Setup dialog box.

❷ Click the Sheet tab if it is not at the front of the dialog box.

❸ Click in the Print **a**rea text box and type the range to print: **A3:A18,E3:E18**. Note that the two individual ranges are separated by a comma. Use commas to separate nonadjacent range specifications.

❹ Print the worksheet. Only the range you defined as the print area will print.

❺ Choose **F**ile, Prin**t** Area, **C**lear Print Area.

The print area is cleared so that in the future the entire worksheet will be printed.

Keep the workbook open for the following tutorial.

You can also use the mouse to select a part of the worksheet to print.

Defining a Print Area Using the Mouse

To print part of the 1st Quarter worksheet of the 1997 Quarterly Sales workbook, follow these steps:

❶ Select cells A3:B18 by clicking and dragging.

❷ Choose **F**ile, **P**rint to display the Print dialog box.

❸ In the Print what area, click the Selectio**n** option button.

❹ Click OK to print the selected print area.

Keep the workbook open for the next tutorial.

5

Objective 7: Add Headers and Footers

You can add headers or footers to a printout of your worksheet by using the Header/Footer tab in the Page Setup dialog box (see Figure 5.16). A header or footer creates a consistent look across all the pages of a document. You can use a header, for example, to place a title at the top of each page, and you can use a footer to automatically number each page at the bottom. Headers and footers appear one-half inch from the top or bottom of the paper.

A header or footer can include items, such as text, a page number, the current date and time, and formatting, such as boldface and italic. Excel's default header, as you have seen on your printouts, is the name of the worksheet being printed. The default footer is the page number. You can delete both of these if you choose. You change the default header or footer by clicking either the **C**ustomize Header or **C**ustomize Footer button.

Figure 5.16

The Header/Footer tab of the Page Setup dialog box.

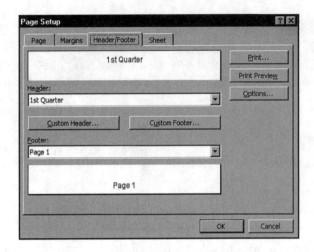

When you indicate that you want a custom header or footer by clicking the appropriate button, the Footer or the Header dialog box is displayed (see Figure 5.17). Each dialog box has three sections in which you enter header (or footer) information that will print on each page. The left section inserts information aligned with the left page margin; the center section inserts information centered on the page; and the right section inserts information aligned with the right margin.

Figure 5.17

The Header dialog box.

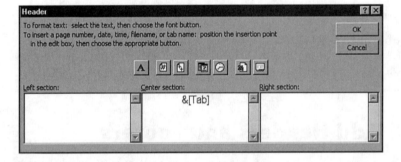

When you enter text in one of these three sections and click the appropriate icon button, Excel includes the information specified by the icon at the top or bottom of each page and left-aligns, centers, or right-aligns the text. By clicking the Font icon button in the Header or Footer dialog box, you can format the header or footer in various fonts.

Excel uses codes to assign formatting. When you click an icon in the Header or Footer dialog box, a code is inserted (and displayed) in the appropriate section. This code tells Excel what to print at that location on the page. All codes begin with an ampersand (&) and are followed by a character code. The default header setting is a &[Tab], which prints the worksheet tab name centered at the top of the page. The default footer setting is Page &[Page], which prints the word *Page* followed by the page number centered at the bottom of the page. Table 5.3 shows the other header and footer icons.

Table 5.3 Header and Footer Icons

Icon	Description
	Enables you to choose a font and other formatting options for selected header or footer text.
	Inserts page number; &[Page].
	Indicates the total number of pages in document; &[Pages].
	Inserts date; &[Date].
	Inserts time; &[Time].
	Inserts file name; &[File].
	Inserts the sheet name from the sheet's workbook tab; &[Tab].

Creating and Printing a Custom Header

To create and print a custom header in the 1st Quarter worksheet of the 1997 Quarterly Sales workbook, follow these steps:

1 Choose **F**ile, Page Set**u**p to display the Page Setup tabbed dialog box.

2 Click the Header/Footer tab.

3 Click the **C**ustom header button to display the Header dialog box (refer to Figure 5.17).

4 Type your name; it will appear in the **L**eft section window.

5 Double-click in the **C**enter section window to select the default header code.

6 Press Del to remove the code and choose OK to close the Header dialog box.

7 Choose OK to close the Page Setup dialog box.

8 Print the worksheet. You will see the revised header displaying only your name.

9 Save your changes and keep the workbook open for the next tutorial.

Footers are often useful when you print a worksheet. In the following tutorial, you learn how to create a custom footer.

Creating and Printing a Custom Footer

To create and print a custom footer in the 1st Quarter worksheet of the 1997 Quarterly Sales workbook, follow these steps:

1 Choose **F**ile, Page Set**u**p to display the Page Setup dialog box.

2 Click the Header/Footer tab.

3 Click the **Cu**stom footer button to display the Footer dialog box.

4 Click in the **R**ight section window.

5 Click the Date icon button; then press the spacebar.

6 Click the Time icon button.

7 In the **C**enter section window, select Page &[Page].

8 Press [Del].

9 Choose OK to close the Footer dialog box.

10 Choose OK to close the Page Setup dialog box.

11 Print the worksheet to see the revised footer.

12 Save your changes and keep the workbook open for the next tutorial.

Objective 8: Use Print Preview

Because a worksheet is actually one large grid of cells, you may have difficulty visualizing what a sheet will look like when you print it. Choose the **F**ile, Print Pre**v**iew command, or click the Print Preview button on the Standard toolbar whenever you want to see how a worksheet will look when you print it. The sheet will be displayed in the Print Preview window (see Figure 5.18). Excel's **F**ile, Print Pre**v**iew command enables you to view and arrange your sheet (or a print area) before you print it.

Figure 5.18
The Print Preview window.

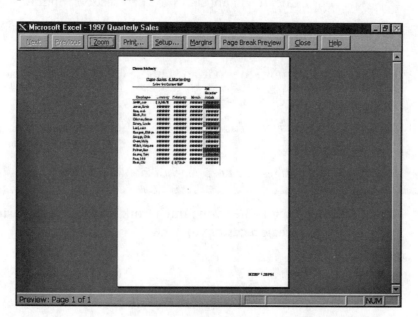

Note

Defining a print area is necessary only if you choose to print just selected areas of an entire worksheet. In the Print Preview window, you see what the document will look like when printed. The Print Preview window also includes buttons that enable you to change the margins of the document, change column width, and zoom in on a section of the document to view a section up close. Table 5.4 lists the functions of the buttons displayed at the top of the Print Preview window.

Table 5.4   The Print Preview Window Buttons

Button	Function
Next	View following page (if available).
Previous	View preceding page (if available).
Zoom	Magnify or reduce the view of the page.
Prin**t**	Display the Print dialog box.
Setup	Display the Page Setup dialog box.
Margins	Display or hide the adjusting handles to change the margins or column widths.
Page Break Pre**v**iew	View page break preview in which you can adjust the page breaks on the active worksheet.
Close	Return to the active sheet.
Help	Obtain help about using Print Preview.

Scrolling in Preview Mode

Print Preview mode
Mode in which you see an overview of the print area showing you what the page will look like when printed.

The **N**ext and **P**revious buttons located at the top of the Print Preview window enable you to move from one page to the next in *Print Preview mode*. If you are previewing a one-page document, the **N**ext and **P**revious buttons are dimmed. If you are previewing multiple pages, the **N**ext button is available only if a page follows the page you are viewing. The **P**revious button is available only if a page precedes the page you are viewing.

Zooming in Print Preview Mode

In Print Preview mode, you may not be able to see the exact detail of your document. If you need a close-up view of the document, you can zoom in and view enlarged sections of it.

Previewing and Zooming Your Worksheet

To preview and zoom in on the 1st Quarter worksheet of the 1997 Quarterly Sales workbook to see how it will look before you print it, follow these steps:

❶ Choose **F**ile, Print Pre**v**iew to display the document in the Print Preview window. Notice that the mouse pointer changes to a magnifying glass when positioned over any part of the worksheet.

(continues)

Previewing and Zooming Your Worksheet (continued)

2 Position the mouse pointer over the section you want to see enlarged and click once.

3 Use the vertical and horizontal scroll bars to move to other sections while maintaining the enlarged view.

4 Click the left mouse button once to return to the full-page view.

5 Choose the **C**lose button to exit Preview mode and return to the active worksheet.

6 Keep the workbook open for the next tutorial.

While in Print Preview, you can adjust the top margin of a worksheet and see how the new margin will look. There are two methods you can use. One method is to select the **S**etup button to display the Page Setup dialog box, and the other method is to drag the margin line. This technique is illustrated in the following tutorial.

Adjusting the Top Margin

To adjust the top margin of the 1st Quarter worksheet of the 1997 Quarterly Sales workbook in Print Preview mode, follow these steps:

1 Choose **F**ile, Print Pre**v**iew to display the worksheet in the Print Preview window.

2 Click the **M**argins button to display the margin lines on-screen (see Figure 5.19).

Figure 5.19

The margin lines in Print Preview mode.

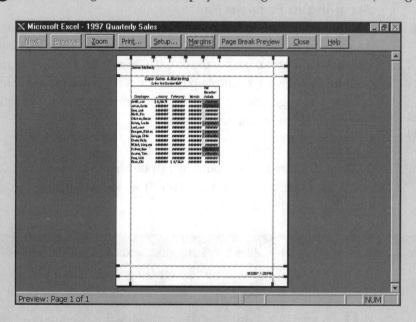

3 Place the mouse pointer on the top margin line. The pointer changes shape to a black double-headed arrow.

④ With the mouse pointer on the handle, press and hold down the left mouse button while you drag the handle down two or three inches. Release the mouse button. Notice that the status bar shows the margin measurement as you drag.

⑤ Click the Print button to see how changing the top margin changes the location of the worksheet on the printout.

⑥ Keep the workbook open for the next tutorial.

Objective 9: Insert Manual Page Breaks

Manual page break
Determines the end of a page, inserted with a command.

When printing, if you select an area that cannot fit on a single page, Excel inserts automatic page breaks to divide the worksheet into separate pages based on the left, right, top, and bottom margins. A page break is displayed on-screen as a dashed line between the end of one page and the beginning of the next page. If you are not satisfied with the location of the automatic page break, you have the option of inserting *manual page breaks*. A manual page break enables you to control where a page ends. After you insert a manual page break, the automatic page breaks readjust for the following pages. To insert a page break, you select the cell below and to the right of the location where you want the page to break. The selected cell becomes the upper-left corner of a new page. After you choose the Insert, Page Break command, a manual page break appears above and to the left of the active cell. Manual page breaks are displayed on-screen as boldface dashed lines.

To insert a horizontal page break only, you select a cell within the row or the entire row that you want at the top edge of a new page. (Click the row number heading to select the entire row.) The page break is inserted above the selected row. To insert a vertical page break only, you select a cell within the column or the entire column that is to the right of where you want to insert the page break. (Click the column letter heading to select the entire column.) The selected column will be placed at the left edge of the next page.

You can delete a manual page break by selecting the cell below or to the right of the page break intersection. If the correct cell is selected, the Insert menu displays the Remove Page Break command rather than the Page Break command. An automatic page break cannot be removed.

Inserting a Horizontal Page Break

To insert a horizontal page break between rows 3 and 4 in the 1st Quarter worksheet of the 1997 Quarterly Sales workbook, follow these steps:

❶ Click the row 3 heading number to select the entire row. This is the row that will be immediately below the inserted page break.

(continues)

Inserting a Horizontal Page Break (continued)

❷ Choose **I**nsert, Page **B**reak. A page break is inserted between rows 2 and 3.

❸ To remove the horizontal page break, select the entire row below where you inserted the page break—in this case, row 3. Choose **I**nsert, Remove Page **B**reak.

❹ Save your changes and keep the workbook open for the next tutorial.

You insert and remove vertical page breaks using a similar technique.

Inserting a Vertical Page Break

To insert a vertical page break between columns A and B in the 1st Quarter worksheet of the 1997 Quarterly Sales workbook, follow these steps:

❶ Click the column B heading to select the entire column. This is where you want to insert the page break.

❷ Choose **I**nsert, Page **B**reak.

❸ To remove the vertical page break, select the entire column to the right of where you inserted the page break—in this case, column B. Choose **I**nsert, Remove Page **B**reak.

❹ Save your changes and keep the workbook open for the next tutorial.

You can remove all manual page breaks in a worksheet after the entire worksheet is selected. Select the entire worksheet by clicking the Select All button on the worksheet. This button is located above the row 1 heading and to the left of the column A heading. Open the **I**nsert menu and choose the Remove Page **B**reak command. All manual page breaks disappear.

Objective 10: Print Worksheets

After setting up the printer and document, you are ready to print your worksheet. You can control the number of copies you want to print, the specific pages you want to print, and the quality of the printing in the Print dialog box. The default print setting is to print one copy of all pages in the worksheet. The Print options are described in Table 5.5.

Table 5.5   Print Options

Option	Description
Selection	Prints a selected range.
Selected Sheet(s)	Prints the selected worksheet(s), usually the worksheet you are working on.
Entire Workbook	Prints all the sheets in the workbook.
Copies	Specifies number of copies to print.
All	Prints all the pages indicated in the Print What area (usually what you want to do).
Pages from and to	Text boxes that enable you to define the first page you want to print (from) through the last page (to).

A shortcut for printing is the Print button on the Standard toolbar. You can bypass the Print dialog box and print one copy of the active sheet by clicking this button.

Printing Multiple Copies of Your Worksheet

To print two copies of the 1st Quarter worksheet of the 1997 Quarterly Sales workbook, follow these steps:

1 Make sure that the 1st Quarter worksheet of the 1997 Quarterly Sales workbook is open on your screen.

2 Choose File, Print to display the Print dialog box (see Figure 5.20).

Figure 5.20
The Print
dialog box.

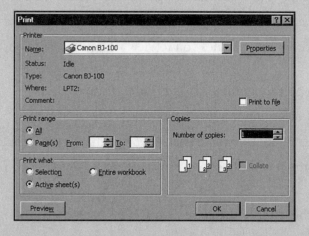

3 Click the Number of copies up arrow to change the number in the box to 2.

4 To print, choose OK. Keep one copy of your printout and give one to your instructor.

5 Save the changes and close the workbook.

5

Chapter Summary

In this chapter, you learned to rename, move, copy, add, and delete worksheets in workbooks. This chapter also introduced you to many aspects of viewing and printing in Excel. You learned to use the zoom feature to magnify or reduce the size of the type on your screen, to control the way a page is set up before you print, to insert and remove manual page breaks, define print areas, and add headers and footers to a document. You also learned about Print Preview and the options included in Preview mode for zooming.

The following chapter introduces you to charting, which is one of Excel's most exciting and powerful features. In Chapter 6, "Creating Charts and Maps," you learn how to create a chart as a separate document and how to create a chart on a worksheet. You also learn how to create maps.

Checking Your Skills

True/False

For each of the following statements, circle *T* or *F* to indicate whether the statement is true or false.

T F **1.** Using the **W**indow, **Z**oom command changes the way a worksheet prints.

T F **2.** You cannot have two workbooks open at the same time in Excel.

T F **3.** Before you can print a portion of a worksheet, you must first define that portion as a print area.

T F **4.** A page break in your worksheet is displayed on-screen as a solid double line.

T F **5.** Manual page breaks cannot be removed.

T F **6.** The Zoom command enables you to view a larger area of your worksheet on-screen.

T F **7.** The default print orientation in Excel is landscape.

T F **8.** You cannot delete automatic page breaks.

T F **9.** The **F**ile, Page Set**u**p command enables you to change the default Top Margin setting.

T F **10.** Excel can print a worksheet only on standard 8.5-by-11-inch paper.

Multiple Choice

In the blank provided, write the letter of the correct answer for each of the following.

1. The **P**rint command is found in the _____ menu.

   a. Window

   b. Output

   c. Options

   d. File

2. Worksheet names can be changed by _____.

   a. using the Format menu

   b. using a shortcut menu

   c. double-clicking the worksheet name

   d. any of the above

3. The _____ command enables you to specify the number of copies you print.

    a. Options, **O**utput

    b. Worksheet, **C**opies

    c. File, **P**rint

    d. none of the above

4. If you cannot print all the columns in your worksheet on one page, you should select _____ orientation.

    a. Landscape

    b. Portrait

    c. wrap

    d. 50% Zoom

5. Automatic page breaks cannot be _____.

    a. seen on-screen

    b. removed

    c. defaulted

    d. none of the above

6. Worksheets can be moved by _____.

    a. using a shortcut menu

    b. using the **E**dit menu

    c. pressing Ctrl as you drag a sheet tab

    d. any of the above

7. _____ are the horizontal and vertical lines on a worksheet.

    a. Borders

    b. Outlines

    c. Grid lines

    d. Graph lines

8. Which of the following would you insert in the Print area text box to print ranges A3 through A18 and D3 through D18?

    a. A3:D18

    b. A3:D3

    c. A3:A18,D3:D18

    d. A18:D18

9. Which command in Print Preview enables you to see your document enlarged?

    a. Enlarge

    b. Magnify

    c. Enhance

    d. none of the above

10. Which of the following header/footer codes will display the workbook name?

    a. &[Name]

    b. &[Tab]

    c. &[File]

    d. &[Workbook]

5

Fill in the Blank

In the blank provided, write the correct answer for each of the following statements.

1. A workbook can contain up to _____ worksheets.

2. A(n) _____ is information that prints in the top margin of a worksheet printout.

3. The horizontal lines between the rows are called _____.

4. To see what a worksheet will look like before you print it, you can use the _____ command.

5. You can move among open workbooks that you have previously saved on disk by clicking their names in the _____ or _____ menu.

6. Before you can print a portion of a worksheet, you must first define that portion as a print _____.

7. _____ page breaks cannot be removed.

8. By default, Excel 97 workbooks contain _____ worksheets.

9. The print orientation that enables you to print the most columns on one page is the _____ orientation.

10. Excel's Print _____ command enables you to view your document before you print it.

Applying Your Skills

Review Exercises

Exercise 1: Printing a Worksheet with Modified Print Settings

In this exercise, you use the Page Setup command to alter print settings of a workbook.

1. Open Chap0502 and save it as **Coastal 2**.

2. Print one copy of the worksheet without gridlines.

3. Print one copy of the worksheet with gridlines and column letters and row numbers displayed on the printout.

4. Print one copy without gridlines and column letters in landscape orientation.

5. Close the workbook.

Exercise 2: Printing a Worksheet with Manual Page Breaks

In this exercise, you insert manual page breaks in a worksheet.

1. Open Chap0503 and save it as **Beverages 2**.

2. Print the worksheet with a vertical page break between columns B and C.

3. Remove the vertical page break and print the worksheet with a horizontal page break between the TOTAL rows and the Mar Cola Drink row.

4. Remove the horizontal page break; then print two copies of the worksheet—one to keep and one to turn in to your instructor.

5. Close the workbook.

Exercise 3: Using the Sheet Tab Shortcut menu

In this exercise, you practice using the sheet tab shortcut menu.

1. Open Chap0504 and save it as **Cape Sales 2**.

2. Insert a sheet between sheets 3 and 4 and name the sheet 1st **Quarter Summary**.

3. Rename sheets 1 through 6 as **January Sales**, **February Sales**, **March Sales**, **April Sales**, **May Sales**, and **June Sales**.

4. Print two copies (one to keep and one to turn in to your instructor) of the entire workbook using the **F**ile, **P**rint command. Hint: be sure to select **A**ll in the Print range area.

5. Copy the June Sales worksheet so that it appears before the January Sales worksheet.

6. Print the June Sales (2) worksheet.

7. Delete the June Sales (2) worksheet.

8. Move the March Sales worksheet so that it appears before the January Sales worksheet.

9. Move the February Sales worksheet so that it appears before the January Sales worksheet.

10. Print two copies (one to keep and one to turn in to your instructor) of the entire workbook. Hint: be sure to select **A**ll in the Print range area of the Print dialog box.

11. Save and then close the workbook.

Exercise 4: Inserting Headers and Footers into a Worksheet

In this exercise, you practice inserting headers and footers into a worksheet.

1. Open Chap0505 and save it as **Six Months Sales**.

2. Insert a custom header that includes the following information: **L**eft section = Student's Name; **C**enter section = File name; **R**ight section = current date.

3. Make sure that the footer includes the following information: **C**enter section = the word *Page* and the Page Number.

4. Print two copies of the worksheet—one to keep and one to turn in to your instructor.

5. Save and then close the workbook.

Exercise 5: Defining a Print Area and Inserting a Manual Page Break

In this exercise, you practice defining a print area in a worksheet and insert a manual page break.

1. Open Chap0506 and save it as **Loan**.

2. Insert a manual page break before Year 4.

3. Using the **F**ile, Page Set**u**p command, insert a Print **a**rea of A8:F72.

4. In the **R**ows to repeat at the top in the Print titles section, enter **A1:F7**.

5. Click **P**rint and then click OK to print the worksheet. Notice that the information in cells A1:F7 is displayed at the top of each page of the printout.

6. Save and then close the workbook.

Continuing Projects

Project 1: Applying Page Setup Features to a Worksheet

Open Chap0507 and save it as **Real Estate 5**. Rename the sheet with the name **Sales**. Insert gridlines on the worksheet. Change the print orientation to landscape. Use page setup commands to assign a print area and allow the first three rows to be repeated at the top of each page of the print-out. Insert a custom header that includes the following information: **L**eft section = Student's Name; **C**enter section = File name; **R**ight section = current date. Be sure that the footer includes the following information: **C**enter section = the word *Page* and the page number. Preview the worksheet and then print two copies—one to keep and one to turn in to your instructor. Save and then close the worksheet.

Project 2: Applying Page Setup Features to a Worksheet

Open Chap0508 and save it as **Employee 5**. Rename the sheet with the name **Employees**. Use page setup commands to assign a print area and allow the first nine rows to be repeated at the top of each page of the printout. Insert a custom header that includes the following information: **L**eft section = Student's Name; **C**enter section = File name; **R**ight section = current date and time. Be sure that the footer includes the following information: **C**enter section = the word *Page* and the page number. Preview the printout of the worksheet, and then print two copies—one to keep and one to turn in to your instructor. Save and then close the worksheet.

Project 3: Renaming Sheets in a Workbook

Open Chap0509 and save it as **Vehicle Mileage 5**. Rename sheets 1 through sheet 6 as **Weekly**, **Monday**, **Tuesday**, **Wednesday**, **Thursday**, and **Friday**. Insert custom headers for each worksheet that includes the following information: **L**eft section = Student's Name; **C**enter section = File name and Workbook name; **R**ight section = current date. Be sure that no footer exists. Preview the printout of the worksheet and then print two copies—one to keep and one to turn in to your instructor. Save and then close the worksheet.

Chapter 6

Creating Charts and Maps

Worksheet data can be understood and interpreted much more quickly when the data is represented graphically. A chart provides a graphical format that has a greater visual impact than rows of numbers in a worksheet. A chart can communicate results that are recognizable at a glance. Without a chart, the viewer must analyze each piece of data to draw a conclusion. Charts show the big picture. Because charts are also fun to create in Excel, you're going to enjoy this chapter.

Chart Wizard
A charting tool used to guide you through creating, formatting, and modifying a chart.

Charting the data in an Excel worksheet is a simple process, and Excel offers two ways to create a chart. You can create a chart as a separate sheet in your workbook, or you can create a chart that is included on the same sheet (workbook page) that provides data for the chart. Charts within a worksheet are called embedded charts. You create and embed them in a worksheet by using Excel's *Chart Wizard*, a charting tool that guides you step-by-step through the process.

Excel builds your chart from the worksheet data you select. The chart is a graph of that data and is linked to the selected data in your worksheet. If you change the underlying worksheet data, the chart updates automatically to reflect the change. After a chart is created, Excel offers many capabilities for enhancing and editing the chart. You can choose from among many different chart types, including column, bar, area, line, pie, scatter, radar, and surface charts. Excel also offers three-dimensional chart types. Each chart type has variations in format. This chapter covers the steps involved in creating a chart, selecting a chart type, and enhancing, formatting, modifying, and printing a chart.

Instead of charts, maps may be a more appropriate way to display data associated with geographic regions. Maps are useful for charting information that is defined by state, country, or province. As you learn in this chapter, maps are similar to charts in the way they are created, modified, and formatted.

Objectives

By the time you have finished this chapter, you will have learned to

1. Create Separate and Embedded Charts

2. Move and Resize an Embedded Chart in a Worksheet

3. Create Different Types of Charts

4. Enhance and Format Charts

5. Print a Chart

6. Create and Modify a Map

Objective 1: Create Separate and Embedded Charts

Charts come in a variety of basic types, and within these types are still more variations. Excel can produce 14 types of standard charts with variations and 20 types of custom charts. In business, the most commonly used types of charts are line, column, bar, and pie charts (see Figure 6.1). This chapter concentrates on these four types of charts.

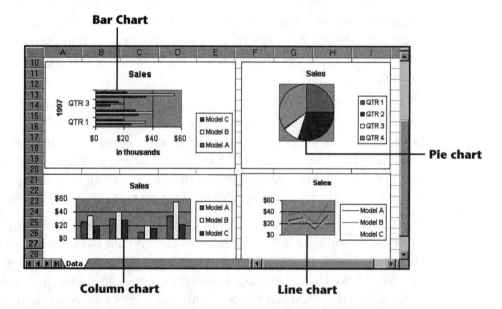

Figure 6.1
Popular chart types.

Line, column, and bar charts can show multiple sets of data and usually are used to show trends or cycles over time or to make comparisons between two or more sets of data. For example, you can use line charts to compare monthly sales in two different years or to compare the budgets of three or four departments in an organization. Line charts are best used when the amount of data is large, such as sales on the New York Stock Exchange. Column charts are useful for making comparisons of smaller amounts of data. Bar charts are helpful when the data has both negative and positive values. Pie charts can chart only one set of values, such as monthly sales for one year. Pie charts, however, are especially useful for showing how various parts (shown as slices of the pie) contribute to a whole.

Default chart type
The chart that Excel automatically creates based on the selected data.

Charts are based on selected data in a worksheet. After you select the data, creating a chart in a separate chart sheet can be as simple as pressing a single key. Excel displays the selected data in a column chart, the *default chart type*. Excel automatically decides how to plot the chart and how to set up the x- and y-axes. Excel plots the chart based on the numbers in the worksheet and the layout of the selected worksheet data. Later in this chapter, you learn how to change the default chart type and layout and use the chart shortcut menus to enhance your chart with formatting. You can keep Excel charts on separate chart sheets in a workbook, or you can embed them in the worksheet that contains the data from which the chart was produced.

If you need to leave your computer before you complete your work in this chapter, be sure to save your work and close the file you have been using. You can then reopen the file with the saved changes when you want to continue this chapter.

Identifying the X- and Y-Axes and the Plot Area

X-axis

The horizontal (category) axis on a chart.

Y-axis

The vertical (value) axis on a chart.

Line, column, and bar charts are charted using two solid lines that are marked off in units. The horizontal axis is called the *x-axis* (or the category axis). In business charts, the x-axis usually represents units of time, such as days, months, and years. These units are often referred to as the x-axis labels. The *y-axis* is the vertical (or value) axis. It shows measured units, such as dollars, number of employees, or units of a product produced. Three-dimensional charts have a third axis, the z-axis.

Plot area

The area on the chart containing the pie, lines, columns, or bars.

Legend

A guide, displayed near the chart, that identifies the data in the chart.

The space on a chart in which the pie, lines, columns, or bars are drawn or plotted is called the *plot area*. Charts usually have a main chart title, and the x- and y-axes can also have titles. When multiple groups of data are being plotted on the same graph—for example, monthly sales in each of the last three years—a *legend* explaining what each set of bars or lines represents is helpful and usually included. Pie charts are not plotted with x- and y-axes. Pie charts are sometimes exploded (slices are pulled out of the pie to emphasize them). With Excel, you can create all these charts. Figure 6.2 shows a column chart and Figure 6.3 shows an exploded pie chart created using Excel.

Figure 6.2
A column chart created in Excel.

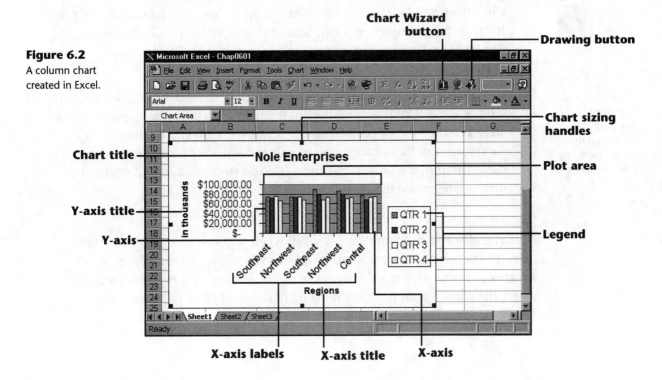

6

Figure 6.3

An exploded pie chart created in Excel.

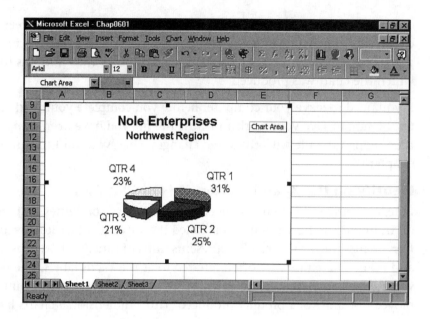

Understanding the General Procedure for Creating Charts

To create a chart, you always follow these general steps:

1. Select the worksheet data you want to chart.

Chart sheet
A workbook sheet that contains a chart but not a worksheet.

2. Decide whether you want the Excel default chart and orientation or a customized chart (something you learn from experience). Second, decide whether you want an embedded chart or a separate *chart sheet*.

3. Press F11 if you want Excel to create a chart using the default chart type.

   Or

   Click the Chart Wizard button on the Standard toolbar (refer to Figure 6.2) to create an embedded or a customized chart. When the Chart Wizard is displayed, enter your preferences, and then click the Chart Wizard Finish button.

Sizing handles
The black squares on the border enclosing a selected chart.

4. If you want to change the finished chart, select the chart by clicking. Chart *sizing handles* appear around the chart and the worksheet range used in the chart is outlined by a colored border. Click the right mouse button for the shortcut menu that enables you to edit and enhance your chart. Where you click determines which menu appears. Excel displays different shortcut menus when you click a gridline, a chart axis, or a plot area.

Saving Charts

A chart embedded in a worksheet is saved when you save the workbook that contains the worksheet. A separate chart is saved when you save the related workbook. If you have made changes in the worksheet data on which a chart is based, the chart is automatically updated (changed) before it is saved.

Creating a Chart Using Excel's Charting Defaults

To create a default chart on a separate page (chart sheet) in a workbook, follow these steps:

1 Open Chap0601 and save the workbook as **Nole-2**.

2 Select the range of cells from A3 to F8.

3 Press F11.

The chart is created using the default settings and is placed on a new chart sheet called Chart1 (see Figure 6.4). This new chart is linked to the data from which it was created and changes when you change the worksheet data.

Figure 6.4
The default chart for the selected data in the worksheet.

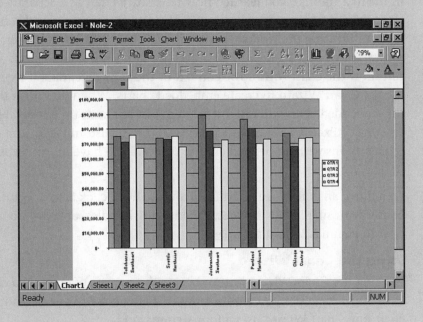

4 Save your changes and keep the workbook open for the next tutorial.

Understanding Excel's Rules for Creating a Default Chart

Excel draws a chart for you from the data you select in your worksheet. To draw the chart, Excel uses certain rules based on how the data is laid out (oriented) in the worksheet. These rules produce the default chart type. The data orientation determines which cells Excel uses for the category axis (the labels along the bottom, or x-axis) and which cells are used for the legend. In most cases, Excel charts come out correctly without intervention from you.

Excel charts the selected data based on the following assumptions:

- The category (x-) axis runs along the longest side of the selection. If your selection is taller than it is wide (more rows than columns), the category labels are taken from the left-most column in the selection. If the selection is wider than it is tall (more columns than rows), the category labels are taken from the first row of the selection.

- If Excel is not sure how to lay out and plot the selected data, a dialog box is displayed and requests more information about plotting data.

Because you are just beginning to chart, don't worry about memorizing the rules; they will mean more to you after you have created some charts. If you don't like the default, just use it as a first draft of a chart. You can always modify the default chart with the Chart Wizard or the charting shortcut menus. If necessary, you can delete the chart and start over. To delete an embedded chart, click it to select it, and press Del. To delete a chart on a separate chart sheet, click the chart sheet tab, right-click, and choose Delete from the shortcut menu.

Creating an Embedded Chart on a Worksheet

In the first tutorial, you learned how to create a chart as a separate chart sheet. A chart on a separate page is more suitable for a presentation and can be printed without printing the worksheet data as well. Many times, however, you will want to have your worksheet data and its chart on the same page. This way you can show the chart within the context of the worksheet data it represents. You use the Chart Wizard to create embedded charts. When you print the worksheet, the embedded chart will also be printed. Just as charts on a separate sheet can be any one of Excel's 14 standard chart types or 20 custom types, you have the same options with embedded charts. You can also have many embedded charts in one worksheet.

To remove an embedded chart from a worksheet, click it to select the chart (a border with small black squares, called sizing handles, appears around the chart, refer to Figure 6.2), and press Del.

Using the Chart Wizard

Clicking the Chart Wizard button begins the process of creating a chart. The Chart Wizard guides you with a series of dialog boxes. When creating a new chart, the Chart Wizard uses a four-step method.

Step 1 displays a dialog box with two tabs, one for selecting a standard type chart and subchart and another for selecting a custom type chart. To see what a chart type will look like, click the standard chart type and select the Press and hold to **v**iew sample option button. In the three remaining steps, the Chart Wizard prompts you to select a data range, to select chart options, and to indicate where the chart will be located.

The four steps of the Chart Wizard are as follows:

- Step 1 displays standard and custom chart types from which you can choose (see Figure 6.5).

Figure 6.5

Step 1 of the Chart Wizard: Selecting a chart type.

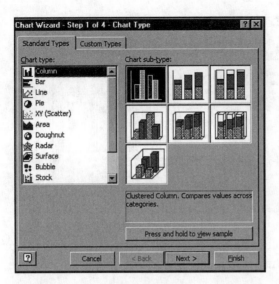

If you click the **F**inish button, the chart is produced using all the default settings, just as if you had pressed F11, except that the chart appears in the worksheet, not in a separate sheet.

- Step 2 displays the range of selected data to chart (see Figure 6.6). If necessary, you can revise the range.

Figure 6.6

Step 2 of the Chart Wizard: Verifying the data range.

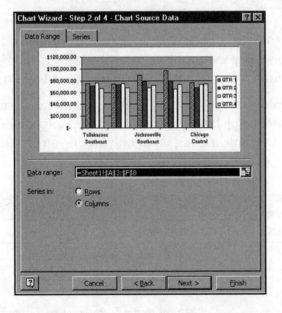

- Step 3 prompts you to select options from a six-tab dialog box. If you want to add a title, click the appropriate text box, and type the title. Be sure to check the chart preview to be sure that it is as you want it (see Figure 6.7).

Figure 6.7

Step 3 of the Chart Wizard: Selecting chart options.

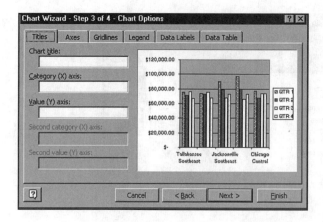

• Step 4 enables you to determine where the chart will appear, on a chart sheet or on the sheet where the worksheet data is located (see Figure 6.8).

Figure 6.8

Step 4 of the Chart Wizard: Indicating where the chart will appear.

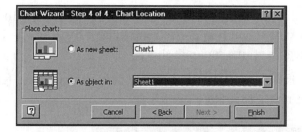

When the Chart Wizard is finished, the chart is embedded on the worksheet or on a separate sheet, depending on the selection chosen in Step 4. Later in this chapter, you learn how to use the Chart Wizard to edit an existing chart.

Each Chart Wizard window contains buttons you can use to move around in the four Chart Wizard dialog boxes. Table 6.1 lists the function of each Chart Wizard button. The OK button is displayed only when you are using the Chart Wizard to modify an existing chart.

Table 6.1 Chart Wizard Buttons

Button	Function
Office Assistant	Gets instructions about Chart Wizard options.
Cancel	Stops the Chart Wizard and returns to your worksheet without creating a chart.
Back	Returns to the preceding Chart Wizard step.
Next	Moves to the next Chart Wizard step.
Finish	Creates the chart displayed in the Chart Wizard sample area and exits the Chart Wizard. (This button, available in each step and in the early steps, creates a chart according to the default or uses any choices that have been selected.)

Creating an Embedded Chart by Using the Chart Wizard

To create an embedded chart in the Sheet1 worksheet of the Nole-2 workbook using the Chart Wizard, follow these steps:

1 Select the Sheet 1 tab, if necessary, to display the Nole Enterprises data.

2 Select the range A3:F8.

3 Click the Chart Wizard button on the Standard toolbar. The Step 1 of 4 Chart Wizard dialog box is displayed (refer to Figure 6.5), along with the Office Assistant.

4 Choose the Next button in the Step 1, Step 2, and Step 3 dialog boxes. Because no changes are being made, you could have just clicked the Finish button in Step 1, but this way you had an opportunity to see all four dialog boxes.

5 Click the Finish button in the Step 4 window to close the Chart Wizard and view the finished chart.

The chart is displayed (see Figure 6.9). Notice that it is the same chart you created on a separate chart sheet in the previous tutorial—only the size is different because it has an entire sheet on which to be displayed and Excel defaults to the chart sheet size.

Figure 6.9
An embedded chart.

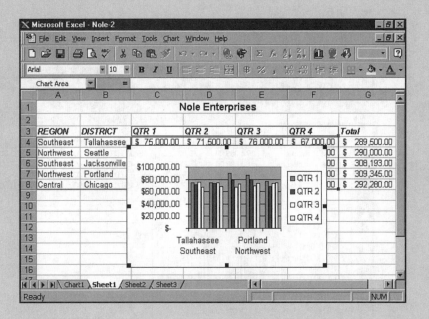

6 Save your changes and keep the workbook open for the next tutorial.

If you have problems... You may find that the y-axis numbers and the x-axis labels in your embedded chart differ from those in the figures; the reason is that changing the height and width of a chart also changes the numbers on the y-axis and the labels on the x-axis. You can alter the appearance of the numbers and labels by resizing the chart so that all labels and values are displayed.

Note

Because you accepted all the charting defaults, you could have clicked the **F**inish button in
Step 1. However, seeing all four of the screens is important.

Usually, when you create the chart area for an embedded chart, you are not sure
exactly where the chart should appear in your worksheet or how big the chart
should be. This situation is not a problem because you can easily select an embedded chart and move it to a new location or change its size. In fact, because
you can have many different charts embedded in the same worksheet, you will
often want to move or resize charts.

Moving a Chart to a New Location in the Worksheet

To move a chart to a new location, follow these steps:

1 On Sheet1 of the Nole-2 workbook, select the chart, if it isn't already selected. (Black sizing handles should appear around the edges of the chart.)

2 Place the mouse pointer in the chart area of the selected chart; press and
hold down the left mouse button and drag the chart so that its top left edge
is in cell A10 of the worksheet. Notice that tips appear next to the mouse
pointer to identify the various chart components, such as the chart area
and the plot area.

3 Release the mouse button. The chart is in its new position (see Figure 6.10).

Figure 6.10
The chart in its
new location in
the worksheet.

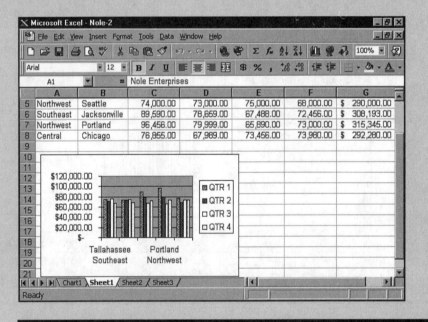

Note

By using drag-and-drop, you can move an embedded chart to any location in the
worksheet.

Notice that you moved the chart; you didn't make a copy of the same chart. To make a copy of the same chart, select the chart and then press Ctrl while dragging the chart to another location.

❹ Save your changes and keep the workbook open for the next tutorial.

Resizing a Chart

As mentioned earlier, when you select an embedded chart, the chart is enclosed by a border with black sizing handles. You use the sizing handles for sizing the chart area. You use the corner sizing handles to resize the chart height and width proportionally, and you use the sizing handles in the middle to increase or decrease the chart size horizontally or vertically. Changing the chart size often changes the appearance of the chart, as well as the display of the labels on the x-axis and the scaling of the y-axis. If labels on the x-axis are vertical or broken into two or more layers (scrunched together), expanding the horizontal size (width) of the chart makes the labels more readable.

Changing the Size of a Chart

To change the size of the embedded chart in the Sheet1 worksheet of the Nole-2 workbook, follow these steps:

❶ If necessary, select the chart.

❷ Place the mouse pointer on the handle in the middle of the right edge of the selected chart. This step requires some careful moving of the mouse; the mouse pointer becomes a double-headed arrow when it is positioned properly on the handle.

❸ Press and hold down the left mouse button, and drag to column G of the worksheet.

❹ Release the mouse button.

❺ Place the mouse pointer on the handle in the middle of the bottom edge of the selected chart.

❻ Press and hold down the mouse button, and drag up to row 20.

❼ Release the mouse button. Your chart should resemble Figure 6.11.

(continues)

6

Changing the Size of a Chart (continued)

Figure 6.11
The embedded chart resized.

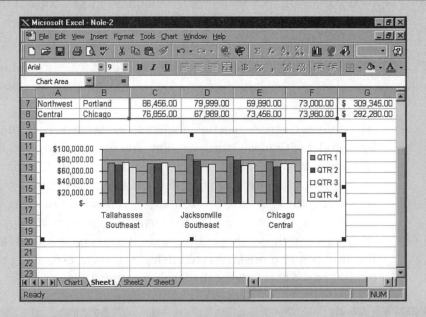

Note

Both the width and height of the selection change when you drag a corner handle of the selection.

❽ Save your changes and keep the workbook open for the next tutorial.

Because a chart is a graphical representation of worksheet data, a chart changes when the underlying worksheet data changes.

Charts change as the worksheet data that produces them changes. Charts on separate sheets are also linked to their worksheet data and change to reflect changes in their worksheet data.

Changing the Worksheet Data on Which a Chart Is Based

To change the worksheet data in the Nole-2 workbook and see the change in the chart, follow these steps:

❶ Take a good look at the chart. Notice the relative height of the columns and the scale of the y-axis.

❷ In cell C8, type the value **96685** and watch the chart as you press ↵Enter. Notice the change in the chart (see Figure 6.12).

Figure 6.12
The revised chart with updated value in cell C8.

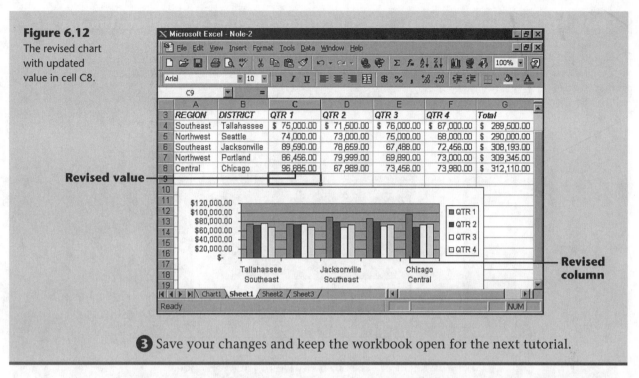

Revised value

Revised column

❸ Save your changes and keep the workbook open for the next tutorial.

With the Chart Wizard, you can create embedded charts, as you have learned. You can also create charts on separate chart sheets, as the following tutorial illustrates.

Creating a Chart on a Separate Sheet by Using the Chart Wizard

Follow these steps to create a chart on a separate sheet of the Nole-2 workbook using the Chart Wizard.

❶ On Sheet1, select the range A3:F8.

❷ Right-click the Sheet1 sheet tab.

❸ From the shortcut menu, choose **I**nsert to display the Insert dialog box.

❹ Click the Chart icon and choose OK to display the Step 1 Chart Wizard dialog box.

❺ In the **C**hart Type list box, select Line; then click the Next button.

❻ In the Chart sub-type section, click the far left chart in the top row and click the Next button.

A line chart is inserted into your workbook on the Chart2 sheet (see Figure 6.13).

(continues)

6

Creating a Chart on a Separate Sheet by Using the Chart Wizard (continued)

Figure 6.13
The inserted line chart in sheet Chart2.

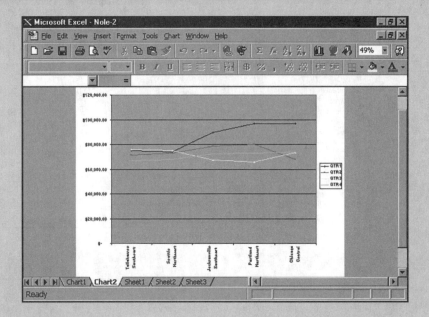

7 Click the Sheet1 sheet tab to move to the worksheet.

8 Save your changes and keep the workbook open for the next tutorial.

You can create a chart on a separate sheet using the Chart Wizard and edit it using the shortcut menus just as easily as you can create and edit an embedded chart; the techniques are the same. In this book, you learn many of the chart-building techniques using an embedded chart, but you can use the same skills with separate chart sheets.

After you have created a separate chart, you can embed it in a worksheet and vice versa. Excel does not limit you to either embedded or separate charts.

Copying an Embedded Chart to a Separate Worksheet

To copy the embedded chart from Sheet1 to another sheet in the Nole-2 workbook, follow these steps:

1 Click the embedded chart to select it.

2 Click the Copy button on the Standard toolbar.

3 Click the Sheet2 sheet tab (the sheet to which you want to copy the chart).

4 Click the Paste button on the Standard toolbar.

The embedded chart is displayed in the new worksheet and can be sized and printed if you like.

5 Save your changes and keep the workbook open for the next tutorial.

Charting Data Stored in Nonadjoining Areas of a Worksheet

The easiest kind of worksheet data to chart is data in a continuous block of rows and columns. You simply select the block, and Excel creates the chart. But what if you need to graph data that is in two or more nonadjoining ranges on a worksheet?

Suppose that you are want to have a column chart of the quarterly sales of the Central Region in Sheet1 of the Nole-2 workbook. The labels for the columns are in row 3, but the Central Region data, in row 8, is separated from these labels by several rows of data that you don't want in the chart. In the following tutorial, you learn how to select nonadjacent ranges to chart.

Selecting Nonadjacent Ranges to Chart

To select nonadjacent ranges to chart in the Sheet1 worksheet of the Nole-2 workbook, follow these steps:

1 To delete the embedded chart in Sheet1, select the chart and press Del.

2 Select the first set of data—the range A3:F3.

3 To select the second set of data, press and hold down Ctrl while you drag from cell A8 to cell F8. Then release the mouse button and Ctrl. You should see both blocks of data selected on-screen.

4 To display the nonadjacent data in a new chart sheet, press F11. Notice that a new sheet tab—Chart3—is displayed (see Figure 6.14).

Figure 6.14
The new chart sheet displaying the selected nonadjacent data.

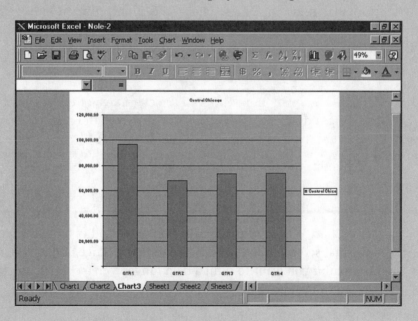

5 Save your changes and keep the workbook open for the next tutorial.

6

Data series

A collection of data from a worksheet; the data your chart represents.

Changing the Excel Default Chart Orientation

Earlier in this chapter, you learned that Excel follows several rules to design the layout of your chart. But what if you want to change Excel's default chart orientation? You can easily change a chart orientation when you create a chart using the Step 2 of 4 Chart Wizard dialog box. Simply click the unselected option button in the Series in section. You then see Excel's alternative chart displayed in the Sample Chart window. (The selected *data series* is the data used to create the chart.) The two option buttons in the Series in section control the way the data series is charted. Click the Next button to continue creating your chart.

Changing the Excel Default Chart Orientation Using Chart Wizard

To change the default chart orientation in the Nole-2 workbook, follow these steps:

1 Delete the embedded chart in Sheet1 by selecting the chart and pressing ⌨Del. Then select the range A3:F8.

 2 Click the Chart Wizard button to display the Step 1 of 4 Chart Wizard dialog box.

3 Click the Next button to display the Step 2 dialog box. Notice the default chart orientation in the Sample Chart window.

4 In the Series in section, click the **R**ows option button. The alternative chart is displayed in the Sample Chart window.

You may find it helpful to click the Co**l**umns option button, study the default chart, and then click the **R**ows option button again so that the differences between the charts become clear to you.

5 In the Step 3 dialog box, choose **F**inish.

6 Place the mouse pointer in the chart area of the selected chart; press and hold down the left mouse button as you drag the chart so that its top edge is in row 10 (column A) of the worksheet.

7 Resize the chart so that its top-right edge is in cell G10.

8 Save your changes and keep the workbook open for the next tutorial.

Two Chart Wizard screens are available to modify an existing embedded chart. The first screen enables you to redefine the range of data you want to chart. This is useful if you want to omit a data range from a chart. You use the second screen to change the default orientation of the chart.

Using Chart Wizard to Modify the Orientation of an Embedded Chart

To use the Chart Wizard to modify the orientation of an embedded chart in the Nole-2 workbook, follow these steps:

❶ With the chart selected on Sheet1, click the Chart Wizard button to display the Step 1 Chart Wizard dialog box.

❷ Click the Next button to display the Step 2 Chart Wizard dialog box. The Chart Preview shows the chart as it currently appears in your worksheet.

Notice that the quarters label the x-axis and the columns represent the different Regions and Districts.

❸ If not already selected, click the **R**ows option button in the Series in area. Notice that the sales in different regions and districts now label the y-axis and the quarters are columns in the chart.

❹ Click **F**inish to see the modified chart.

❺ Perform steps 1 through 3 again.

❻ Click the Series In Co**l**umns option button and then click **F**inish.

❼ Save your changes and keep the workbook open for the next tutorial.

Objective 2: Create Different Types of Charts

Excel has the capacity to produce 14 types of custom charts—either embedded or in a separate sheet. These 14 types of charts are displayed in the Step 1 Chart Wizard dialog box when you are creating a chart. Available variations in the format of the basic chart type you select in Step 1 are shown in the Chart Wizard. Not all types of worksheet data can produce all 14 types of charts, but you will find that you always have enough charting power at your fingertips for any Excel worksheet data. An explanation of all 14 chart types is available in Excel's **H**elp menu.

Changing the Chart Type

Up to this point, you have created a column chart and a line chart—but column and line charts are not the only types of charts available in Excel. To find out which chart type presents your data best, you should take some time to explore the various types of charts. In the following tutorials, you learn how to do this. You also use the chart shortcut menus.

6

Changing the Chart Type of an Embedded Chart

To change the Sheet1 embedded chart in the Nole-2 workbook from a column chart to a line chart, follow these steps:

1 Select the chart, if necessary, and place the mouse pointer in a clear area of the chart.

2 Right-click the chart to display a chart shortcut menu (see Figure 6.15).

Figure 6.15
The chart shortcut menu.

3 Choose Chart **T**ype to display the Chart Type dialog box (see Figure 6.16).

Figure 6.16
The Chart Type dialog box.

4 Select Line from the **C**hart type list. In the Chart sub-**t**ype section, select the top-left chart and click OK. The chart changes from a column chart to a line chart; the charted data is the same—only its representation changes (see Figure 6.17).

Figure 6.17
The line chart.

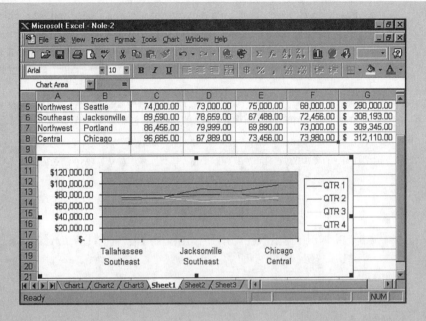

⑤ Place the mouse pointer in the line chart area and right-click.

⑥ Choose Chart **T**ype to display the Chart Type dialog box.

⑦ Select Bar from the **C**hart type list (the first one in the second row). Notice that when you click a chart type, the box below it describes the chart.

⑧ In the Chart sub-**t**ype section, click the clustered bar with a 3-D visual effect option (second row, far left) and click OK.

If the chart is too large to be displayed in the chart area, you need to increase the size of the chart area by using the top or bottom middle handle.

Your screen should look similar to Figure 6.18.

6

Figure 6.18
The 3-D clustered bar chart.

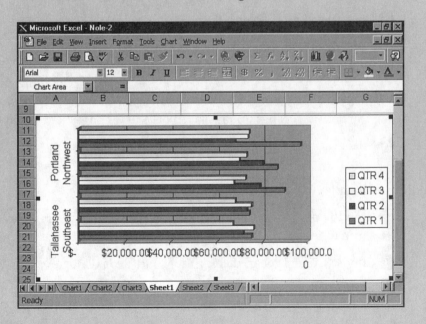

⑨ Save your changes and keep the workbook open for the next tutorial.

> **If you have problems...** If you click on a different part of the chart than is specified in a tutorial, you will see a different shortcut menu. If this happens, click outside the shortcut menu to close it and position the mouse pointer again before clicking.

Changing the Type of a Chart on a Separate Sheet

To use the Sheet1 worksheet of the Nole-2 workbook to create a 2-D pie chart and then change it to a 3-D pie chart, follow these steps:

1 Select the range A3:F8.

2 Right-click the Sheet1 sheet tab.

3 From the shortcut menu, choose **I**nsert to display the Insert tabbed dialog box (see Figure 6.19).

Figure 6.19
The Insert tabbed dialog box.

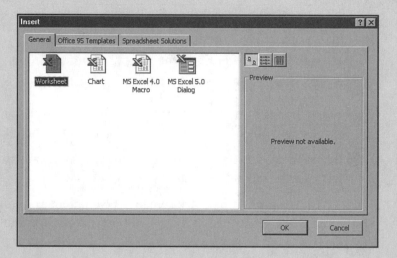

4 Click the Chart icon and then click OK.

The Step 1 Chart Wizard dialog box is displayed.

5 In the **C**hart type list box, click Pie and then click the **F**inish button.

A pie chart is inserted into your workbook (see Figure 6.20). The chart is created using the default settings and is placed on a new chart sheet called Chart5.

6 Select the pie chart; place the mouse pointer in the middle of any slice, and click the left mouse button.

Sizing handles surround the pie slice.

7 Keep the pointer in the middle of the pie slice, and right-click to display a shortcut menu.

8 Choose Chart Type to display the Chart Type dialog box.

9 In the Options section, make sure that no check marks are displayed. If there is a check mark, click the selection again to remove the check mark.

Figure 6.20
The inserted pie chart.

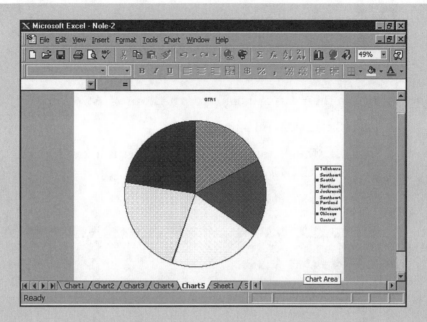

⑩ In the Chart sub-**t**ype section of the Chart Type dialog box, click the 3-D option in the top row (middle pie) and click OK.

The chart becomes a 3-D pie chart; however, the worksheet data that underlies the chart has not changed.

⑪ Click the Sheet1 sheet tab; save your changes and keep the workbook open for the next tutorial.

Objective 3: Enhance and Format Charts

6

Chart object
An item on a chart (such as an arrow) that can be moved, sized, and formatted.

After you have created a chart, you can modify and enhance it. You can insert a new data series into a chart, and you can delete data series from a chart. You can add text notes and *chart objects*, such as arrows, to your chart. You can also format text, change the colors used in the plotting of a chart, and change the color of text in the chart. Start the following tutorials with a new chart.

Formatting a Chart

To format a new chart in the Sheet1 worksheet of the Nole-2 workbook, follow these steps:

❶ With Sheet1 displayed on your screen, select the existing chart and press Del.

❷ Select the range A3:F8, if necessary, and click the Chart Wizard button.

❸ In the Step 1 and Step 2 Chart Wizard dialog boxes, click the Next button.

❹ In the Step 3 dialog box, click the Titles tab.

(continues)

Formatting a Chart (continued)

⑤ In the Chart **t**itle text box, type **Nole Enterprises**.

⑥ In the Category (X) axis text box, type **1997**.

⑦ In the Y axis text box, type **in thousands**.

⑧ Click the **F**inish button.

⑨ Drag the chart so that its top-left edge is in cell A10 and the top-right edge is in cell G10.

Your screen should now resemble Figure 6.21.

Figure 6.21
The new chart with titles.

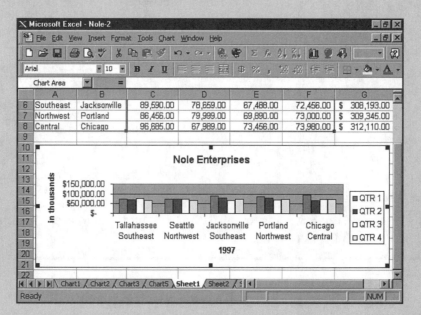

⑩ Save your changes and keep the workbook open for the next tutorial.

If you decide that your chart contains too much data and looks cluttered, you can easily delete one or more data series from the chart.

Deleting a Data Series From a Chart

To delete a data series directly from the chart you created in the Nole-2 workbook in the preceding tutorial, follow these steps:

❶ Select the chart on Sheet1 if it isn't already selected.

❷ Click one of the columns that represents QTR 4. All of the QTR 4 columns become selected.

❸ Press ⌦ to delete all the QTR 4 columns (see Figure 6.22).

Figure 6.22
The chart with QTR 4 data deleted.

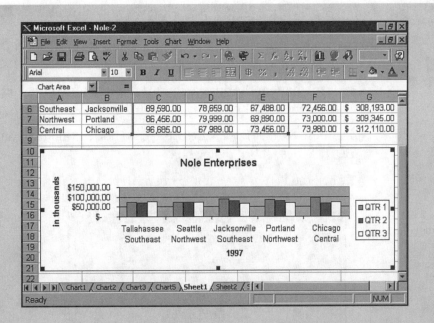

④ Save your changes and keep the workbook open for the next tutorial.

Occasionally, you will create charts that do not contain all of the data located in a worksheet. After you have created a chart, you may decide that you need to include the additional data from the worksheet. You can do this by selecting the worksheet cells that contain the additional data and dragging and dropping them onto your chart. The chart will then be updated to show the new data.

Adding a Data Series to a Chart

To add the QTR 4 data back into your chart in the Nole-2 workbook, follow these steps:

❶ On Sheet1, select the range F3:F8.

❷ Place the mouse pointer on the right edge of the selection; then press and hold the left mouse button, and drag the data over the chart. Note that a plus symbol is added to the mouse pointer.

❸ Release the mouse button when the data is anywhere over the chart to drop the data onto the chart. The chart now contains the additional data and should look like the original chart shown in Figure 6.21.

❹ Save your changes and keep the workbook open for the next tutorial.

At some point, you may want to change the color of a set of columns in a chart to emphasize that data series. If you have a color printer, you may find a set of chart colors that looks especially striking in a presentation.

6

Changing the Color of a Data Series in a Chart

To change the color used for the QTR 1 series of the chart in the Nole-2 workbook, follow these steps:

1 Make sure that the Sheet1 chart is selected for editing and then right-click any of the QTR 1 columns.

2 Choose Format Data Series from the shortcut menu to display the Format Data Series tabbed dialog box.

3 Click the Patterns tab if it is not at the front (see Figure 6.23).

Figure 6.23
The Patterns tab of the Format Data Series dialog box.

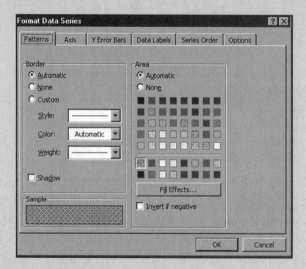

4 Click the bright blue square in the second row of the color palette (third from the right) and click OK.

The QTR 1 columns change to a bright blue color.

5 Click the worksheet area to deselect the columns.

6 Save your changes and keep the workbook open for the next tutorial.

Adding Text to a Chart

In the Chart Wizard, as you have seen, you can add a chart title and you can attach titles to the category (x-) and vertical (y-) axes. You can also include additional explanatory text in an Excel chart. You place explanatory text in a chart by using a text box. The Text Box button, is found on the Drawing toolbar.

Note

You can use the chart spell checker to check the spelling of all text in the chart.

Unattached text

Text in a text box on a chart that can be selected and moved to different locations on the chart.

Some charts may require you to include text you can move and position on the chart. You enter this text in a text box as *unattached text*. For example, you may want to position text in the form of a brief note or label to explain a specific point on the chart. You can move this text box wherever you like on the chart.

To delete the text, you select it so that sizing handles appear around the text area and then press [Del]. You can also format, move, and size other chart objects, such as arrows.

Adding Explanatory Text to Your Chart

To display the Drawing toolbar and add explanatory text to the chart in the Nole-2 workbook, follow these steps:

❶ Click the Drawing button on the Standard toolbar to display the Drawing toolbar at the bottom of the Excel window (see Figure 6.24).

Figure 6.24
The Drawing toolbar displayed at the bottom of the Excel window.

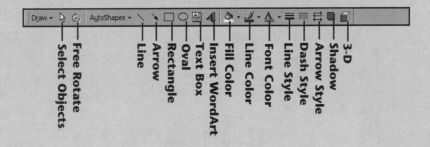

❷ Click the Text Box button. The pointer changes into a cross hair, so you can add a text box.

❸ Place the pointer to the right of the chart title.

❹ Press the left mouse button, and drag down and to the right until you have created a box about 2 inches wide and 1 inch high. Release the mouse button.

❺ Type **New district in Southeast region**.

❻ Click outside the text box.

❼ Save your changes and keep the workbook open for the next tutorial.

6

Creating an Arrow That Points to Data in Your Chart

To create an arrow pointing from the text box you completed in the preceding tutorial to the chart columns representing the Tallahassee district in the Nole-2 workbook, follow these steps:

❶ With the Sheet1 chart selected, click the Arrow button on the Drawing toolbar.

The mousepointer changes to a cross hair, so you can draw an arrow.

❷ Move the cross hair to a point just below the left-top edge of the text box note—New district in Southeast region.

(continues)

Creating an Arrow That Points to Data in Your Chart (continued)

❸ Press and hold down the left mouse button. Drag the mouse pointer until it is just above the Tallahassee Southeast columns; then release the left mouse button.

An arrow appears on your chart pointing to the sales figures for the Tallahassee district of the Southeast region (see Figure 6.25).

Figure 6.25
The arrow object connecting text to a chart area.

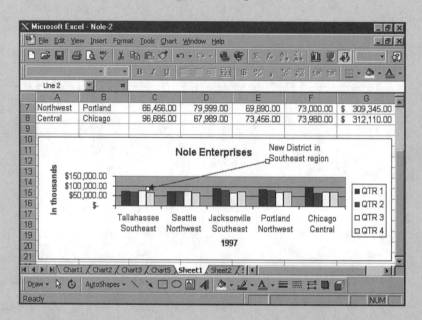

Note

You can resize, move, or delete an arrow by selecting it and clicking and dragging the sizing handles.

❹ Click outside the chart area to deselect the arrow.

 Close the Drawing toolbar by clicking the Drawing button on the standard toolbar.

Note

Don't worry about placing the text box in exactly the right location. You can click it and drag it to a new location later. If the text box is too small to display all the text, select the text box and drag a handle to make the box larger. You can delete a text box by clicking it to select the box and then pressing Del.

❺ Save your changes and keep the workbook open for the next tutorial.

Just as you can format the text in a worksheet, you can also format the text in a chart. You can format text by changing the font, point size, or style, or by adding a border, pattern, or color. To format text in a chart, you can right-click the text to display a shortcut menu. A formatting tabbed dialog box enables you to make a variety of formatting changes to the text. The following tutorial illustrates techniques for formatting text.

Formatting Text in Your Chart

To make formatting changes to the text in the chart title of the Sheet1 worksheet of the Nole-2 workbook, follow these steps:

1 If necessary, click the chart to select it for editing and right-click to display a shortcut menu.

2 Choose Format Chart Area to display the Format Chart Title tabbed dialog box.

3 Click the Font tab to bring it to the front.

4 In the Size list box, scroll down and select 14.

5 Click the Patterns tab to bring it to the front.

6 In the Border section, click the Color drop-down arrow, and select the dark blue color located in the first row (third from the right).

7 Click the Custom option button, if it is not already selected.

8 Click the Shadow check box.

9 In the Area section, click the yellow square in the fourth row of the color palette and then click OK.

10 Deselect the chart to see the changes.

11 Save your changes and keep the workbook open for the next tutorial.

6

Formatting the Plot Area of a Chart

A Plot Area shortcut menu enables you to make formatting changes to the plot area. In the final tutorial for this objective, you use this menu to change the background pattern of the plot area. Recall that the plot area on the chart contains the pie, lines, columns, or bars.

Using the Plot Area ShortCut Menu

To use the Plot Area shortcut menu to format the plot area of the Sheet1 chart of the Nole-2 workbook, follow these steps:

1 Click the plot area (refer to Figure 6.2). Sizing handles are displayed around the plot area to show that it is selected.

2 Keep the mouse pointer in the same position and right-click to display a shortcut menu (see Figure 6.26).

(continues)

Using the Plot Area ShortCut Menu (continued)

Figure 6.26
The plot area
shortcut menu.

Format Plot Area...

Chart Type...
Source Data...
Chart Options...
Location...

3-D View...
Chart Window

Clear

3 Choose Format Plot Area to display the Format Plot Area dialog box.

4 In the Area section, select yellow from the fourth row, second from the left; then click OK. The plot area background color is changed.

5 Click in the worksheet area to deselect the chart.

6 Save your changes and keep the workbook open for the next tutorial.

Objective 4: Print a Chart

Printing charts is similar to printing worksheets. You can print immediately from the Excel workbook screen by clicking the Print button on the Standard toolbar or by choosing the **F**ile, **P**rint command. You also can preview the chart before printing. Previewing a chart gives you a more accurate view of how the chart will appear when printed. By using Print Preview and Page Setup (refer to Chapter 5, "Managing Workbooks," you can make adjustments to the page margins that control the size of the chart when it is printed.

Printing Embedded Charts

Charts embedded on worksheets print with the worksheets. To print an embedded chart, simply print the worksheet in which the chart is embedded. You need to remember that if Excel cannot print all of a worksheet on one page, it will print the rest on a second page. To avoid this from happening, you can move or resize the chart so that it fits on one page. You can also use manual page breaks to control printing (refer to Chapter 5). A useful tip for printing only the embedded chart without the worksheet is to click the chart to activate it; then click the Print button on the Standard toolbar.

Printing a separate chart is not much different than printing a worksheet. You do not, however, have to define a print area when you print a chart.

Printing a Separate Chart

To print a chart in the Nole-2 workbook, follow these steps:

1 Click the Chart1 sheet tab to make the sheet active.

2 Click the Print button on the Standard toolbar.

Keep the workbook open for the next tutorial.

In the following tutorial, you print a worksheet and its embedded chart.

Printing a Worksheet and Its Embedded Chart

To print the Sheet1 worksheet of the Nole-2 workbook with its embedded chart, follow these steps:

1. Click the Sheet1 tab if the worksheet is not active.

2. Move and size the chart so that the chart and worksheet fit on one page. You can use Print Preview to see how your printout will look.

3. Click outside the chart to deselect it and then click the Print button on the Standard toolbar to print the worksheet and chart.

Keep the workbook open for the following tutorial.

You can also print only the embedded chart. In the following tutorial, you print the chart without printing the worksheet.

Printing Only an Embedded Chart

To print only the embedded chart in the Sheet1 worksheet of the Nole-2 workbook, follow these steps:

1. Click the embedded chart to select it.

2. Click the Print button.

Only your chart prints.

3. Save and close the Nole-2 workbook.

Objective 5: Create a Map

Excel maps are useful for graphically displaying information that is defined by state, country, or province. Maps can help you visualize your worksheet information graphically. Like charts, maps are based on selected data in a worksheet. Printing maps is similar to printing worksheets. You can print immediately from the Excel workbook screen by clicking the Print button or choosing the **F**ile, **P**rint command. You also can preview a map before printing. Previewing a map gives you a more accurate view of how the map will appear when printed.

If you have problems... You must install Microsoft Map to use the mapping capability of Excel. If you don't see the Map button on the standard toolbar, rerun the Setup program to install Microsoft Map.

Creating a Map

To create a map using the data in a new workbook, follow these steps:

1 Open Chap0602 and save the workbook with the name **Nole-3**.

2 Select the range of cells A6:B12.

3 Click the Map button on the Standard toolbar.

4 Click and then drag the mouse pointer (looks like a crosshair) over cells C3:F19 to define the location for the map. Release the mouse button.

5 When the Multiple Maps Available dialog box is displayed, select United States (AK & HI Inset) and click OK.

6 When the Microsoft Map Control dialog box is displayed, click the Close button located at the top-right corner of the title bar.

The map is displayed (see Figure 6.27). Note that menus and toolbars show Data Map menu commands and toolbar buttons when a map is active (see Figure 6.28).

Figure 6.27
An Excel map.

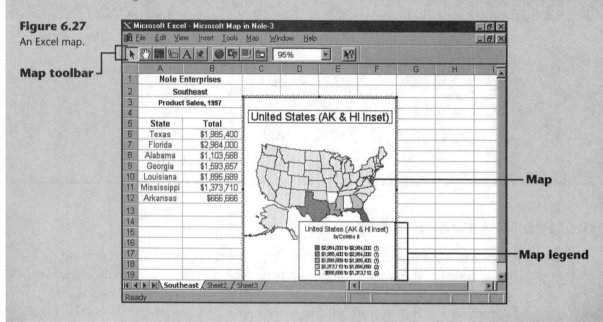

Figure 6.28
The Excel Data Map menu bar and toolbar.

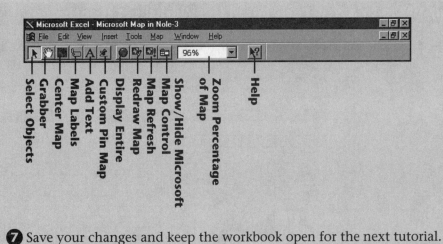

7 Save your changes and keep the workbook open for the next tutorial.

Usually, when you create the map area, you are not sure exactly where the map should appear in your worksheet or how big the map should be. This situation is not a problem because you can easily select the map and move it to a new location or change its size. In fact, because you can have many different maps in the same worksheet, you will often want to move or resize maps.

Moving a Map to a New Location in the Worksheet

To move the map in the Nole-3 workbook, follow these steps:

1 Click in the worksheet area to deselect the map.

2 Place the mouse pointer in the map area of the selected map. When the map sizing handles are displayed around the map area, press and hold down the left mouse button.

3 Drag the map so that its top edge is in row 14 (column A) of the worksheet and release the mouse button. The map is now in its new location (see Figure 6.29).

(continues)

6

Moving a Map to a New Location in the Worksheet (continued)

Figure 6.29
The map in its new location.

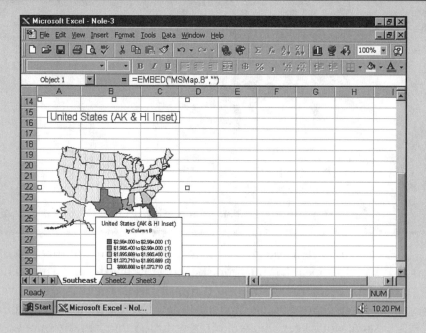

④ To move the map higher so that it is not covered by the legend, double-click the map. Notice the Data Map toolbar that is displayed below the menu bar.

 ⑤ Click the Grabber button on the Data Map toolbar. The mouse pointer changes shape to a small hand.

⑥ Position the Grabber in the middle of the United States area and drag to move the map image higher so that the legend is not covered (see Figure 6.30).

Figure 6.30
The map area in its new location.

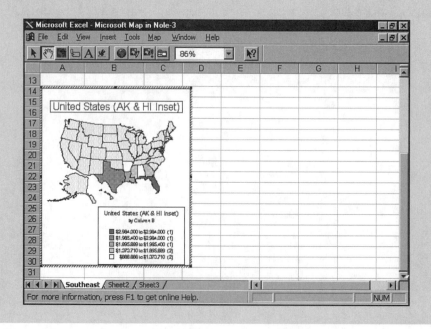

> **Note**
>
> By using drag-and-drop, you can move an embedded map to any location in the worksheet.

> **Note**
>
> To make a copy of the same map, select the map and press Ctrl while you drag the map to another location.

7 Save your changes and keep the workbook open for the next tutorial.

Sizing a Map

When an embedded map is selected, the map is enclosed by boundary lines with eight small black squares called sizing handles. You use the sizing handles for resizing the map area. You use the corner sizing handles to size the map height and width proportionally, and you use the sizing handles in the middle to increase or decrease the size of the map horizontally or vertically. Changing the map size often changes the appearance of the map as well as the display of the labels. If labels are vertical or broken into two or more layers (scrunched together), expanding the horizontal size (width) of the map makes the labels more readable.

Changing the Size of a Map

To change the size of the embedded map in the Nole-3 workbook, follow these steps:

1 Select the map by clicking it. The black square selection sizing handles are displayed.

2 Place the mouse pointer on the handle in the middle of the right edge of the selected map. The mouse pointer becomes a double-headed arrow when it is positioned properly on the handle.

3 Press and hold down the left mouse button and drag to column G of the worksheet.

4 Release the mouse button.

5 Place the mouse pointer on the handle in the middle of the bottom edge of the selected map.

6 Release the mouse button. Your screen should now resemble Figure 6.31.

(continues)

6

Changing the Size of a Map (continued)

Figure 6.31
The resized map.

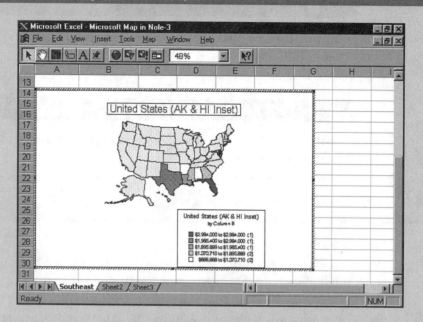

Note

Both the width and height of the selection change when you drag a corner handle of the selection.

7 Save your changes and keep the workbook open for the next tutorial.

Because a map is a graphical representation of worksheet data, a map changes when the underlying worksheet data changes. The following tutorial illustrates this concept.

Changing the Worksheet Data on Which a Map Is Based

To see the chart in the Nole-3 workbook change as its data changes, follow these steps:

1 Take a good look at your map. Notice the values displayed in the map legend.

2 In cell B12, type the value **9668590**.

3 Double-click the map so that the thick, rope-like border appears around the map.

4 Double-click the legend to display a Microsoft Map warning box that indicates that MS Map has detected that data has changed and that the map must be refereshed before the operation can proceed.

5 Click OK to refresh the map legend area. Notice the change in the legend based on changing the value in cell B12 (see Figure 6.32).

Figure 6.32
The revised chart with the updated legend.

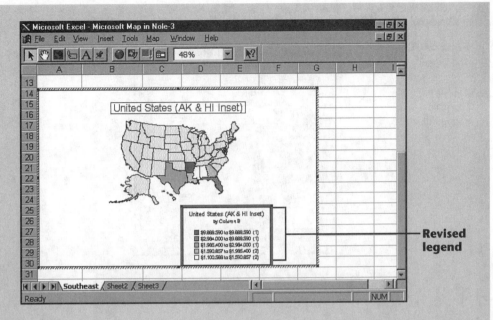

Revised legend

⓺ Change the value in cell B12 to **1,363,700**. Notice the change in the map legend.

⓻ Save your changes and keep the workbook open for the next tutorial.

After you have created a map, you can modify and enhance it. You can also format text, change the colors used in the plotting of a map, and change the color of text in the chart.

Enhancing and Formatting Maps

6

To modify the map legend, map title, and map subtitle in the Nole-3 workbook, follow these steps:

❶ Double-click the map. The border should be thick and rope-like. The Data Map toolbar should display below the menu bar.

❷ Click in the middle of the legend. A heavy border is displayed around the legend.

❸ Right-click to display a map shortcut menu.

❹ Choose **E**dit to display the Format Properties dialog box.

❺ Select the Legend Options tab.

❻ In the Title text box, type **Nole Enterprises**.

❼ In the Subtitle text box, type **Regional Sales** (see Figure 6.33).

(continues)

Enhancing and Formatting Maps (continued)

Figure 6.33
The Legend
Options tab of
the Format
Properties
dialog box.

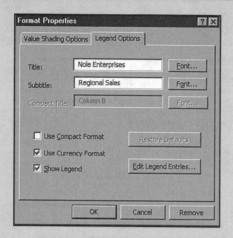

8 Click OK to close the dialog box. The data map is displayed with the new legend titles.

9 Click in the middle of the map title. A heavy border is displayed around the title.

10 Right-click to display a map shortcut menu.

11 Choose **H**ide to hide the default title from the chart.

12 Select the Add Text button on the Data Map toolbar.

13 Click in the top-left corner of the map area and type **Nole Enterprises**; then press ⏎Enter.

14 Click the Select Objects button on the Data Map toolbar.

15 Click the title. A heavy outlined border surrounds the title to show that it is selected.

16 Enlarge the title by dragging the bottom-right corner sizing handle.

Your map should now resemble Figure 6.34.

In addition to the previous formatting techniques, you can also add or change map color.

17 Click the Show/Hide Microsoft Map Color button on the Data Map toolbar.

18 In the Microsoft Map Control dialog box, drag the Category Shading icon to the left of column B in the bottom half of the dialog box (see Figure 6.35).

Figure 6.34
The revised map showing a new enlarged title.

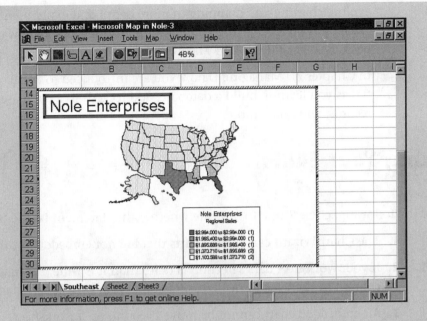

Figure 6.35
The Microsoft Map Control dialog box.

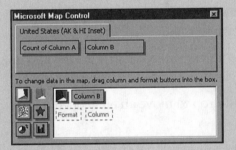

⑲ Close the dialog box by clicking the Close button located at the top-right corner of the title bar.

Note that the states named in the worksheet data range are displayed in different colors in the map, corresponding to the colors in the legend.

⑳ Print two copies of the worksheet—one to keep and one to turn in to your instructor.

㉑ Save and then close the workbook.

Chapter Summary

In this chapter, you have been introduced to many components of charting and mapping. This chapter covers topics related to creating and formatting a chart and a map. You have learned how to create a chart in a separate chart sheet and how to create a chart in a worksheet. This chapter also explains how to add titles, arrows, and text boxes to enhance the appearance of a chart and a map. You have learned to format all chart and map objects using the shortcut menus and various dialog boxes. Charting and mapping is a major feature in Excel. This chapter has focused primarily on charting and mapping basics. If you want to explore charting and mapping in more depth and experiment with some of Excel's advanced charting and mapping features, you may want to read Que's book, *Special Edition, Using Microsoft Excel 97.*

In Chapter 7, "Managing Data," you are introduced to Excel's database capabilities as you learn to build a database, add records to a database, sort data, find records, and much more.

Checking Your Skills

True/False

For each of the following, circle *T* or *F* to indicate whether the statement is true or false.

T F **1.** The Chart Wizard can create charts that are not embedded in the worksheet.

T F **2.** If your worksheet data selection is taller than it is wide, the labels in the left-most column of the selection will, by default, appear on a chart's y-axis.

T F **3.** An embedded chart cannot be moved around on a worksheet.

T F **4.** When you change the data in a worksheet, a chart embedded in the worksheet also changes to show the new data.

T F **5.** When you have selected an embedded chart, clicking and dragging a black handle changes the size of the chart.

T F **6.** You cannot use drag-and-drop to move an embedded map to any location in the worksheet.

T F **7.** Excel does not create three-dimensional charts.

T F **8.** Text used as the chart title can be moved on the chart.

T F **9.** A button on the Standard toolbar can be used to place an arrow in your chart.

T F **10.** Changing the chart size often changes the appearance of the chart as well as the display of the labels on the x-axis and the scaling of the y-axis.

Multiple Choice

In the blank provided, write the letter of the correct answer for each of the following.

1. When you right-click a chart object, _____ is displayed.

   a. an arrow

   b. a shortcut menu

   c. a legend

   d. the Chart Wizard

2. To change the type of chart displayed in a worksheet, you select a new chart type from the _____ menu.

   a. Chart

   b. Format

   c. Gallery

   d. none of the above

3. The default chart type is a 2-D _____ chart.

    a. bar

    b. column

    c. line

    d. pie

4. Which of the following is/are example(s) of attached text?

    a. a chart title

    b. a value axis title

    c. a category axis title

    d. all the above

5. Which dialog box enables you to control the type of border applied to a selected chart object?

    a. Format

    b. Patterns

    c. Text

    d. none of the above

6. A _____ is used to identify the data in a chart.

    a. legend

    b. gallery

    c. Chart Wizard

    d. none of the above

7. The vertical axis on a chart is the _____-axis.

    a. x

    b. y

    c. z

    d. category

8. A collection of data in a worksheet that is used as the basis for a chart is called a(n) _____.

    a. data series

    b. array

    c. A-range

    d. none of the above

9. If the worksheet data selection you are charting is taller than it is wide, by default the x-axis labels are taken from the _____ of the selection.

    a. top row

    b. bottom row

    c. left-most column

    d. right-most column

10. The title of the y-axis is an example of _____ text.

    a. attached

    b. unattached

    c. nonformattable

    d. border

6

Fill in the Blank

In the blank provided, write the correct answer for each of the following statements.

1. By default, Excel uses the data along the _____ side of your selection as labels for the x-axis.

2. Text in a chart text box can be formatted by using the _____ command in the shortcut menu.

3. When creating a(n) _____, click and then drag the mouse pointer (looks like a crosshair) over the cells in which you want the object to display.

4. The two ways to create a chart from selected data in Excel are by pressing _____ and using the _____.

5. To select nonadjoining areas in your worksheet, you use both the mouse and the _____ key.

6. When an embedded chart is selected on a worksheet, the chart appears enclosed by boundary lines with eight black squares called _____.

7. To select an embedded chart, place the mouse pointer on the chart, and _____.

8. Colors used in a map are also used in the map's _____.

9. To make copies of a map, press _____ while dragging the map to another location.

10. The arrow that can be used to point to a column in a chart is found on the _____ toolbar.

Applying Your Skills

Review Exercises

Exercise 1: Creating an Embedded Area Chart

In this exercise, you create an embedded area chart.

1. Open Chap0603 and save it as **Coastal 3**.

2. Create an embedded area chart using the nonadjacent data range of A3:D3 and A7:D11.

3. Position the chart below the data area (rows 16 through 35).

4. Use the **Chart, Chart Options** command to insert a chart title, an x-axis title, and a y-axis title. The chart title is **1ˢᵗ Quarter Expenses**. The x-axis title is **Office Expenses**, and the y-axis title is **in dollars**.

5. Print two copies of the worksheet and chart—one to keep and one to turn in to your instructor.

6. Save and then close the workbook.

Exercise 2: Printing a Line Chart on a Chart Sheet

In this exercise, you create a line chart on a separate chart sheet.

1. Open Chap0604 and save it as **Beverages 3**.

2. Create a line chart using the nonadjacent data range of A4:D4 and A6:D8.

3. Position the chart on a separate worksheet.

4. Use the **C**hart, Chart **O**ptions command to insert a chart title and an x-axis title. The chart title is **1ˢᵗ Quarter Sales**. The x-axis title is **Beverage Sales**.

5. Print two copies of the worksheet and chart—one to keep and one to turn in to your instructor.

6. Save and then close the workbook.

Exercise 3: Creating a 3-D Pie Chart

In this exercise, you create an embedded pie chart.

1. Open Chap0605 and save it as **July Sales**.

2. Create a 3-D pie chart using the data range of A5:B11.

3. Position the chart in rows 14 through 25 below the data area.

4. Insert a chart title, **July Sales**.

5. Use the Chart Options dialog box to add data labels that show percent of sales for sales agent.

6. Print two copies of the worksheet and chart—one to keep and one to turn in to your instructor.

7. Save and then close the workbook.

Exercise 4: Creating a Map

In this exercise, you create an embedded map.

1. Open Chap0606 and save it as **Sales Map**.

2. Select the range A6:B18.

3. Click the Map icon on the Standard toolbar.

4. Click and then drag the mouse pointer (the crosshair) over cells A20:D42 to define the location for the map. Release the mouse button.

5. Select the United States (AK & HI Inset) map style.

6. Use the Show/Hide Microsoft Map Color button on the Data Map toolbar to drag the Category Shading icon to the left of Column B.

7. Use the Format Properties Legend Options tab to change the legend title to **1997 Sales** and change the legend subtitle to **by State**.

8. Drag the legend to the lower-left side of the map.

9. Change the map title to **Acme Sports Equipment**.

10. Print two copies of the worksheet and map—one to keep and one to turn in to your instructor.

11. Save and then close the workbook.

Exercise 5: Formatting a Column Chart
In this exercise, you format an existing column chart.

1. Open Chap0607 and save it as **Formatted Chart**.

2. Position the chart below the data area (rows 10 through 22).

3. Use the **C**hart, Chart **O**ptions command to insert a chart title and an x-axis title. The chart title is **Sales**. The x-axis title is **1997** and the y-axis title is **in thousands**.

4. Select the Model B data series and change the color to yellow.

5. Select the Model C data series and change the color to red.

6. Change the chart type to bar.

7. Print two copies of the worksheet and chart—one to keep and one to turn in to your instructor.

8. Save and then close the workbook.

Continuing Projects

Project 1: Creating and Formatting a Map
Open Chap0608 and name the workbook the **Real Estate 6**. Create a map using State and Agents data columns. Add the map title **Cape Sales and Marketing**. Revise the legend title to **Agents** and the subtitle to **by State**. Use Microsoft Map Control to display the legend in color and display the map in color. Finally, save and print two copies of the worksheet and map—one to keep and one to turn in to your instructor.

Project 2: Creating and Formatting a Chart
Open the Chap0609 and name the workbook **Employee 6**. Create a column chart using the data in columns A and B. Move the chart to the range A15:E30. Add a chart title of **Kipper Industries**. Print two copies of this chart. Change the chart type to cylinder. Print two copies of the worksheet; save and then close the workbook.

Project 3: Creating Several Embedded Charts on One Worksheet
Open Chap0610 and save the workbook with the name **Vehicle Mileage 6**. Create six embedded column charts, one for each car in the motor pool. Include appropriate titles for the x-axis and y-axis and the chart title. Print two copies of the worksheet. Save and then close the workbook.

Chapter 7

Managing Data

Database
A collection of related information about a subject organized in a useful manner.

You are probably familiar with lists of information. Maintaining records for inventories of office equipment, sales prospects, plaintiffs in a lawsuit, client billings, or subscribers to a newsletter can become a real headache when you use pencil and paper or a card file. A computer can help you with this record keeping if you set up a *database* (a list) using Excel. An Excel list is like an automated card file. With Excel, you can easily enter, edit, find, and delete database information. When the information in your worksheet is organized into a list, you can use database commands to locate and extract data that meets certain criteria. You can also sort a database to organize the data into a specific order.

This chapter helps you learn skills you can use to manage a corporate database of 600, or even 6,000, records. Without database software, you can't just look at large databases to easily find what you need. Nor can you verify that you have sorted or searched the database properly. You simply cannot catch your own errors because of the amount of data.

Here, you practice with a small database so that you can check your results to verify that you have followed the correct procedures. With only a few fields and records, you can immediately see any errors and so perfect your skills. Then you can confidently work with large databases because you will know exactly what you are doing. Huge amounts of data aren't a problem for Excel. If you issue the right commands, Excel always gives you the correct results.

This chapter explains what a database is and tells you how to create a database using Excel. You learn to enter, edit, delete, and find data using a data form. You sort a database using one or more fields, search for records meeting specified criteria, and extract from database records that meet specific criteria. This chapter also explains how to use the AutoFilter. The AutoFilter enables you to extract (filter out) the records that meet your selection criteria.

If you need to leave your computer before you complete your work in this chapter, be sure to save your work and close the file you have been using. You can then reopen the file with the saved changes when you want to continue this chapter.

Objectives

By the time you have finished this chapter, you will have learned to

1. Understand Databases

2. Build a Database

3. View Database Records Using the Data Form

4. Add New Database Records

5. Delete Records

6. Sort Records

7. Use the Data Form to Search for Records

8. Find Records in a Database by Using AutoFilter

Objective 1: Understand Databases

Record
A row of cells containing fields of related information in a database.

A database stores information in an organized manner. A telephone directory and the cards in a card file are examples of a database. Each entry in a telephone directory is a *record*, and each record contains the same items of information. Each record contains a person's last name, followed by a first name or initial, an address, and a phone number.

Field names
Labels (the column headings) that identify the contents of a column in a database.

In Excel, you construct a database from a worksheet. The database is a range of cells in a worksheet and consists of a row of *field names* followed by rows of data records. A row in a database worksheet represents a record, and the worksheet's columns are the *fields* of the record. A record contains related information. The information on each line in a telephone directory, for example, is related because the information refers to the same person or organization. Excel uses the term *list* to refer to worksheets organized as databases.

Field
A column in a database; each column contains one type of information.

All the records in a database contain the same fields. Each column represents a field. The fields in a database identify the items of information that are required in each record. The first row of a database must contain labels that identify what the database fields are. These labels are referred to as field names. Each field name is entered in a separate column in the top row of the database (the column headings). The field names must each be different. In a telephone directory database, the field names would be Last Name, First Name, Street, and Phone (see Figure 7.1).

Figure 7.1
A telephone
directory database.

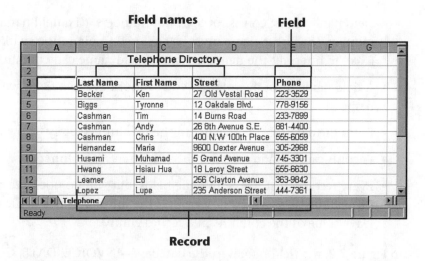

Data records (data rows) immediately follow the row of field names—no blank rows should appear between the row of field names and the first data record. Do not insert a row of dashes (or any other characters) under the row of field names. Normally, you enter the records into the database one after the other without any blank rows in the database range.

After you have entered all the data records, you select the worksheet range that contains the field names and records and defines them as a database. When the database is defined, you can use Excel's database commands to add new records; to edit or delete existing records; and to search, sort, and extract the data. Excel lists (databases) containing thousands of records are not uncommon. In this chapter, you work with a small database.

Objective 2: Build a Database

When you create a database in an existing worksheet or set up a new worksheet to be used as a database, you should follow certain guidelines:

- Consider where you will position the database. If you create a database within an existing worksheet, you must position the database where you can insert and delete additional columns and rows without disturbing the rest of the worksheet. When a column or row is inserted or deleted, it is inserted or deleted through the entire worksheet.

- The first row of the database must contain field names. Field names can be entered in several rows if the column widths are not wide enough to hold the complete heading. However, only the contents of the cells in the bottom row of the headings are actually used by Excel as the database field names. Take for example the field name *Accounts Receivable: Accounts* is on one row and *Receivable* is on the line below; Excel would use only *Receivable* (the name immediately above the data list), as the field name.

- A field name should be descriptive of the field's contents, and it can contain up to 255 characters. As a rule, you should keep field names brief.

7

- Field names must consist of text, not numbers. (If a field name contains a number, the entire name must be enclosed in quotation marks in order for Excel to interpret the name as text.) A field name can contain spaces (blanks).

- A field name must be unique—you cannot have two fields with the same field name.

- Enter the data records starting in the row immediately below the field names.

- Records can include text, numbers, formulas, and functions.

- Every record must have the same fields, but you do not have to enter data into all the fields for every record. If the information is not available, you can leave some of the columns in a record empty.

In Figure 7.2, the field names in the database—INVOICE, DATE, COMPANY, DUE DATE, and AMOUNT—are entered in row 5. Five records have been entered in rows 6 through 10. The data entered in the records includes dates, text, numbers, and formulas. The formula takes the DATE field in column C and adds 60 days to calculate the DUE DATE.

Figure 7.2
A database of outstanding invoices.

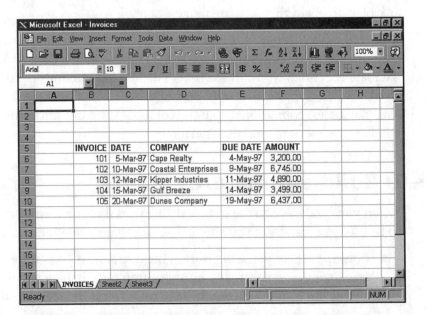

For the first tutorials in this chapter, you use the data shown in Figure 7.2. When you are setting up a worksheet to be used as a list, you enter the field names and data using the same worksheet entry techniques you learned in earlier chapters.

Entering Field Names and Records

To enter the field names and records in a new workbook, follow these steps:

1 Click the New button on the Standard toolbar to start a new workbook.

2 Enter the field names and data as shown in Figure 7.2. The DUE DATE field contains a formula that adds 60 days to the corresponding DATE field. In cell E6, enter the formula **=C6+60**.

3 Complete the worksheet and name the sheet tab **INVOICES**.

4 Use the Best Fit feature to set the width of columns B through F.

5 Save the workbook as **Invoices**.

Keep the workbook open for the following tutorial.

After you have entered the field names and the data records, you define the database (an Excel list). You give the database a name, which Excel uses (refers to) whenever you issue a database command.

Defining Your Database

To define a range of cells as a database, use the Invoices workbook from the previous tutorial and follow these steps:

1 Select the range B5:F10 (the entire range of the database).

2 Choose **I**nsert, **N**ame, **D**efine. The Define Name dialog box is displayed (see Figure 7.3).

Figure 7.3
The Define Name dialog box.

3 In the Names in **w**orkbook text box, type **Database** to replace the suggested name (INVOICE).

4 Click OK. Notice that the word Database appears on the left side of the formula bar to show that the range of cells is defined as a database.

5 Save your changes and keep the workbook open for the next tutorial.

Objective 3: View Database Records Using the Data Form

Data form
Displays field names, text boxes, and buttons for adding, deleting, and finding records in your database.

Usually, each record in a database has more fields than can be displayed across your screen at one time. Consequently, you are forced to constantly scroll left and right in a record to see all the information. This scrolling is both inefficient and hard on your eyes. To avoid such problems, you should use Excel's *data form*. This on-screen form provides a way for you to see all the fields of a long record at the same time. The data form shows the contents of all the fields in one data record. The data form displays the field names in the database; if the field is not a calculated field, a text box appears to the right of each field name (see Figure 7.4).

Figure 7.4
A record containing many fields viewed in the data form.

Using the data form is also an efficient technique for adding, editing, deleting, and searching records. You use the data form frequently in the tutorials in this chapter. Because your sample database is small, the benefits of using the data form may not be apparent to you now. When you encounter your first big database, however, you will immediately appreciate the data form.

Viewing Records Using the Data Form

To view the database records in the Invoices workbook using the data form, follow these steps:

❶ Choose **Data, Form** to display the data form.

The data form displays the contents of the first database record (see Figure 7.5). Observe that Excel automatically adds hot keys (the underlined letters) to each field name. The DATE field is displayed as you entered it (unformatted). Note that the DUE DATE field's contents are not displayed in a text box because this field is calculated by Excel, not entered by you.

Figure 7.5
The first database
record shown in
the data form.

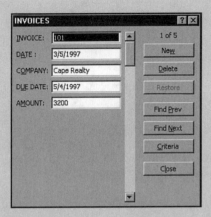

② Use the Find **N**ext and the Find **P**rev buttons, or the scroll bar, to move up and down through the records.

> **Note**
>
> Find **N**ext displays the next record in the list unless you are on the last record in the list. Find **P**rev displays the previous record in the list unless you are on the first record in the list.

③ Click **Cl**ose to close the data form.

Keep the workbook open for the following tutorial.

Objective 4: Add New Database Records

Excel offers two methods for adding records to a database. You can add records into blank cells or rows as you usually do in a worksheet. If you use this method, remember to insert the records within the defined database range. You can also use the data form method to enter new records into a defined database. Because the data form presents an organized view of the data and makes data entry easier and more accurate, this method is highly recommended. You use the data form in this chapter to add new records to your database; the database automatically expands to include the new record(s).

Entering a Formula into a Database

When you use a formula in a database (such as the formula that calculates DUE DATE in the sample database), you must first enter the formula into the worksheet. You cannot use the data form to enter or edit a formula. After you set the database and choose the **D**ata, **Fo**rm command, any field containing a formula appears in the data form as a fixed entry; the field name will not have a text box next to it. When you add a new record to the database using the **D**ata, **F**orm, Ne**w** command, the field containing the formula is automatically calculated when you enter the new record.

7

Adding a Record Using the Data Form

To use the data form to add a record to the Invoices workbook database, follow these steps:

1 Choose **D**ata, **F**orm to display the data form containing data for your first record (refer to Figure 7.5).

2 Click the New button. A New Record data form is displayed.

The DUE DATE field is a fixed entry on the data form because the field contains a formula. Excel enters this result for you.

3 Enter **106** in the **I**NVOICE field and press ⟨Tab⟩ to move to the D**A**TE field.

4 Enter **3/27/97** in the DATE field, **Scouting, Inc.**, in the C**O**MPANY field, and **2300** in the AMOUNT field. Press ⟨Tab⟩ to move down to a new field.

> ### Note
>
> Pressing ⟨Shift⟩+⟨Tab⟩ moves one field up in a form. You can also click in a field to move directly to that field.
>
> To enter another new record, press ⟨Enter⟩ when you finish a record. A new blank data form is displayed.

5 Click the Close button to clear the form and add the record to your database (see Figure 7.6).

Figure 7.6
The new record added to the database.

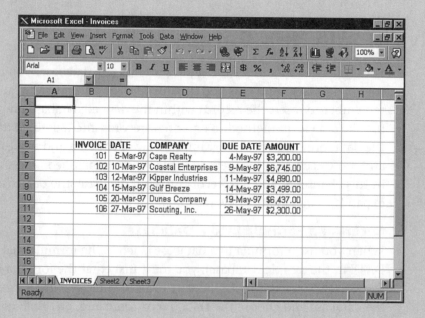

6 Save your changes and keep the workbook open for the next tutorial.

Objective 5: Delete Records

You can edit a database using the data form, or you can edit directly on the worksheet. When you are deleting database records, the data form is usually the easiest and most accurate method. When you use the form, however, you are limited to deleting one record at a time. The worksheet method (selecting the records and choosing **E**dit, **D**elete) enables you to select more than one record to delete, but you may inadvertently select a record you do not want to delete. The recommended method is always to use the data form when deleting records. In the following tutorial, you delete a record using the data form.

Caution

You cannot undelete or recover a deleted record.

Deleting a Record Using the Data Form

To use the data form to delete a record in the Invoices workbook, follow these steps:

❶ Choose **D**ata, **F**orm to display the data form.

❷ Choose Find **N**ext until the record for INVOICE 104 is displayed in the data form (see Figure 7.7).

Figure 7.7
The record to be deleted.

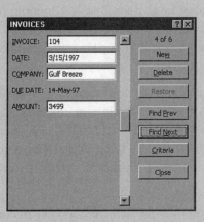

❸ Choose **D**elete. A warning box appears to remind you that the displayed record will be permanently deleted (see Figure 7.8).

(continues)

Deleting a Record Using the Data Form (continued)

Figure 7.8
The warning box for deleting a record.

❹ Choose OK to delete the record and close the warning dialog box.

The records below the deleted record are renumbered to account for the deleted record.

❺ Choose Close to return to the worksheet.

❻ Save your changes and keep the workbook open for the next tutorial.

Objective 6: Sort Records

Sort field

The field specified to control the reordering of a database.

Excel sorts databases by fields. You can use any field name in the database as a *sort field* for reordering the database. You may, for example, want to sort the records in a telephone directory database according to last name.

When you use Excel's sort capability, you can specify second and third sort fields so that you can perform a sort within a sort. If, for example, you are sorting names in a telephone directory database and several people have the same last name, you can base your second sort on the first name field. If several people have the same last name and the same first name, you can base the third sort on the address.

You can sort the database in ascending or descending order. The **A**scending option in the Sort dialog box sorts the rows alphabetically from A to Z. The **De**scending option reverses this order and sorts from Z to A. Numbers are sorted from the lowest negative number to the largest positive number with the **As**cending option, the default selection. Numbers always sort as less than (before) letters.

To avoid accidentally messing up your database, always make sure that you use the **F**ile, Save **A**s command to make another copy of the document with another name before performing a sort. You can work with one copy while the other copy remains intact. If you accidentally do something disastrous to your database, you always have that backup copy.

Note

If you ever perform a sort that is incorrect, immediately choose the **E**dit, **U**ndo Sort command to reverse the sort and return to the original database list.

One of the most common sorting errors occurs when selecting the range in the worksheet to sort. Excel sorts only the selected columns of the records. If you do not select all the records or all the fields within the records, the sort can create a disaster. For example, if you perform a sort and you don't select the last column containing the invoice amount, the sorted data will not align with the correct invoice amounts. The selected data is reorganized when a sort is performed, but the unselected data remains in its original order. Remember to select all fields and all the records.

Fortunately, Excel 97 automatically recognizes a list as a database if you select the first cell in the sort range before choosing the Sort command. Excel 97 uses the following list elements to organize the data:

- The columns in the list are the fields in the database

- The column labels in the list are the field names in the database

- Each row in the list is a record in the database

You should always check to make certain that the default selected range is the correct range for your sort.

Caution

If Excel 97 cannot identify a sort range when you choose the **D**ata, **S**ort command, a warning box is displayed (see Figure 7.9).

Figure 7.9
An Excel warning box.

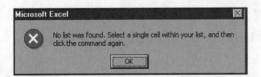

Sorting Records in Your Database Using One Field

To sort records in the Invoices workbook database so that they appear in order of increasing amount, follow these steps:

❶ Select the range B5:F10. Make sure that both the field names and all the records you want to sort are selected.

❷ Choose **D**ata, **S**ort to display the Sort dialog box (see Figure 7.10).

Figure 7.10
The Sort dialog box.

7

(continues)

Sorting Records in Your Database Using One Field (continued)

3 In the My list has section, click the Header **r**ow option to indicate that you have included the row of field names (header row) in the selected range (list of data) to sort.

4 Click the Sort by drop-down arrow to display the field name list (see Figure 7.11). You indicate the field that you want to sort by clicking that field's name in the list.

Figure 7.11
The Sort Dialog box showing the field name list.

5 Click AMOUNT in the field name list.

6 Click the **A**scending option button, if necessary.

7 Because you are sorting on only one field, choose OK.

The selected cells are sorted according to the amount from low to high.

8 Save your changes and keep the workbook open for the next tutorial.

To sort on multiple fields, you follow the same procedure as when you sort one field, except that you also select a second and often a third sort field and indicate whether the sort(s) should be in ascending or descending order.

Sorting Records in Your Database by Using Three Fields

To sort the database in the Invoices workbook using three sort fields, follow these steps:

1 Make sure that the range of cells B5:F10 is selected.

2 Choose **D**ata, **S**ort to display the Sort dialog box.

3 Click the Sort by drop-down arrow and select AMOUNT from the field name list.

4 Click the first Then by drop-down arrow and select COMPANY from the field name list.

5 Click the second Then by drop-down arrow and select DATE.

6 Make sure that the Header **r**ow option button is selected.

7 Click OK to perform the sort.

The data is sorted in a new order, first by amount, then by company, and then by date.

8 Save your changes and keep the workbook open for the next tutorial.

In the following tutorial, you return the database records to their original order. You again practice performing a sort.

Returning Sorted Records to Their Original Order

To return the data in the Invoices workbook to its original order, do the following:

1 Make sure that the range B5:F10 is selected.

2 Choose **D**ata, **S**ort to display the Sort dialog box.

3 Click the Sort by drop-down arrow and select INVOICE.

4 Click the first Then by drop-down arrow and select (none).

5 Click the second Then by drop-down arrow and select (none).

6 Make sure that the Header **r**ow option button is selected.

7 Click OK to perform the sort so that the data is in its original order (in order of increasing invoice number (101 to 106)).

8 Save your changes and keep the workbook open for the next tutorial.

Objective 7: Use the Data Form to Search for Records

Criteria
Specified tests for the contents of the fields in a record; test conditions used to find records in a database.

Sometimes you will want to search a database for records that meet a specified criterion. *Criteria* provide a pattern or the specific details that help you find certain records. After you establish criteria, you can use Excel commands to locate records that match the criteria. These commands are useful when you are searching a database that contains many records.

7

Finding Records

You can define the criteria you want a record to match by using either the data form or the **D**ata, **F**ilter command. The data form provides a quick and easy method for finding and displaying each record that satisfies your selection criteria. In this lesson, you learn how to specify your criteria and find records by using the data form.

The criteria data form gives you several options. To search forward through the list and find the next record that meets the criteria, you choose the Find **N**ext button. To search backward through the list and display the previous record that meets the criteria, you use the Find **P**rev button. To enter new criteria, you choose the **C**riteria button. The **R**estore button cancels any changes you have made to a record. When you are finished, you choose the C**l**ose button.

When you enter numeric selection criteria where you search for a range of values, such as all records with INVOICE field values higher than 125, you use comparison operators (special symbols). Table 7.1 lists these operators.

Table 7.1	**The Comparison Operators**
Operator	**Meaning**
>	Greater than
<	Less than
>=	Greater than or equal to
<=	Less than or equal to
<>	Not equal to

Finding Records Using the Data Form

To find the records with an AMOUNT field value greater than 3,500 using the data form, make sure that the Invoices workbook is open, and then follow these steps:

❶ Choose **D**ata, **F**orm to display the data form.

❷ Choose **C**riteria to display a blank criteria data form (see Figure 7.12).

Figure 7.12
A blank criteria data form.

You select a text box by clicking it. Then you enter the criterion or pattern for which you want to search.

❸ Click in the A**M**OUNT text box, and type **>3500**.

The search criterion is an amount greater than 3,500.

❹ Choose the Find **N**ext button. The first record to match the defined criterion is displayed in the criteria data form (see Figure 7.13). If no matches exist, you hear a beep.

Figure 7.13
The first record matching the search criterion.

Note

Remember that the search for a record that matches the selection criteria starts from the next record below the record that is current when you first click Find **N**ext. You need to click Find **P**rev to find the current record and any records above the current record that match the criteria.

⑤ Choose C**l**ose to close the criteria data form and return to the worksheet.

Keep the workbook open for the following tutorial.

Key field
A field that can be used to find a particular record in a database because each record contains a unique value in that field.

Searching by Using an Identifier Field

If each record in your database has a unique identifier (sometimes called a *key field*), such as a Social Security number or the invoice number in the sample database, Excel can quickly search even large databases and find and display the record. Although the sample database doesn't contain many records, the next tutorial illustrates the search technique.

Finding a Specific Record Using the Data Form

To find the record with an INVOICE number of 103 in the Invoices database workbook, follow these steps:

❶ Choose **D**ata, **F**orm to display the data form.

❷ Choose Criteria to display a blank criteria data form.

❸ Type **103** in the **I**NVOICE text box and click the Find **N**ext button. The record matching the defined criteria is shown in the criteria data form.

❹ Choose Close to close the data form and return to the worksheet.

Keep the workbook open for the next tutorial.

Defining Multiple Selection Criteria

You can specify multiple search criteria. For example, you can search for records that have a specified amount and that have a certain due date. This capability enables you to conduct more specific searches and to find all the records you want in a single search operation.

> **Note**
>
> A limitation of the Criteria data form is that you cannot use the data form if you are looking for records that match either one criteria or the other. To find records in which one criteria or the other is met, you must use the commands in the Data Filter submenu (discussed in Objective 8, "Find Records in a Database by Using AutoFilter").

Finding Records Using the Data Form

To use multiple criteria to find all records that are due after May 15 and have an invoice amount greater than or equal to $3,000, make sure that the Invoices workbook is open and follow these steps:

1 Choose **D**ata, **F**orm.

2 In the data form, choose **C**riteria to display a blank Criteria data form.

3 Click the text box to the right of DUE DATE, and type **>5/15/97**.

4 Click the text box to the right of A**M**OUNT, and type **>=3000**.

5 Click the Find **N**ext button. The first record that matches the criteria is displayed (see Figure 7.14).

Figure 7.14
The first recorded match.

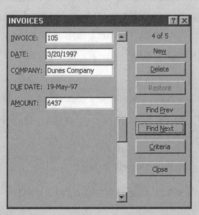

6 Use the Find **N**ext and Find **P**rev buttons to see all the records that match the multiple criteria.

7 Choose C**l**ose to clear the criteria data form.

8 Close the workbook.

Objective 8: Find Records in a Database by Using AutoFilter

Filter

The criteria that tell Excel which database records to display.

If you want to find records that match more complex criteria, or if you want to print the records, you must use the **D**ata, **F**ilter command. This command displays a submenu with two *filtering* options: AutoFilter and **A**dvanced Filter.

> **Note**
>
> For specifying very complex criteria, you use the Advanced Filter command, which is beyond the scope of this text. To learn more about specifying complex selection criteria, read Que's book *Special Edition Using Microsoft Excel 97*.

In this objective, you learn how to specify a filter for a list (a database) to show only the data you want to see. To select your list for filtering, click any cell in the list. Then you choose the **D**ata, **F**ilter, AutoFilter command. Filter arrows appear next to the field names in your list (see Figure 7.15).

Figure 7.15

The filter arrows provided by the AutoFilter command.

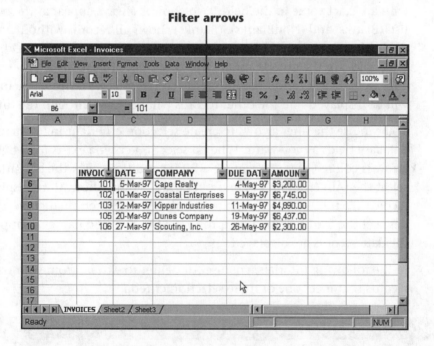

When you click a filter arrow, a list of criteria is displayed under the arrow (see Figure 7.16). Six choices always appear in your list of criteria. Three of the choices, (All), (Top 10), and (Custom), are always displayed at the top of the list. (All), the default, shows all the records without using the field to filter out records. You can choose (All) when you want to remove any filtering criteria you have previously established for a field. (Top 10) enables you to filter a specified amount of numeric data, either by percent or by number of items, from the top or bottom of a list. (Custom) enables you to specify multiple selection conditions in an AND or OR relationship. When you choose Custom, you can use the comparison operators (shown in Table 7.1) in your criteria.

Figure 7.16
The options
provided by
the AutoFilter
command.

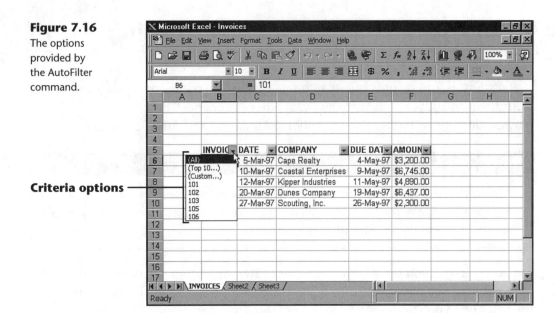

Criteria options ──────────

Next, exact values display in the drop-down list that enable you to select records with an exact value in the field. Two choices always appear at the bottom of the list, (Blanks) and (NonBlanks). (Blanks) shows all records without an entry for a field. (NonBlanks) shows only records that have an entry for a field. The remaining choices in the criteria list are the data values in the field. When you choose a data value as a criterion (a filter), only the records with this value in the field will be displayed—all the other records will not pass through the filter.

You can use the filter arrows to create selection criteria using as many of the database fields as you want. When a selection criteria exists for a field, its filter arrow is colored blue. To remove a filter condition, click the blue filter arrow and select the (All) criterion or choose the Data, Filter, **S**how All to display all records. To turn off the AutoFilter, choose **D**ata, **F**ilter; then choose Auto**F**ilter to deselect the feature. The filter arrows next to the field names disappear, and all the data records are displayed.

In the following tutorials, you use AutoFilter to extract from your database the records that meet one or more selection criteria.

Filtering Records Using One Filter Criterion

To extract records using only one filter criterion, follow these steps:

1 Open Chap0701 and save the workbook with the name **Coastal Oil 1**.

2 Click cell A3 to select the entire list.

Only the cell you click appears to be selected, but all the cells in the list are now selected.

3 Choose the **D**ata, **F**ilter, Auto**F**ilter command to display the filter arrows next to the field names.

4 Click the filter arrow in cell B3. Notice that the filter arror for the Location field is colored blue to indicate that the Location field has been used to filter data.

5 From the drop-down list, select TX.

Only the records from the TX location are extracted and displayed (see Figure 7.17).

Figure 7.17

The extracted database records.

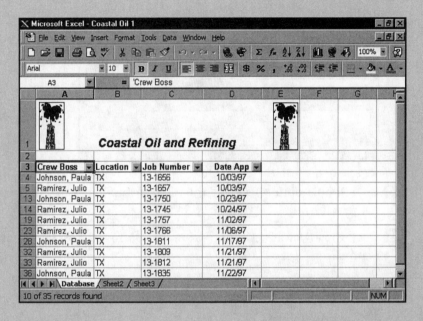

6 Click the Print button on the Standard toolbar to print the extracted records.

7 Click the blue filter arrow in cell B3 and select (All).

This removes the filtering condition that uses this field. The filter arrow in cell B3 is no longer blue; no records are filtered out.

Keep the workbook open for the following tutorial.

In the next tutorial, you use the Custom AutoFilter dialog box to display only those records that meet either one condition or another condition. In this dialog box, you build your selection criteria. The dialog box contains two criterion text boxes so that you can use multiple selection conditions. To the left of each crite-rion box is a drop-down arrow that enables you to select an operator (equals, does not equal, is greater than, is greater than or equal to, is less than, is less than or equal to, begins with, does not begin with, ends with, does not end with, contains, and does not contain). If you set two selection conditions, you can make them work in an AND or an OR relationship by clicking the appropri-ate option in the dialog box.

Filtering Records Using an OR Relation in One Field

To use a custom filter to see only the jobs in TX or FL in the Coastal Oil 1 workbook, follow these steps:

❶ Click the filter arrow in cell B3.

❷ From the list, click (Custom) to display the Custom AutoFilter dialog box.

❸ Click the top-right criterion drop-down arrow and select TX (see Figure 7.18).

Figure 7.18
The Custom AutoFilter dialog box.

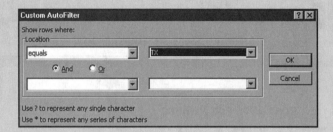

❹ Click the **Or** option to make the relationship between the two criteria an OR relationship.

❺ Click the lower-left criterion drop-down arrow to display the relational operators (see Figure 7.19).

Figure 7.19
The list of relational operators.

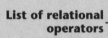
List of relational operators

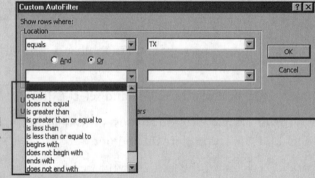

❻ Select the equals operator.

❼ Click the lower-right criterion drop-down arrow and select FL from the list of data values.

❽ Make sure that the **Or** option is selected.

Your dialog box should now look like Figure 7.20.

Figure 7.20

The completed Custom Auto-Filter dialog box.

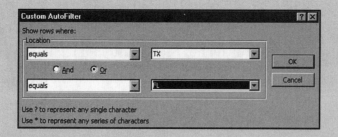

9 Click OK. The records of jobs in either TX or FL are extracted (see Figure 7.21).

Figure 7.21

The extracted database records.

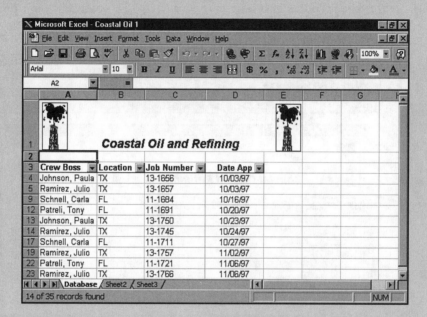

10 Click the filter arrow in cell B3 and choose (All) to remove the filtering condition.

Keep the workbook open for the following tutorial.

Note

Removing all old filtering conditions before you set new filtering conditions is always a good idea. Otherwise, you may forget a previously set filtering condition that is still affecting a more recent search.

7

Filtering Records Using Two Fields in an AND Relation

To see the records in the Coastal Oil 1 workbook for Crew Boss = Ramirez, Julio with Job Locations in TX, you do not need a custom filter; follow these steps:

❶ Click the filter arrow in cell B3 and select TX from the drop-down list.

All the TX jobs are displayed. Now you add the additional filter that will filter out all TX records that don't have one specific crew boss.

❷ Click the filter arrow in cell A3 and select Ramirez, Julio from the list.

Your screen should now look like Figure 7.22. Note that two of the filter arrows on your screen are blue because you are using two fields in your criteria. These filters will keep filtering until you remove them or leave the AutoFilter.

Figure 7.22
The extracted database records.

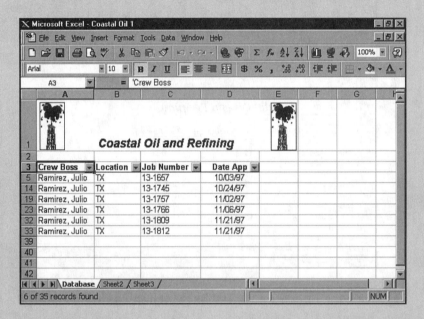

❸ Remove both filters by clicking each blue filter arrow and clicking (All) in the list.

Now all the records should be displayed because you have removed the filters. Remember to remove old filters that you are not going to use again before you set up new filters.

Keep the workbook open for the following tutorial.

As you can see, there are several ways to view information using the AutoFilter command. In the next tutorial, you learn how to filter out a range of values.

Using Filters to Filter Out a Range of Values

To find the location with a crew boss named Johnson, Paula, and job number(s) greater than 13-0000 in the Coastal Oil 1 workbook, follow these steps:

1 Click the filter arrow in cell A3 and select (Custom) from the list. The Custom AutoFilter dialog box is displayed.

2 In the top-right criterion box, click the drop-down arrow and select Johnson, Paula.

3 Click OK to show only those records showing Johnson, Paula.

4 Click the filter arrow in cell C3 and select (Custom) to display the Custom AutoFilter dialog box.

5 Click the top-left criterion box drop-down arrow and select is greater than.

6 Click the top-right criterion box drop-down arrow and select 13-1750.

7 Click OK.

Your screen should now look like Figure 7.23. Notice that all the extracted records have Johnson, Paula as the crew boss and have a job number greater than 13-0000.

Figure 7.23
The extracted database records.

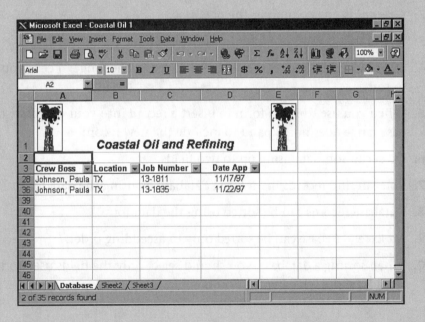

8 Choose **D**ata, **F**ilter, AutoFilter to clear the filter conditions.

9 Close the workbook.

7

Chapter Summary

This chapter introduced you to fundamental database concepts. You learned what a database is and how to create a database in an Excel worksheet. Other topics in the chapter included entering data into a database and using the data form to add and delete records. You also learned how to sort your database. Additionally, you learned to define criteria and find records that match the criteria by using the data form and the AutoFilter.

If you want to explore databases in more depth and experiment with some of Excel's advanced database features, you may want to read Que's book *Special Edition Using Microsoft Excel 97*. It includes instructions on how to use Excel's SQL feature, which enables you to access external databases and bring the data into an Excel worksheet.

Checking Your Skills

True/False

For each of the following, circle *T* or *F* to indicate whether the statement is true or false.

T   F   **1.** Each database field name can occupy only one cell.

T   F   **2.** A record is one column in the database.

T   F   **3.** A field that is used as a filter in AutoFilter has a red arrow.

T   F   **4.** The row of field names should be included in the range of cells you are going to sort.

T   F   **5.** When you use the data form to insert a record into your database, the database range does not expand to include the new record.

T   F   **6.** Excel can sort data using up to two fields.

T   F   **7.** You can find records in an Excel database by using the data form.

T   F   **8.** Database records can be sorted using the data form.

T   F   **9.** An Excel database can be sorted only in ascending order.

T   F   **10.** When sorting a database, you should select only the fields used to sort the records before selecting the Sort command.

Multiple Choice

In the blank provided, write the letter of the correct answer for each of the following.

1. Which relationship(s) can be used in a Custom AutoFilter criteria?

    a. AND

    b. OR

    c. both AND and OR

    d. none of the above

2. Which of the following menus contains the command that enables you to delete a record from a database?

    a. File

    b. Data

    c. Tools

    d. none of the above

3. Which of the following menus contains the command that enables you to define a criteria?

    a. Edit

    b. Data

    c. Selection

    d. none of the above

4. Excel enables you to sort up to _____ different fields.

    a. two

    b. three

    c. four

    d. five

5. Which option in the criteria list, displayed when you click a filter arrow, removes any filters for that field?

    a. (Blank)

    b. <>

    c. (All)

    d. none of the above

6. Field names in a database can consist of up to _____ row(s).

    a. one

    b. two

    c. three

    d. four

7. The symbol for the criterion less than is _____.

    a. <

    b. >

    c. |

    d. .LT

8. The best way to add records to a database is to use the _____ command.

    a. Edit Add

    b. Edit Insert

    c. Data Insert

    d. none of the above

9. If you perform a sort that is incorrect, choose the _____ command to return to the record order of the original database.

    a. Edit, Undo Sort

    b. Data, Resort

    c. Data, Undo Sort

    d. Data, Restore

10. Which of the following buttons do you click in the data form to find the records that match a search condition in the database?

    a. Search

    b. Seek

    c. Criteria

    d. none of the above

7

Fill in the Blank

In the blank provided, write the correct answer for each of the following statements.

1. To establish a filter to search a database for records with a PAYMENT field value of less than 100, the criteria is _____.

2. The best way to add records to an existing database is by using the data _____.

3. When you have finished finding records using the Data Filter command, you can return to the normal worksheet mode by _____.

4. To find records in a database in which one criteria OR the other is met, you use the _____.

5. To find a record in the database with an invoice number less than 130, you enter _____ in the **I**NVOICE field of the data form.

6. The _____ names indicate the information contained in each record.

7. The first row of a database must contain _____.

8. A(n) _____ is a pattern or the specific details you are looking for in a database record.

9. In an ascending Excel sort, _____ will be sorted before letters.

10. An Excel database is also referred to as an Excel _____.

Applying Your Skills

Review Exercises

Exercise 1: Sorting a Database

In this exercise, you sort a database.

1. Open Chap0702 and save it as **Coastal Oil 2**.

2. Sort the database worksheet in ascending order by the Last Name and First Name fields.

3. Save the database worksheet and print two copies—one to keep and one to turn in to your instructor.

Exercise 2: Adding Records Using the Data Form

In this exercise, you use the data form to add records to a database list, then you sort the list.

1. Open Chap0703 and save it as **Contacts**.

2. Use the Data form to add the following two records to the database:

John Andrews	**Elisa Lane**
(317)555-1234	**(317)555-3222**
954 Marion Blvd.	**65 Monroe Ave.**
Indianapolis	**Carmel**
IN	**IN**
46523	**46522**

3. Print two copies of the workbook—one to keep and one to turn in to your instructor.

4. Sort the database worksheet in ascending order by the Last Name field.

5. Print two copies of the sorted database—one to keep and one to turn in to your instructor.

6. Save and then close the workbook.

Exercise 3: Finding Records Using the Data Form

In this exercise, you use the data form to find records.

1. Open Chap0704 and save it as **Allied Loan**.

2. Use the data form criteria feature to count the number of records meeting the following conditions:

    Loan Officer = Johnson, Paula

    Location = IL

3. How many records meet the criteria? Record your answer in cell E1.

4. Sort the list in ascending order by using three fields—Loan Officer, Location, and Loan Number.

5. Save and print two copies of the worksheet—one to keep and one to turn in to your instructor.

7

Exercise 4: Finding Records by Using AutoFilter

In this exercise, you use the data form to find records.

1. Open Chap0705 and save it as **Coastal Cellular Communications**.

2. Use the AutoFilter to display all records for Region = South.

3. Print two copies of the worksheet (one to keep and one to turn in to your instructor). Then remove the filtering condition.

4. Use the AutoFilter to display the Top 10 in the Dollars field.

5. Print two copies of the worksheet—one to keep and one to turn in to your instructor. Then remove the filtering condition.

6. Use the AutoFilter to create a custom filter that will display the records with 11 or more employees.

7. Print two copies of the worksheet—one to keep and one to turn in to your instructor. Then remove the filtering condition.

8. Save and then close the workbook.

Exercise 5: Finding Records by Using Two or More AutoFiltering Conditions

In this exercise, you use the data form to find records.

1. Open Chap0706 and save it as **Clearwater**.

2. Sort the database in ascending order by Last Name.

3. Use the AutoFilter to create a filter that displays all records possessing the following characteristics:

   Department = Engineering

   Shift = 2

   Salary = is greater than 60000 (or) is less than 30000

4. Print two copies of the worksheet—one to keep and one to turn in to your instructor.

5. Save and then close the workbook.

Continuing Projects

Project 1: Finding Records Using AutoFilter

Open the Chap0707 database and rename it **Real Estate 7**. Use AutoFilter to display the records of all the listings that meet the following conditions: Suburban Location = SE, Price < 150,000, and the number of bedrooms is >2. Print two copies—one to keep and one to turn in to your instructor. Then save the workbook.

Project 2: Finding and Sorting Records

Open the Chap0708 database and rename it **Employee 7**. Sort the list by the INVOICE field. Use AutoFilter to display all records for Carr. Print two copies of the worksheet—one to keep and one to turn in to your instructor. Then clear the autofilter condition. Use AutoFilter to display the top 10 amounts sorted by salesperson. Print two copies of the worksheet again. Then save the workbook.

Project 3: Using the Data Form to Add Records

Open Chap0709 and rename it **Vehicle Mileage 7**. Use the data form to add the following records to the Coastal Sales Motor Pool list:

Car #7	34	45	33	65	22
Car #8	54	23	34	33	89
Car #9	59	65	37	49	46

Use AutoFilter to display all records for the Monday that have mileage greater than 50 or less than 30. Print two copies of the worksheet—one to keep and one to turn in to your instructor. Save and then close the workbook.

7

Chapter 8

Using Excel Macros to Automate Repetitive Tasks

Procedure
A macro; a series of Visual Basic statements you create using the Macro Recorder and store together.

Macro
A stored list of commands and keystrokes that are automatically executed by Excel.

Visual Basic for Applications
A programming language; the Excel Macro Recorder creates macros consisting of Visual Basic statements.

Modules
Where Excel places the recorded commands. Modules can be viewed through the Visual Basic Editor.

In the preceding chapters, you learned how to use Excel to perform a variety of tasks. Whenever you find yourself performing the same series of actions again and again in Excel, you should consider using Excel's Macro Recorder. When you use the Macro Recorder to record your actions and commands, Excel creates a Visual Basic *procedure* (called a *macro* in Excel). After a procedure has been created, you never have to enter the same commands or perform the sequence of mouse actions again; you simply instruct Excel to run the recorded procedure. Simple macros can duplicate the tasks you find yourself performing repeatedly, such as changing fonts, entering the same data in several locations, and changing page setup commands.

There are two methods to create macros. You can use the Macro Recorder or you can write the macro using Visual Basic. In this chapter, you learn to create macros using the Macro Recorder, although you will have an opportunity to view the macro in Visual Basic.

These procedures function in the same way as the macros you may have used in earlier versions of Excel or in another spreadsheet program, such as Lotus 1-2-3. *Visual Basic for Applications* is the Microsoft programming language used in the newest Microsoft products. You don't, however, have to be a programmer or even understand Visual Basic to create procedures. You simply instruct Excel to record your actions and then save the procedure. In this way, you can automate repetitive tasks. The Visual Basic procedures you record are then stored in workbook *modules*.

A macro is a great time-saver for performing a repetitive task in a worksheet. Excel macros can automatically perform such tasks as entering keystrokes, formatting, and issuing commands. Using macros may sound complicated, but it is really easy—as you will see.

To create a macro, you turn on the Excel Macro Recorder, perform the sequence of actions that you want to record, and then turn off the Macro Recorder. As Excel records your actions, they are immediately translated into a Visual Basic procedure. You can then use the macro in any worksheet in the workbook. To have a macro accessible in any workbook, save the macro to the Personal macro workbook, instead of the current workbook. The secret to creating these automated procedures is a little planning and some practice.

If you need to leave your computer before you complete your work in this chapter, be sure to save your work and close the file you have been using. You can then reopen the file with the saved changes when you want to continue this chapter.

Objectives

By the time you have finished this chapter, you will have learned to

1. Create a Macro by Using the Macro Recorder

2. Run a Macro

3. Create a Button to Run Your Macro

4. Delete a Macro from a Workbook

Objective 1: Create a Macro by Using the Macro Recorder

Before you start the Macro Recorder, plan exactly what you want to do in the worksheet and the order in which you want to take the actions. Then run through the steps in the procedure to verify that they work exactly as you planned. As a rule, planning and then recording the macro in one session is the best way because you will make fewer mistakes. You should also decide on a name, without spaces or periods, for the macro; the name should reflect the actions the macro performs. If the name is more than one word and you want to separate the words, use an underscore (_) rather than a space.

After you have planned the steps in the procedure and decided on a name, your next step is to prepare to record the macro. Before starting the Macro Recorder, prepare the worksheet by doing everything you do not want included in the macro. This preparation may include such things as opening a new worksheet or scrolling to a specific location.

After you start the Macro Recorder, every action you take—every cell you select, every character you type, and every command you choose—is recorded and becomes part of the Visual Basic procedure. When you run the macro, the results are the same as if you had entered all the keystrokes, formatting, and commands yourself. The macro is faster, however, and you don't have to worry about making a typing error. Compare the Macro Recorder to a tape recorder. All keystrokes are recorded after the Macro Recorder is turned on until the Recorder is turned off.

Automate
To create a Visual Basic Procedure (a macro) to perform repetitive worksheet tasks automatically.

In this chapter, you first familiarize yourself with using the Excel Recorder by creating a macro that *automates* the creation of a simple worksheet. This worksheet has an input cell and a calculated output cell. You enter a cost in the input cell, and the output cell calculates the discounted cost. The discount rate is displayed in a third cell.

Preparing to Record a Macro

To prepare your worksheet and display the Record Macro dialog box, follow these steps:

1 Click the New button on the Standard toolbar to open a new workbook.

2 Choose the **T**ools, **M**acro, **R**ecord New Macro command (see Figure 8.1) to display the Record Macro dialog box (see Figure 8.2).

Figure 8.1
The menu choices to begin recording a new macro.

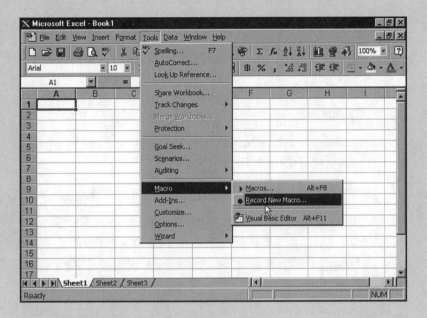

Figure 8.2
The Record Macro dialog box.

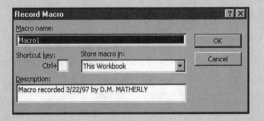

Keep the Record Macro dialog box on-screen for the next tutorial.

The Record Macro dialog box is where you enter information used by the Macro Recorder. You use the **M**acro name and **D**escription text boxes to name your macro and add a short description of the purpose of the macro. In addition, you can use this dialog box to enter a shortcut key combination for a macro. When you want to run a macro, you can use just two keystrokes—Ctrl and a designated letter of the alphabet or Ctrl+◆Shift and a letter.

It is important to include a complete but brief description so that you will remember what the macro does when you want to use it. Excel usually suggests a description that includes the date and the name of the purchaser of the copy of Excel you are using. You can delete this default description and enter your own description.

8

> ### Caution
>
> Remember, no spaces are allowed in a macro name.

Starting the Macro Recorder

To enter a macro name and description in the Record Macro dialog box and start the Macro Recorder, follow these steps:

1 In the **M**acro name text box, type **DiscountCalculator**.

2 Delete the text in the **D**escription text box and type **A macro to create a discount calculator**. Always remember to include a clear description of what the macro does.

3 Click OK.

The Stop Recording Macro button is displayed as the only button in a floating toolbar (see Figure 8.3).

Figure 8.3
The Stop Recording Macro button.

Stop Recording Macro button

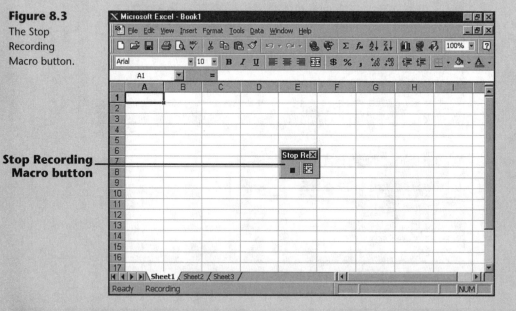

The Macro Recorder now records your actions—all your keystrokes and mouse clicks—until you click the Stop Recording Macro button.

You now record the macro by simply creating the worksheet as you would normally. Read through the steps in the following tutorial before you begin. If you make a mistake, the Recorder will record it, and your macro won't work properly, so work slowly. If you make no mistakes when recording a macro, it will always run correctly regardless of how many complicated steps are in the macro.

> ### Caution
>
> Work slowly and carefully as you record a macro because the Recorder will record any mistakes.

Recording the Macro

To record the macro, follow these steps:

1 Choose **T**ools, **O**ptions to display the Options dialog box.

2 Click the View tab, and click the **G**ridlines check box to turn off the gridlines. Then click OK.

3 In cell B5, type **Retail Price:** and press ⏎Enter.

4 Select cell C5, and choose F**o**rmat, **C**ells.

5 In the Format Cells dialog box, click the Protection tab to bring it to the front and deselect the **L**ocked check box.

This turns off protection for the cell so that later, when you enable protection for the worksheet, you are still able to change the value in this cell.

6 Click the Number tab; select the currency format and click OK.

7 In cell B7, type **Discounted Value:** and press ⏎Enter.

8 In cell B9, enter **Discount Rate:** and press ⏎Enter.

9 Use the Best Fit feature to make column B wide enough so that the label in cell B7 fits within the column.

10 Select cells B5:B9 and choose F**o**rmat, C**e**lls.

11 In the Format Cells dialog box, click the Alignment tab. Click the **H**orizontal drop-down arrow and select Right. Then click OK to right-justify the text in the cells.

12 Select cell C7 and choose F**o**rmat, **C**ells.

13 In the Format Cells dialog box, click the Number tab, select the currency format, and then click OK.

14 In cell C7, type the formula **=(1–C9)*C5** and press ⏎Enter.

15 Select cell C9 and choose F**o**rmat, **C**ells.

16 In the Format Cells dialog box, click the Number tab, select the Percentage format and click OK.

17 Set a discount rate by entering **.05** in cell C9 and pressing ⏎Enter.

18 To protect the cells in the worksheet so that the user cannot type in them, choose the **T**ools, **P**rotection, **P**rotect sheet command. Make sure that check marks appear in all three check boxes in the Protect Sheet dialog box; then click OK.

19 You have finished all the steps in the macro. Click the Stop Macro button in the floating toolbar. The worksheet should now look like Figure 8.4.

(continues)

8

Recording the Macro (continued)

Figure 8.4

The worksheet after you have entered the commands, formatting, and keystrokes.

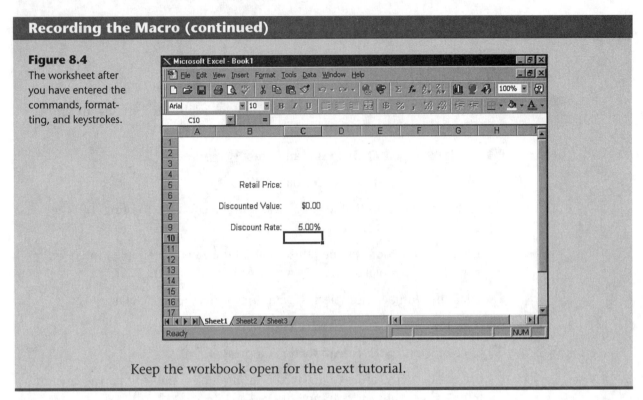

Keep the workbook open for the next tutorial.

The macro is now complete. Your next step is to test the macro to be sure that it works correctly.

Testing the Macro

To test the macro, follow these steps:

❶ In cell C5, enter **10** and press ↵Enter. The amount $9.50 appears in cell C7 (see Figure 8.5).

Figure 8.5

The worksheet as you are testing it.

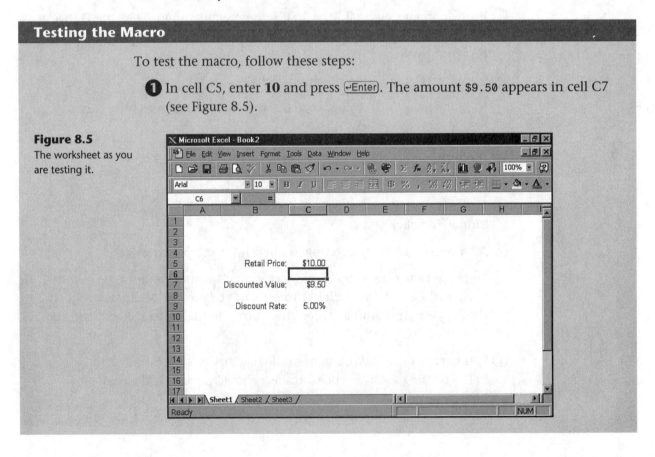

② Try to type anywhere else on the worksheet. Excel displays a warning box telling you that you can't make any changes because the cell is protected (see Figure 8.6). You protected the worksheet cells so that the users can enter data only where they are supposed to—in the input cell.

Figure 8.6
Microsoft Excel
warning box.

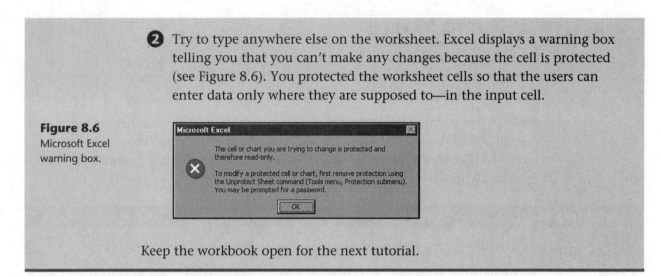

Keep the workbook open for the next tutorial.

Viewing the Macro

You don't need to examine the recorded macro (or even understand it) before you use it. You can, however, easily take a look at the macro, but be careful not to change it accidentally. To examine the procedure, choose the **T**ools, **M**acro, **M**acros command. Select the macro (DiscountCalculator) from the list and choose **E**dit. Your procedure appears on-screen (see Figure 8.7). If necessary, close any other open windows and maximize the macro window.

Figure 8.7
The new macro
procedure.

Some text in the module is displayed in green. These green lines are comment lines. Notice that the macro name and the description are both in green and that each comment line is preceded by an apostrophe. If you use many Visual Basic macros, you can insert your own comments into a macro to document and explain its functions. The beginning and the end of a macro are indicated by blue text. The rest of the macro is black text. Note that the menu bar changes to reflect Visual Basic commands, and below the menu bar is the Visual Basic toolbar, used to alter and test a macro. The alteration of macros is beyond the scope of this text. You are better off letting the Recorder create your macros until you are very familiar with Visual Basic.

8

Objective 2: Run a Macro

Before you run a macro for the first time, you should save a backup copy of your workbook on disk. You could have an error in the macro that erases or alters part of your worksheet or file on your disk.

To run the macro you just created, first move to an unused worksheet in your workbook. If you want to reuse the sheet in which you created the DiscountCalculator macro, be sure to turn off protection before you run the macro because the protected sheet cannot be changed.

Running a Macro

To run the macro you created in the previous tutorials, follow these steps:

❶ In the open workbook, click the Sheet2 sheet tab. The macro will create the discount calculations in this worksheet.

❷ Choose **T**ools, **M**acro, **M**acros.

The Macro dialog box is displayed (see Figure 8.8). This dialog box shows all the procedures (macros) available in this workbook and can be used to run or delete a macro.

Figure 8.8
The Macro dialog box.

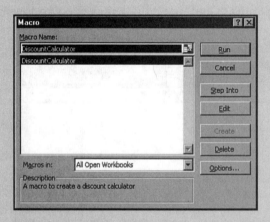

❸ In the **M**acro Name list box, click DiscountCalculator if it is not already selected; then click the **R**un button.

The worksheet is displayed, and the macro runs, setting the contents and the formatting of the worksheet cells.

The completed worksheet is identical to the one you created with the Recorder running. Running the macro is much more efficient than typing all the commands and keystrokes again.

Keep the workbook open for the next tutorial.

If you have problems... Sometimes, a macro may not insert its results in the right place in your worksheet, or a macro may not work at all. Some macros may require you to select a cell (perhaps A1) before you run the macro. When you design a macro, you may want to activate a cell as the first step in the macro itself. Make sure that you make the appropriate cell active before you start the macro.

Objective 3: Create a Button to Run Your Macro

As you have learned, you can run macros by using the **T**ools, **M**acro command. Most people, however, prefer to create a button in their worksheet and attach a macro to the button. The button can be edited to contain the name of the macro; then just clicking that button runs the macro. The tool that you use to create a button is on the Forms toolbar.

In the following tutorial, you create a button in an empty worksheet, attach the DiscountCalculator macro to the button, and then name the button to show which macro it runs. In the second tutorial of this section, you use the button to run the DiscountCalculator macro. In Objective 4, you learn how to delete a button you no longer need from a worksheet.

Creating a Button to Run a Macro

To create a button that can be used to run your macro, follow these steps:

1 In the workbook that contains the DiscountCalculator macro, click the Sheet3 sheet tab.

2 If the Forms toolbar (see Figure 8.9) is not on your screen, choose the **V**iew, **T**oolbars command and select Forms.

You use this toolbar to create a button in your worksheet.

Figure 8.9
The Forms toolbar.

Button tool

3 Click the Button tool.

The mouse pointer changes to a crosshair, ready for you to draw the button.

4 Click and drag over the range of cells G2:I3.

(continues)

8

Creating a Button to Run a Macro (continued)

When you release the left mouse button, the button is created in the range G2:I3 and the Assign Macro dialog box is displayed (see Figure 8.10).

Figure 8.10
The Assign Macro dialog box.

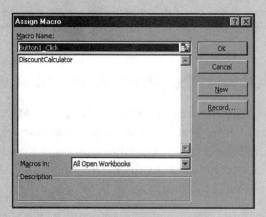

5 In the **M**acro Name list box, click DiscountCalculator; then click OK.

Your screen should now look like Figure 8.11.

Figure 8.11
The new button, labeled Button 1.

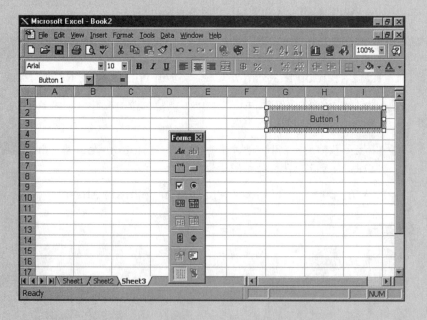

Your next step is to delete the default text in the button and replace it with the name of your macro.

6 Double-click inside the button to place the blinking insertion point inside the button. Delete the default text—Button 1.

7 Make sure that the blinking insertion point is still inside the button; then type **DiscountCalculator**.

8 Click in a cell outside the button to deselect the button.

❾ Click the Forms Close button in the top-right corner of the Forms title bar to close the toolbar.

Your screen should now look like Figure 8.12.

Figure 8.12
The worksheet containing the macro button.

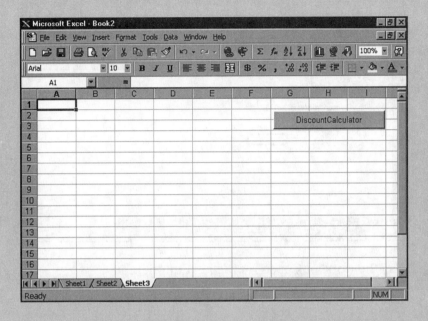

Note

If you print a worksheet containing macro buttons, by default the buttons do not print.

Keep the workbook open for the next tutorial.

If you have problems... Suppose that you make a mistake while creating a button. If the button still has the square selection handles around it, you can press Del to delete the button. If the button does not have the square selection handles around it, press and hold down Ctrl; then click the button. The button is selected (square handles appear); press Del to delete the button. Remember, to select a button without executing its attached macro, hold down ↵Enter when you click the button.

8

Running a Macro Using a Button

To run the macro using the button, follow these steps:

❶ Make sure that Sheet3 of the workbook containing the DiscountCalculator macro is on your screen.

❷ Click the DiscountCalculator button.

The macro creates the Discount Calculator and protects the worksheet (see Figure 8.13).

(continues)

Running a Macro Using a Button (continued)

Figure 8.13
The finished
worksheet with
the macro
button.

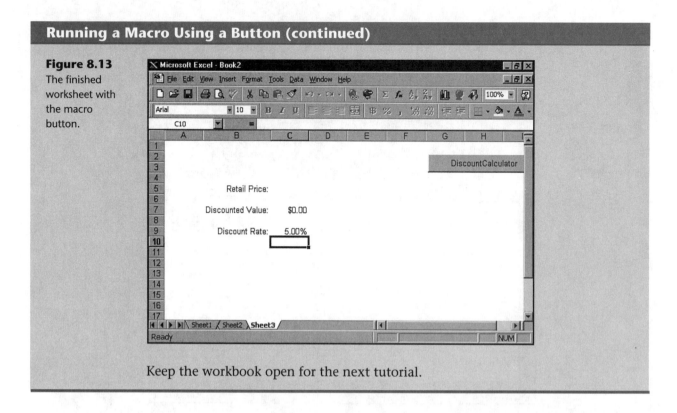

Keep the workbook open for the next tutorial.

Objective 4: Delete a Macro from a Workbook

When you save a workbook, the macros that it contains are also saved. If you
want to delete a macro from the open workbook, you use the **T**ools, **M**acro
command.

Deleting the Discount Calculator Macro

To delete a macro from the open workbook, follow these steps:

❶ Choose **T**ools, **M**acro, **M**acros to display the Macro dialog box (refer to Figure 8.8).

❷ In the **M**acro Name list box, click DiscountCalculator—the macro you want
to delete.

❸ Click the **D**elete button.

Excel displays a warning box (see Figure 8.14).

Figure 8.14
Microsoft Excel
warning box.

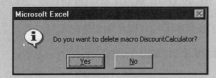

④ Click Yes to delete the macro from the workbook.

Usually, you will also want to delete the button that runs the macro. This button is still in Sheet3. Because the macro turned on worksheet protection in Sheet3, you must turn off worksheet protection before you can delete the button.

⑤ Choose **T**ools, **P**rotection, Un**p**rotect Sheet.

Sheet3 is now unprotected, and you can select and delete the button.

⑥ Press and hold down Ctrl and click the DiscountCalculator button.

Square selection handles appear around the button.

⑦ Press Del to delete the button.

⑧ Save the workbook with the name **Macro 1**.

⑨ Print all worksheets in the workbook and then close the workbook.

Chapter Summary

In this chapter, you learned what an Excel macro is. You learned how to create and run a macro and how to create a button to run the macro. You also learned how to delete a macro and the button that you created to run the macro. In Chapter 9, "Linking, Summarizing, and Consolidating Worksheets," you learn how to link two Excel worksheets and how to link Excel worksheets with other Windows applications.

Checking Your Skills

True/False

For each of the following, circle *T* or *F* to indicate whether the statement is true or false.

T   F   **1.** A macro can be used only in the worksheet in which it was recorded.

T   F   **2.** Macros are stored by Excel in a sheet that it names Macro1.

T   F   **3.** A macro consists of a series of Visual Basic statements.

T   F   **4.** When you have finished creating a macro, the macro recorder automatically stops recording.

T   F   **5.** By default, macro buttons are printed.

T   F   **6.** The Macro Recorder will not record menu choices.

T   F   **7.** A macro name cannot contain a space.

T   F   **8.** A macro name cannot consist of more than eight characters.

T   F   **9.** The Stop Macro button is found on the Drawing toolbar.

T   F   **10.** A macro can contain a maximum of 20 statements.

Multiple Choice

In the blank provided, write the letter of the correct answer for each of the following.

1. To select a macro button, you first press and hold down the _____ key before you click the button.

    a. Alt

    b. Ctrl

    c. Del

    d. Shift

2. To begin recording a macro, you first choose _____ in the menu bar.

    a. Edit

    b. Record

    c. Tools

    d. none of the above

3. The command you choose to display the dialog box that enables you to delete a macro is **Tools,** _____.

    a. Edit

    b. Erase

    c. Macro

    d. View

4. You signal Excel that you have finished recording a macro by clicking the _____ button.

    a. Turn Off Recorder

    b. Stop Recording

    c. Exit

    d. none of the above

5. To display the toolbar that enables you to create a button to run a macro, click the _____ button on the Standard toolbar.

    a. Drawing

    b. Macro

    c. Play

    d. Form

6. The **Locked** check box is found in the _____ dialog box.

    a. Format Cells

    b. Protection

    c. Utilities

    d. none of the above

7. The command that lets you run a macro is found in the _____ menu.

    a. Tools

    b. File

    c. Window

    d. none of the above

8. Which of the following is the default name that Excel gives a button?

    a. Run

    b. Macro

    c. Start

    d. Button 1

9. You attach a macro to a button by using the _____ Macro dialog box.

    a. Assign

    b. Attach

    c. Create

    d. Run

10. You can enter text in a button when the button is _____.

    a. pressed

    b. running the macro

    c. selected

    d. being drawn

Fill in the Blank

In the blank provided, write the correct answer for each of the following statements.

1. When the mouse pointer is placed on a button, the pointer changes shape to a(n) _____.

2. A macro is saved on disk when you save its _____.

3. A macro will work the _____ way every time you run it.

4. The language in which Excel macros are written is _____ for Applications.

5. To delete a selected button, press the _____ key.

6. The command to protect the cells of a worksheet so that a user cannot type in them is found in the _____ menu.

7. A(n) _____ is a series of commands stored in a worksheet.

8. Comments in a macro are colored _____.

9. Before you run a macro, you should _____ your workbook.

10. The first step in creating a macro is to _____ the steps in the macro.

Applying Your Skills

Review Exercises

Exercise 1: Recording and Running a Macro

In this exercise, you create a simple macro to insert column headings in a worksheet.

1. Open a new workbook and choose **T**ools, **M**acro, **R**ecord New Macro to record a macro named Headings and a description of Column headings. Create the macro to place the column heading EMPLOYEE in cell A1, EXTENSION in cell B1, and DEPARTMENT in cell C1.

2. Change the width of column A to 20 and use the Best Fit feature for columns B and C.

3. Make the headings boldface.

4. Switch to an empty worksheet (Sheet2) and run the macro.

5. Print two copies of the workbook—one to keep and one to turn in to your instructor. Then save the workbook with the name **Macro 2**.

Keep the workbook open for the next exercise.

8

Exercise 2: Recording a Macro That Uses a Dialog Box

In this exercise, you create a macro that includes formatting features.

1. Be sure the Macro 2 workbook is open. Choose **T**ools, **M**acro, **R**ecord New Macro to record a macro named Formats and a description of Heading formats. Create the macro to use the F**o**rmat, C**e**lls command to outline the border of cells A1:C1.

2. Switch to an empty worksheet (Sheet3) and run the macro.

3. Print two copies of the workbook—one to keep and one to turn in to your instructor; then save the workbook with the name **Macro 3**.

   Keep the workbook open for the next exercise.

Exercise 3: Creating Macro Buttons

In this exercise, you create two macro buttons to run the macros created in Exercise 1 and Exercise 2.

1. Be sure the Macro 3 workbook is open.

2. Choose **I**nsert, **W**orksheet to insert a new worksheet after Sheet3.

3. On Sheet4, use the Forms toolbar to create buttons to run each of the macros you created in the first two exercises. Name the buttons **Headings** and **Formats**.

4. Run the macros.

5. Save the workbook with the name **Macro 4**.

6. Print, then close Macro 4.

   Keep the workbook open for the next exercise.

Exercise 4: Recording a Page Setup Macro

In this exercise, you create a macro that changes the print orientation.

1. Be sure the Macro 4 workbook is open.

2. Choose **T**ools, **M**acro, **R**ecord New Macro to record a macro named Landscape and a description Landscape orientation. Create the macro to change the page orientation to landscape.

3. Select Sheet1; then run the Landscape macro.

4. Choose **F**ile, Print Pre**v**iew to view the sheet.

5. Save the workbook with the name **Macro 5**.

6. Print, then close Macro 5.

   Keep the workbook open for the next exercise.

Exercise 5: Recording a Print Macro

In this exercise, you create a macro that prints the worksheet created after using the Headings, Format, and Landscape macros.

1. Be sure the Macro 5 workbook is open.

2. Choose **T**ools, **M**acro, **R**ecord New Macro to record a macro named Printing and a description Print. Create the macro to print a worksheet

3. Select Sheet1, then run the Printing macro.

4. Save the workbook with the name **Macro 6**.

Continuing Projects

Project 1: Creating a Macro to Open and Print a Workbook.

Record a macro to open the Chap0801 workbook and print the worksheet in landscape orientation. Run the macro. Save the workbook with the name **Real Estate 8**.

Project 2: Creating a Macro to for Kipper Industries

Record a macro named Letterhead that will display the following information in boldface:

cell A1: Kipper Industries

cell A2: 501 Dogwood Drive

cell A3: Tallahassee, FL 32312

The first line should be in 14-point font. Lines two and three should be in 10-point italicized font. Run the macro in Sheet2 of the workbook. Rename the Sheet2 worksheet **Letterhead**. Print two copies of the Letterhead worksheet—one to keep and one to turn in to your instructor. Save the workbook with the name **Employee 8**.

Project 3: A Macro to Create a Workbook Form

Create a macro named CarPool that sets up a Coastal Sales Motor Pool spreadsheet similar to the one shown in Figure 8.16. You can use this macro every week to create a spreadsheet to tally the mileage records. Run the macro in Sheet2 of the workbook. Save the workbook as **Vehicle Mileage 8**. Print two copies of the worksheet—one to keep and one to turn in to your instructor; then close the workbook.

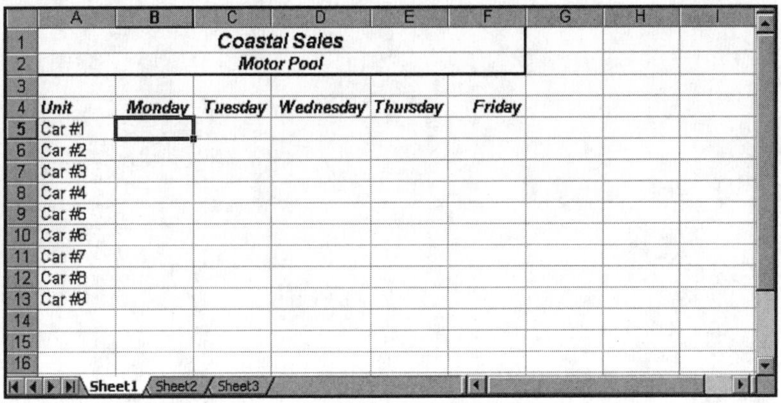

Figure 8.16

The Coastal Sales Motor Pool Mileage worksheet.

8

Chapter 9

Linking, Summarizing, and Consolidating Worksheets

Spreadsheets or databases used by the manager of a retail store have a different level of detail than those used by the regional manager of the retail chain. Generally, at higher levels in an organization, spreadsheets are used to show the big picture without providing extraneous detail. At lower levels of the organization, however, what is needed is detailed information on the operation of the office, department, or retail store.

When you build a higher-level summary worksheet, reentering information that is already in a lower-level worksheet is inefficient. The worksheets used by higher-level managers summarize the detailed data in worksheets used by lower-level managers. Quarterly reports summarize the information from three monthly reports. Excel gives you the capability to extract information (such as sales totals) from multiple detail worksheets in order to create a higher-level summary worksheet.

In this chapter, you learn how to link a cell in one (source) worksheet to a cell in a second (dependent) worksheet, as well as linking cells in one worksheet to cells in a different workbook. When the data in the source worksheet is changed, the data in the dependent worksheet is instantly updated. You learn how to link information in an Excel worksheet to a document in another Windows application. Then you learn how to create summary reports that contain subtotals and averages for groups of related records in a worksheet. In the final section of this chapter, you learn how to consolidate three annual reports into one summary report.

If you need to leave your computer before you complete your work in this chapter, be sure to save your work and close the file you have been using. You can then reopen the file with the saved changes when you want to continue this chapter.

Objectives

By the time you have finished this chapter, you will have learned to

1. Create Links between Worksheets
2. Change and Restore Links

3. Link Data from a Worksheet to a Windows Application

4. Create a Summary Report with Subtotals

5. Create a Consolidated Report

Objective 1: Create Links between Worksheets

Link
A one-way data connection from the source workbook to the dependent workbook.

Dependent workbook
A workbook containing an external reference (a link) to another (source) workbook and therefore dependent on the other workbook for data.

Source workbook
A workbook that supplies data over a link to a dependent workbook.

When you are creating a worksheet, you will sometimes want to use data stored in a different worksheet or workbook. You can copy and paste the data, but if the data changes, you have to copy and paste again. Creating a *link* provides the solution to this problem.

You can create a link between a worksheet in a *dependent workbook*, the workbook that receives data, and a worksheet in a *source workbook*, the workbook that contains the original data. The link carries data from the source workbook to the dependent workbook. A link is like a pipeline between the two; the pipeline carries data in one direction only (from the source workbook to the dependent workbook). Links can also be established between a worksheet in an Excel workbook and a document created by another Windows application.

By default, Excel updates the dependent data automatically when the source data changes. As you will see, you can also instruct Excel not to update the dependent data if you want to retain the older data in the dependent workbook.

You can link one cell or a range of cells. Linked data in a dependent worksheet can be formatted, used in a function or formula, and charted just like the data that is actually entered into the dependent worksheet.

> **Note**
>
> The terminology used to refer to linked (source and dependent) workbooks differs in different Excel textbooks. Sometimes you will see the terms source workbook (or worksheet) and target workbook or supporting workbook and dependent workbook.

Linking enables one workbook to share the data in another workbook. Source workbooks can be on-screen or on disk; the dependent workbook can always get the information it needs through the link. If the source workbook is open when the dependent workbook opens, the target workbook's linked data is automatically updated (read) from the source workbook. If the source workbook is not open when you open the dependent workbook, you have a choice: you can use the data the dependent workbook had when it was saved, or you can have the dependent workbook read in new data from the source workbook on disk.

Linking data enables you to avoid the problems inherent in large, cumbersome workbooks. You can build small worksheets and workbooks to accomplish specific tasks and then link all these components together to form a larger system. Links between workbooks can pass data, numbers, and text to the receiving (dependent) workbook.

In the following tutorials, you set up a dependent worksheet in a workbook. A cell in the dependent worksheet will receive a sales total from an existing source worksheet cell. Next, you display both workbooks side-by-side on your screen to create a link between a cell in the source worksheet and a cell in the dependent worksheet. Finally, you test the link to see that it is functioning properly.

Creating the Dependent Worksheet

To create a dependent worksheet that will receive data from a source worksheet, follow these steps:

1 Make sure that you don't have any workbooks open; then click the New button on the Standard toolbar to open a new workbook—Book1.

This new workbook will be set up as the dependent workbook.

2 Change the width of column A to 16.

3 Enter **Nole Enterprises** in cell A1.

4 Enter **Total Sales** in cell A2.

5 Format cell A4 to currency with two decimal places.

Your worksheet should now look like Figure 9.1. Cell A4 in this worksheet will receive its data from a cell in the source worksheet.

Figure 9.1
The dependent worksheet.

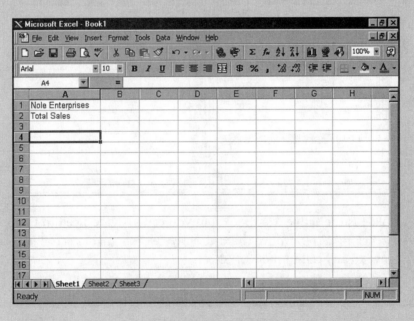

6 Open Chap0901 and save it as **Nole-4**.

7 Change the name of the Sheet1 sheet tab to **1997**.

Keep both workbooks open for the next tutorial.

Creating links between worksheets is easiest when both worksheets are visible on-screen at the same time. In the next tutorial, you arrange your screen so that both worksheets (the source worksheet and the dependent worksheet) are displayed simultaneously.

Displaying the Source and Dependent Worksheets Simultaneously

To display both the source (Nole-4) and dependent (Book1) worksheets simultaneously, follow these steps:

1 Choose **W**indow, **A**rrange to display the Arrange Windows dialog box (see Figure 9.2).

Figure 9.2
The Arrange Windows dialog box.

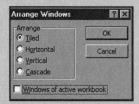

2 Click the **T**iled option button, if necessary, and click OK.

You should now be able to see both worksheets simultaneously (see Figure 9.3).

Figure 9.3
Both the source and the dependent worksheets are displayed simultaneously.

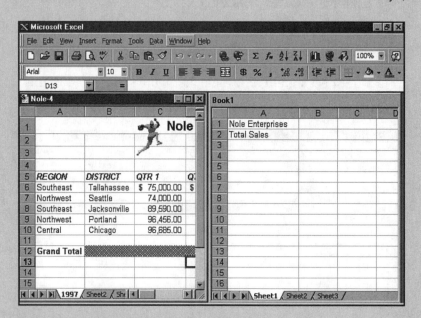

Nole-4 is the active workbook, but you can activate a cell in the Book1 workbook by clicking a cell. Notice that the active workbook has scroll bars so that you can move to any cell in the worksheet.

Keep these workbooks open for the following tutorial.

External reference formula
A reference to a cell or range in another Excel workbook, also called an external reference.

In the next tutorial, you establish a link between these two worksheets. You create an *external reference formula* in cell A4 of the new workbook. This external reference formula is the link that extracts data from the source workbook (Nole-4) and places that data in the new (dependent) workbook.

Linking the Two Worksheets

To create the link between the Nole-4 and Book1 worksheets, follow these steps:

1 In the 1997 worksheet of Nole-4, scroll to cell G12, which contains the Grand Total for Nole Enterprises.

2 Right-click cell G12 to display a shortcut menu (see Figure 9.4).

Figure 9.4
The shortcut menu that displays when copying cell entries.

3 Choose **C**opy. A marquee appears around cell G12.

4 In the Book1 worksheet, right-click cell A4 to display a shortcut menu (see Figure 9.5).

Figure 9.5
The shortcut menu that displays when pasting cell entries.

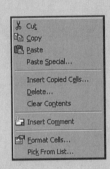

5 Choose Paste **S**pecial. The Paste Special dialog box is displayed (see Figure 9.6).

Figure 9.6
The Paste Special dialog box.

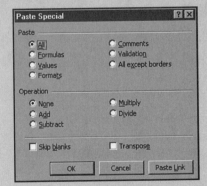

6 In the Paste section, click the **A**ll option button if it isn't already selected.

7 Click the Paste **L**ink button.

(continues)

9

Linking the Two Worksheets (continued)

The external reference formula (='[Nole-4.xls]1997'!$G$12) is placed in cell A4 and displayed in the formula bar. This formula brings data from cell G12 of the 1997 worksheet in the source workbook (Nole-4) into cell A4 of the dependent worksheet. The value, $1,555,148.00, from Nole-4, appears in cell A4 (see Figure 9.7).

Figure 9.7
The linked worksheets.

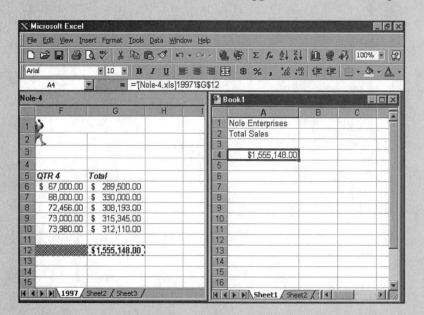

8 Save your changes and keep both workbooks open for the next tutorial.

Now that you have established the link, you can test it. If cell G12 in the Nole-4 workbook did not contain a formula, you could just type a value in cell G12, and cell A4 in Book1 would immediately change to display the new value. When a cell contains a formula, to test the link you must change a value in a cell that is used in the formula.

Testing the New Link

To test the link between cell G12 in the Nole-4 worksheet and cell A4 in the Book1 worksheet, follow these steps:

1 Click cell G12 in Nole-4.

2 Press Esc to return to the Ready mode (and remove the marquee).

The formula in cell G12 sums cells G6:G10. When you change cell F6, the contents of both G12 and cell A4 in the dependent worksheet will change.

3 In cell F6, type **85,000** and press Enter. Your screen should now look like Figure 9.8.

Figure 9.8
The altered
worksheets.

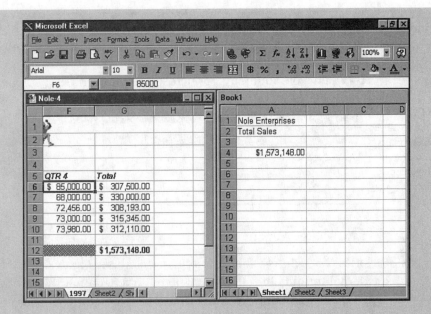

Notice that a new total has been calculated and that it is also shown in cell A4 of the dependent worksheet.

4 Save your changes and keep both workbooks open for the next tutorial.

In the next tutorial, you save the Book1 workbook as Nole Summary and again change the value in cell G12 of Nole-4. What will happen to the contents of cell A4 in the dependent workbook? Actually, the results depend on what you do the next time you open the dependent workbook. Before Excel opens a dependent workbook, Excel gives you the option of updating any links. If you choose not to update the dependent workbook, the dependent workbook will retain the values it had when last saved.

Testing the Link Further

To further test the link by updating the link, follow these steps:

1 Click any cell in the dependent worksheet (Book1) to make the worksheet active; then save it as **Nole Summary**.

> ### Note
>
> Because BOOK1 is a default name that Excel provides when no name is used, it should always be replaced with a more descriptive name.

2 Close Nole Summary by clicking the Close button.

3 Maximize Nole-4 by clicking its Maximize button.

4 Change cell E9 in Nole-4 to **81,000**. The sales total in cell G12 is now $1,588,258.00.

9

(continues)

Testing the Link Further (continued)

5 Save and close Nole-4.

6 Open Nole Summary. A Microsoft Excel warning box appears (see Figure 9.9).

Figure 9.9
The Microsoft Excel warning box prompts you to update the dependent workbook by reestablishing links.

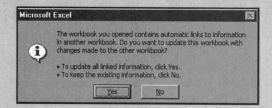

7 Click the **Yes** button.

Notice that cell A4 is immediately updated (see Figure 9.10). Note also that the external formula in cell A4 is changed to reflect that the source workbook is now stored on disk. Your external formula will look different because the formula depends on where the source workbook is stored on your disk.

Figure 9.10
Cell A4 is updated.

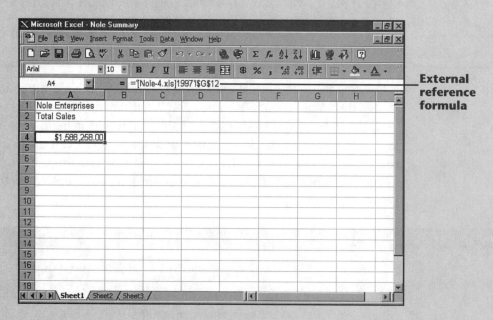

External reference formula

8 Save your changes and keep the workbook open for the next tutorial.

As you have seen in the previous tutorials, creating links enables you to use the same data for more than one worksheet. Also, when the original (source) data changes, the linked data in other worksheets is updated.

Saving Linked Workbooks

You should save any open source workbooks before you save the open dependent workbooks linked to them. Then you can be sure that the formulas in a source workbook have been calculated and that any changed workbook and worksheet names used in the external reference formulas of the dependent workbook are updated.

If you name or rename a source workbook with the **S**ave or Save **A**s command, the dependent workbook must be open for the names in the external reference formula to be updated. Save the source workbook; then resave the dependent workbooks. This procedure ensures that the dependent workbooks record the new path and file names of their source workbooks.

If you move the source workbook to another directory, remember to delete or rename it because when the dependent workbook is closed, the links to your data will be broken.

In the next objective, you learn how to restore a dependent workbook's broken link using the **E**dit, **L**inks command.

Objective 2: Change and Restore Links

External reference formulas are the mechanisms through which a dependent workbook receives data from its source workbook. The actual link between two sheets is created by the external reference formula in the dependent workbook. The formula that links the data from the source sheet to the dependent sheet consists of an equal sign and the external cell reference

='[NOLE-4.XLS]NOLE-4'!$G$12

The linking formula contains an absolute cell address preceded by an exclamation point. The formula also includes the file name and sheet name of the source worksheet. The path name, if the source workbook is in a different directory from the dependent workbook, is also included in the formula. For external cell references, workbook names are always enclosed by square brackets [ ]. If source workbooks are renamed or moved to other directories, dependent workbooks cannot find the needed data. These links are lost and must be reestablished.

Changing and Updating Links

To link the Nole Summary (dependent) workbook to a different source workbook, follow these steps:

❶ Open Nole Summary if it isn't already on your screen.

❷ Choose **E**dit, **L**inks to display the Links dialog box; then select the file links to change or update (see Figure 9.11).

(continues)

9

Changing and Updating Links (continued)

Figure 9.11
The Links dialog box and selected file for which you want to reestablish or change the links.

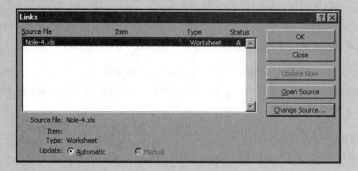

❸ Click the **C**hange Source button to display the Change Links dialog box (see Figure 9.12).

Figure 9.12
Change links using this dialog box.

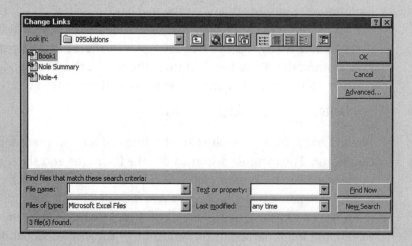

You reestablish the link by selecting a directory and entering a file name to indicate the directory and file name of the new supporting workbook that you want to establish as the source.

❹ Because the current link in this tutorial is the one you want to keep, click Cancel.

❺ In the Links dialog box, click Close.

❻ Save your changes and keep the workbook open for the next tutorial.

Restoring Links

If you move the source workbook file to another directory, rename it, or delete it, the links to your data will be broken. If you have a backup copy of the source file, or if the file is in another directory, you can easily change the link so that your data will appear in the dependent workbook as before. If you need to move a file into a new directory, be sure also to move to the same directory any files linked to the moved file.

> **Note**
>
> If you want to delete a source file and remove any links to it, you can select the linked cells on the dependent worksheet and clear the linking formulas. If you want to retain the information, but not the link, you can copy the cells on the dependent worksheet that contain the linked information, and then use the Paste **S**pecial command to paste only the values in place of the links.

Breaking a Link

To break the link between the source (Nole-4) and the dependent (Nole Summary) workbooks, make sure that both workbooks are open and follow these steps:

1 Save the Nole-4 workbook as **Nole-5**.

2 Switch to Nole Summary and verify that the external reference formula in cell A4 now shows Nole-5 as the source workbook (see Figure 9.13). *Remember:* the actual formula is shown in the formula bar.

Figure 9.13
The external
reference formula.

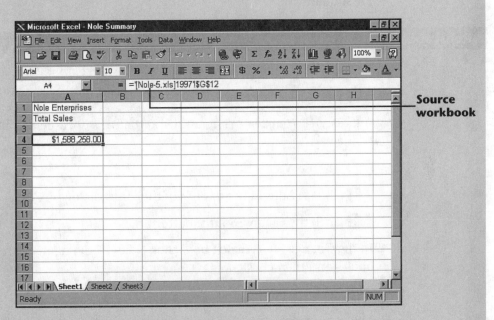

3 Switch to Nole-5 and close the workbook.

4 Save Nole Summary and keep it open.

5 Choose **F**ile, **O**pen. In the Open dialog box, select Nole-5 and press Del.

The Confirm File Delete warning box appears (see Figure 9.14).

(continues)

9

Breaking a Link (continued)

Figure 9.14
The Confirm File
Delete warning box.

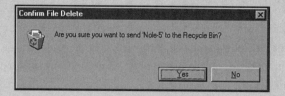

6 Choose **Yes**.

Now the source workbook in the link to Nole Summary is deleted, and the link no longer exists. However, the external reference formula is still in cell A4 of Nole Summary because this is where the value came from.

7 Close the Nole Summary workbook.

If you break a link between a source and dependent file, you can restore the link. Whether you are restoring a link to a source workbook that was moved to another directory or changing a link to point to a new source workbook, the steps are similar.

Reestablishing a Broken Link

To reestablish the link using Nole-4 as the source, follow these steps:

1 Open Nole Summary.

A message box appears to remind you that this document contains links (refer to Figure 9.9).

2 Choose **No**.

3 Choose **Edit**, **Links** to display the Links dialog box (refer to Figure 9.11).

4 Click the **Change Source** button.

In the Change Links dialog box, click Nole-4—the name of the new source workbook—and then click OK.

5 Click OK in the Links dialog box.

The new source workbook is now included in the external reference formula in cell A4 of the dependent workbook Nole Summary (see Figure 9.15). The link will now update automatically.

Figure 9.15
The new external reference formula.

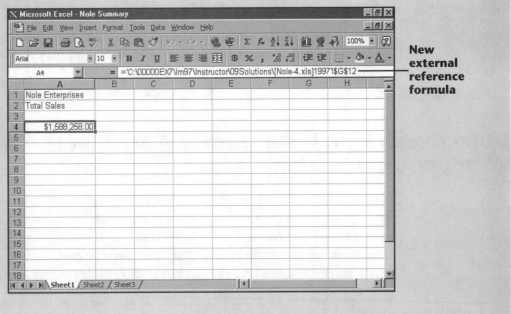

New external reference formula

Keep the Nole Summary workbook open for the next tutorial.

When you no longer want a cell in a dependent workbook to be updated automatically from a source workbook, you can remove the link. Usually, you will want the dependent workbook to retain the most recently updated value from the source workbook. The following tutorial shows you how to remove the link and save the updated value.

Removing a Link

To remove the link and save the most recently updated value in cell A4, follow these steps:

1 Make sure that both the Nole-4 and Nole Summary workbooks are open and tiled on your screen.

2 Click cell A4 in the Nole Summary window to activate it.

3 Choose **E**dit, **C**opy.

4 Choose **E**dit, Paste **S**pecial.

5 In the Paste section of the Paste Special dialog box, click the **V**alues option button and click OK.

6 Press (↵Enter).

The Paste **S**pecial, **V**alues combination places the most recently updated value (not formula) in cell A4. Cell A4 no longer contains an external reference formula (refer to the formula bar).

(continues)

9

Removing a Link (continued)

❼ Verify that the link is broken by making a change in the expenses in Nole-4 and checking to see whether cell A4 in Nole Summary is updated.

❽ Save and close Nole Summary. Keep Nole-4 open for the next tutorial.

Objective 3: Link Data from a Worksheet to another Windows Application

You can copy information from one Windows application into another by using the Clipboard and the Copy and Paste commands. Often, workers preparing reports copy Excel worksheets or Excel charts into word processing documents. Many word processing programs don't give you the capability to lay out a grid of numbers or to create a chart easily, but with Excel these tasks are simple.

When you use the Copy and Paste commands, the current worksheet or the chart is copied into the word processing document. If the data in the worksheet changes, however, the worksheet or chart in the word processing document is not updated. You may not want updating, for example, if you want your report to reflect your organization's data at one point in time and you are sure that you will be aware of any last-minute updates to the worksheet. Sometimes, however, you will want to create a link between the (dependent) word processing document and the (source) Excel worksheet.

In the following tutorials, you create a link between a word processing document and your Excel worksheet. A link to another Windows application functions and is updated just like a link between two Excel workbooks. You use Windows 95 WordPad in these tutorials because it is supplied with Windows 95. The same techniques can be used with any Windows 95 word processing program. If you are not familiar with WordPad, check with your instructor before beginning the following tutorial.

Creating a Link to Display a Worksheet in a WordPad Document

To create a link between part of the Nole-4 worksheet and a WordPad document, follow these steps:

❶ Select the range of cells A5:C10 in the Nole-4 workbook.

❷ Choose **E**dit, **C**opy to place these cells in the Clipboard.

❸ Use the Windows 95 Start button to start the WordPad program. (WordPad is located in the Accessories group.)

❹ In WordPad, type **These are our first quarter sales:** and press ⏎Enter twice.

❺ Choose **E**dit, Paste **S**pecial to display the Paste Special dialog box (see Figure 9.16).

Figure 9.16
The Paste Special
dialog box.

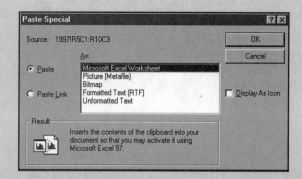

6 Click the Paste **Link** option button and click OK.

The range of selected worksheet cells is pasted into the WordPad document (see Figure 9.17) and linked to the Nole-4 worksheet.

Figure 9.17
The worksheet
cells in the
WordPad
document.

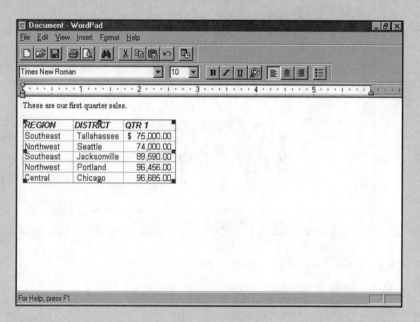

7 In the WordPad document, press ⬇ until the blinking cursor is to the right of the bottom right cell (96,685.00).

8 Press ⏎Enter twice to insert blank rows to prepare for the next tutorial.

9 Save the workbook and keep the workbook and the WordPad document open for the next tutorial.

You can also create a chart in Excel and copy it to a word processing document. Charts help readers see comparisons more easily and give reports a professional appearance.

9

Creating a Link to Display a Chart in a WordPad Document

To create a chart in the Nole-4 worksheet and paste the linked chart into your WordPad document, follow these steps:

1 Switch to the Excel Nole-4 workbook and press Esc to remove the marquee around cells A5:C10.

2 Click the ChartWizard button to create an embedded column chart that shows the first quarter sales.

3 Position the chart in cells A14 to F25 (see Figure 9.18).

Figure 9.18

The ChartWizard chart in Excel.

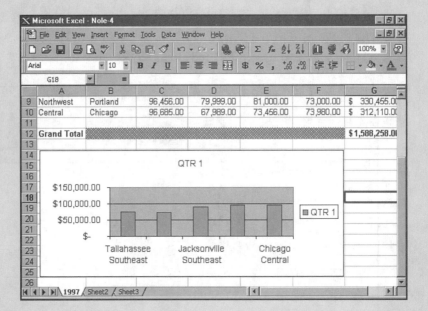

4 Select the chart if it isn't already selected.

5 Choose **E**dit, **C**opy.

6 Switch to the WordPad document.

7 Choose **E**dit, Paste **S**pecial to display the Paste Special dialog box.

8 Click the Paste **L**ink option button and then click OK to insert the chart into the WordPad document (see Figure 9.19).

Figure 9.19

The ChartWizard chart inserted into the WordPad document

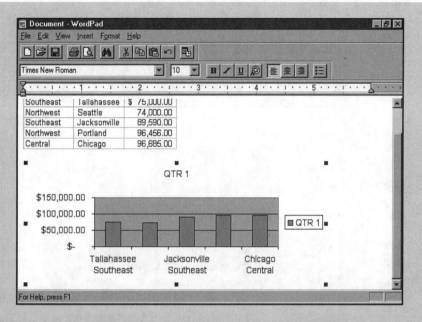

9 Print the WordPad document.

> **Note**
>
> If you are not familiar with WordPad, you first choose the **F**ile, **P**rint command to display the Print dialog box. In the Print dialog box, click OK to print your document. You can click the Print button if the WordPad toolbar is displayed.

10 Save both files and keep both the Nole-4 workbook and the WordPad document open for the next tutorial.

Testing the links between applications is always a good idea. When you have verified the proper functioning of the link, you can be sure of your results. This test is especially important when you have multiple links between applications.

Testing the Link

To test the link to see whether changing the source (Nole-4) will update the dependent WordPad document, follow these steps:

1 In the Nole-4 worksheet, change the first quarter sales in cell C6 to **124,000** and press ↵Enter.

2 Switch back to the WordPad document.

3 If your link was established properly, the chart in the WordPad document should now look like Figure 9.20. Compare Figure 9.20 to Figure 9.19. Scroll to the top and then back to the bottom of your WordPad document. Note that both the (dependent) worksheet selection and chart have been updated through the link. The chart is still the same size, but the data series column for Tallahassee has changed.

9

(continues)

Testing the Link (continued)

Figure 9.20
The linked data in the WordPad document.

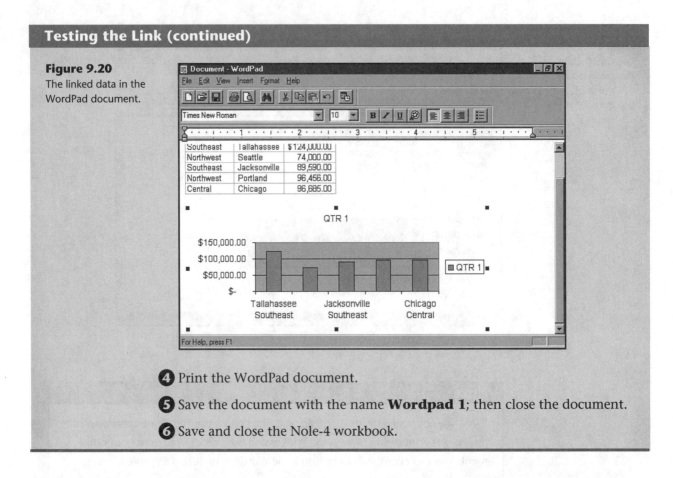

4️⃣ Print the WordPad document.

5️⃣ Save the document with the name **Wordpad 1**; then close the document.

6️⃣ Save and close the Nole-4 workbook.

Objective 4: Create a Summary Report with Subtotals

Summary report
A list in which data is broken into groups and summarized by group subtotals with an overall total given at the bottom of the list.

When you use Excel in an office, you will usually need to share the data in your worksheets. When you prepare a report, or even organize your data for your own use, you often need to prepare a *summary report* of your information. As you learned in Chapter 7, "Managing Data," large amounts of data are stored as records in an Excel list. Subtotals are the standard way of summarizing information in lists of sales, payrolls, expenses, inventories, and other kinds of data. You can easily and quickly summarize the data in a list by creating subtotals in Excel.

Creating a summary report is a two-step process. First, you sort your data into groups; then you use the **D**ata, Sub**t**otals command to produce subtotals, averages, and counts for each group. Excel labels the subtotals, averages, and counts with the appropriate group names. By using this method, you keep the details (the supporting information) in the worksheet and also produce a bottom line summary that managers can use. In the following tutorials, you learn how to create automatic subtotals that summarize the information in a list.

Creating Subtotals of Sales for Each Region

To create subtotals for dollars of sales for each region and a grand total, follow these steps:

❶ Open the Chap0902 and save it as **Coastal Cellular 2**.

❷ Sort the data by Region in ascending order.

This sort groups the data into regions so that Excel can create subtotals.

❸ Click any cell in the list to activate the list for Excel. (For example, click cell A4.)

❹ Choose **D**ata, Su**b**totals to display the Subtotal dialog box (see Figure 9.21).

Figure 9.21
The Subtotal dialog box.

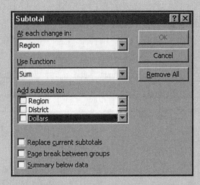

❺ Click the **U**se function drop-down arrow and select SUM, if it is not already selected.

This tells Excel to use the SUM function to create subtotals at the end of each group and then to create a grand total at the end of the summary report.

❻ In the A**d**d subtotal to scroll box, click any of the check boxes that contain a check mark to remove any pre-existing subtotal settings for a field.

❼ Click the Dollars check box so that it is the only field with a check mark (see Figure 9.22). Note that check marks still remain in both the Replace current subtotals check box and the Summary below data check box.

Figure 9.22
The completed Subtotal dialog box.

9

(continues)

Creating Subtotals of Sales for Each Region (continued)

8 Click OK.

Your screen should now look like Figure 9.23. Notice that the subtotals for each region are calculated and labeled with the appropriate region. (When a regional grouping ends, Excel automatically calculates a subtotal.)

Figure 9.23
The Summary
subtotals.

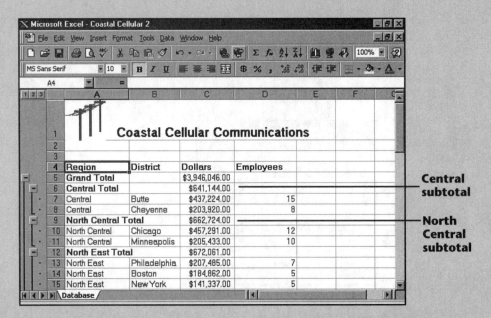

Central
subtotal

North
Central
subtotal

9 Scroll down your screen to see the rest of the records.

10 Print the worksheet.

11 Save your changes and keep the workbook open for the following tutorial.

When you are calculating a series of different subtotals, you must remove the old subtotals before producing the next set of subtotals.

Removing Subtotals

To remove the subtotals in the Coastal Cellular 2 worksheet, follow these steps:

1 Choose **D**ata, Su**b**totals.

2 In the Subtotal dialog box, click the **R**emove All button.

The subtotals are removed, and you see the original sorted list on your screen.

3 Save your changes and keep the workbook open for the next tutorial.

Excel can also calculate averages for subgroups of your data. This capability is useful for many kinds of reports.

Summarizing by Using Averages for Each Region

To find the average dollars of sales and the number of employees in the Coastal Cellular 2 worksheet, follow these steps:

1 Click cell A4 to activate the list.

2 Choose **D**ata, Su**b**totals to display the Subtotal dialog box.

3 Click the **U**se function drop-down arrow and select Average to use the AVERAGE function to produce averages for each group.

4 Use the scroll bar in the A**d**d subtotal to list box to see the available fields.

5 Click the Employees check box. Check to make sure that the Dollars check box also has a check mark in it. Only the check boxes for these two fields should contain a check mark.

6 Click OK.

Your screen should now look like Figure 9.24. Note that the averages are calculated for Dollars of Sales and Employees.

Figure 9.24
The Summary
Report using
averages.

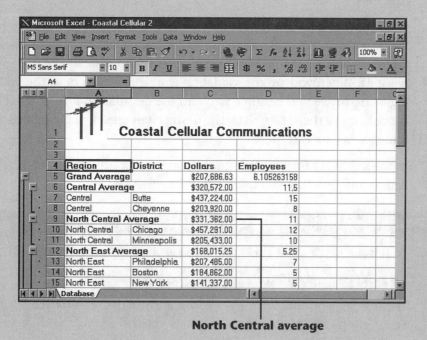

North Central average

7 Print the worksheet.

Next, you remove all subtotals from your list.

8 Choose **D**ata, Su**b**totals.

9 In the Subtotal dialog box, click the **R**emove All button.

10 Save, then close the workbook.

9

Objective 5: Create a Consolidated Report

Consolidated report
A report in which data from multiple source areas (usually different worksheets) is gathered into one worksheet.

Consolidation function
The function (like SUM or AVERAGE) that Excel is to use when it consolidates your data.

Source area
The cell ranges from which the Consolidate command draws data.

Destination area
The range of cells you select to hold data summarized by the Consolidate command.

Suppose that you have three worksheets of sales data and you need to print a report that summarizes them all. When you create a *consolidated report*, you pull all the data together from the three sheets and place the combined data on one sheet. Then you can print your report from that sheet. Excel can create this kind of consolidated worksheet automatically for you by performing calculations on similar data across multiple worksheets and workbooks and placing the results of the calculations in a consolidation worksheet. Excel uses *consolidation functions* to create these reports.

For example, each month you could use the SUM function to consolidate department budgets into one division budget; then you could consolidate the division budgets into one corporate budget. You create the consolidated worksheets from existing data; no additional work is necessary. The consolidation is easiest for Excel if all the worksheets have the same physical layout, as is often the case with budget worksheets. If the layouts are different, Excel can usually figure out what you want it to consolidate by examining the worksheets' row and column headings.

The worksheets (or the ranges in worksheets) that will be consolidated are called the *source area*. You can specify up to 255 source areas to consolidate. The part of the worksheet into which the source areas are consolidated is called the *destination area*. When you are consolidating worksheets, you have the option of creating a link between the source area and the destination area. If you choose to create links to the source data, the destination area data is updated when the source area data is changed.

In the following tutorial, you consolidate six monthly sales reports. The consolidation function that you use is the SUM function.

Selecting a Destination Sheet and a Consolidation Function

To select a destination sheet and a consolidation function, follow these steps:

❶ Open Chap0903 and save it as **Acme Summary**.

The first six worksheets in this workbook contain data that is laid out similarly. You consolidate the data in these six sheets into a seventh sheet (Consolidated Sales).

❷ Switch to the Consolidated Sales sheet by clicking its sheet tab.

❸ Select cell B7.

❹ Choose **D**ata, Co**n**solidate to display the Consolidate dialog box (see Figure 9.26).

Figure 9.25
The Consolidate
dialog box.

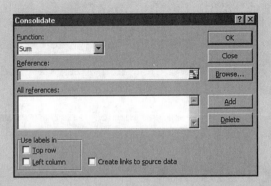

5 In the **F**unction drop-down list box, make sure that Sum is the function selected.

Keep the Consolidate dialog box open for the following tutorial.

In the following tutorial, you use the Consolidate dialog box to specify the consolidation function, the source areas to consolidate, and the row and column labels you want Excel to use in the consolidated report.

Selecting the Information to Consolidate

To select the worksheets in the Acme Summary workbook to be consolidated, follow these steps:

1 In the Consolidate dialog box, click the **R**eference text box (refer to Figure 9.25).

2 Click the January sheet tab.

3 Drag the Consolidate dialog box out of the way (if necessary); then click and drag to select cells B7:B19 in the January sheet.

4 Click the **A**dd button in the Consolidate dialog box.

Now your dialog box should look like Figure 9.26. The Reference box contains the sheet name and the cell references of the selection.

Figure 9.26
The Consolidate
dialog box with
partial details.

9

5 Click the February sheet tab. (Use the scroll buttons at the left of the sheet tabs to move to the sheet.)

(continues)

Selecting the Information to Consolidate (continued)

6 The corresponding cells, B7:B19, are already selected. Click the **Add** button.

7 Repeat steps 5 and 6 to select the March, April, May, and June sheets and add the data ranges (B7:B19) to the All **r**eferences list.

Now the six consolation ranges appear in the All **r**eferences list of the Consolidate dialog box (see Figure 9.27).

Figure 9.27
The Consolidate dialog box lists all three ranges.

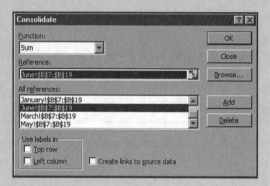

8 Click OK. The six sheets are consolidated in your worksheet (see Figure 9.28).

Figure 9.28
The consolidated worksheet.

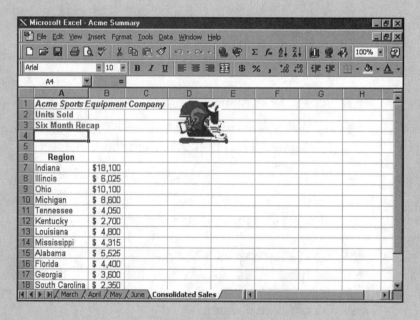

9 Save, then close the workbook.

Chapter Summary

In this chapter, you have learned how to link two Excel worksheets and how to repair a link that has been destroyed. You have learned how to link an Excel worksheet or chart into another application. You also learned how to produce a summary report with subtotals and how to consolidate multiple worksheets into one overall report.

In Chapter 10, "Analyzing Worksheet Data," you learn how to perform a what-if analysis by creating scenarios with the Scenario Manager.

Checking Your Skills

True/False

For each of the following, circle *T* or *F* to indicate whether the statement is true or false.

T   F   **1.** Managers at higher levels in an organization need more details in a worksheet.

T   F   **2.** A source workbook is the workbook that supplies the data that is sent on a link.

T   F   **3.** A link carries data in two directions: source to dependent and dependent back to source.

T   F   **4.** By default, Excel always automatically updates the linked data in a dependent workbook.

T   F   **5.** Dependent worksheets are also called target worksheets.

T   F   **6.** You can link one cell or a range of cells.

T   F   **7.** Source workbooks in a link must be on-screen for the link to update the dependent workbook properly.

T   F   **8.** You cannot format linked data in a dependent workbook.

T   F   **9.** After a link has been lost, it cannot be reestablished.

T   F   **10.** A link between a source workbook and another Windows application will not update automatically.

Multiple Choice

In the blank provided, write the letter of the correct answer for each of the following.

1. Which of the following can be passed over a link between workbooks?

    a. numbers

    b. text

    c. ranges of cells

    d. all the above

2. Between which of the following can you establish links?

    a. worksheets

    b. workbooks

    c. Excel and another Windows application

    d. all the above

3. To display two worksheets simultaneously on your screen, you use the **W**indow _____ command.

    a. **A**rrange

    b. **S**plit

    c. **D**ouble

    d. none of the above

4. To create a link between the source and the dependent worksheets, you use the _____ command.

    a. **P**aste

    b. Paste **O**bject

    c. Paste **L**ink

    d. none of the above

9

5. The actual cell reference in an external reference formula is always preceded by _____.

    a. {

    b. [

    c. @

    d. !

6. Worksheets that will be consolidated are called the _____ area.

    a. input

    b. source

    c. target

    d. consolidation

7. When you are consolidating worksheets, you have the option of creating a _____.

    a. link

    b. destination

    c. function

    d. none of the above

8. When you are selecting the information to consolidate, you use the _____ dialog box.

    a. Consolidate

    b. Select

    c. Source

    d. Summarize

9. You can specify up to _____ source areas to consolidate.

    a. 10

    b. 124

    c. 142

    d. 255

10. To remove summary subtotals from a list you use the _____, Subtotals command.

    a. **D**ata

    b. **R**emove

    c. **T**ools

    d. none of the above

Fill in the Blank

In the blank provided, write the correct answer for each of the following statements.

1. The part of the link that actually extracts the data from the source workbook and places it into the dependent workbook is the _____.

2. You should usually save the link's _____ workbook before you save the link's _____ workbook.

3. The command you use to restore broken links is the _____ command.

4. To remove a link between two sheets, you must delete the _____ from the linked cells in the dependent worksheet.

5. The _____ command enables you to create subtotals.

6. A link is a(n) _____-way connection between the source worksheet and the dependent worksheet.

7. A dependent workbook contains a(n) _____ reference to another workbook.

8. If a source workbook is _____ when the dependent workbook opens, the dependent workbook's linked data is automatically updated from the source workbook.

9. A(n) _____ report is a worksheet in which list data is broken into groups and summarized by group subtotals with an overall total at the bottom.

10. A(n) _____ report is one in which data from multiple source areas is gathered into one worksheet.

Applying Your Skills

Review Exercises

Exercise 1: Linking the Nole-4 Worksheet to a Dependent Worksheet

In this exercise, you link data between worksheets.

1. Open Chap0904 and save it as **Linking 1**.

2. Open a new workbook (the dependent workbook).

3. In the first three rows of the new workbook, enter the titles found in the first three rows of the Linking 1 workbook.

4. In cell A5 of the dependent workbook, type **July Sales**.

5. Link cell B5 of the new workbook to cell B12 of the Linking 1 workbook (the source workbook).

   Hints: 1.) activate cell B12 in Linking 1; then right-click and choose **C**opy; 2.) activate cell B5 in the dependent workbook; then right-click and choose Paste **S**pecial.

6. Test the link by changing the sales in cell B8 of Linking 1. Does cell B5 in the new workbook change?

7. Save the dependent workbook with the name **Linking 2**.

8. Save the Linking 1 workbook.

9. Print two copies of both workbooks—one to keep and one to turn in to your instructor.

10. Keep both workbooks open for the next exercise.

Exercise 2: Removing a Link Between Two Linked Workbooks

In this exercise, you remove a link between workbooks, while retaining the linked value in the destination workbook.

1. Be sure that both the Linking 1 and Linking 2 workbooks are open.

2. Remove the link that you established in Exercise 1 by using the **C**opy and Paste **S**pecial commands in the Linking 2 worksheet.

3. Test to see that the link has been removed by entering a new sales value in cell B8; cell B5 in the new workbook should not change.

4. Close both workbooks, without saving your changes.

9

Exercise 3: Linking an Excel Worksheet Chart into a WordPad Document

In this exercise, you create a chart using the data in one worksheet and then link the chart to a WordPad document.

1. Open Chap0904 and save it as **Linking 3**.

2. Create a column chart using the data in the Linking 3 worksheet (use the range A5:B12).

3. Use the **C**opy and Paste **S**pecial commands to link the chart into a WordPad document.

4. Save the WordPad document with the name **Wordpad 2**.

5. Verify that when you change data in Linking 3, the chart in the WordPad document is updated.

6. Print two copies of both the Linking 3 workbook and the Wordpad 2 document—one to keep and one to turn in to your instructor.

7. Save and then close both files.

Exercise 4: Creating Subtotals by Using the SUM Function

In this exercise, you create subtotals using the SUM function.

1. Open Chap0905 and save it as **Subtotals 1**.

2. Sort the data in ascending order by the Agents field.

3. Use the **D**ata, Su**b**totals command to create AGENT subtotals, using the SUM function for the PRICE field.

4. Print two copies of the worksheet (one to keep and one to turn in to your instructor) with the subtotals displayed.

5. Save and then close the workbook.

Exercise 5: Creating Subtotals by Using the AVERAGE Function

In this exercise, you create subtotals using the AVERAGE function.

1. Open Chap0906 and save it as **Subtotals 2**.

2. Use the **D**ata, Su**b**totals command to create LOCATION subtotals, using the AVERAGE function for the SQ. FEET field.

3. Print two copies of the worksheet (one to keep and one to turn in to your instructor) with the subtotals displayed.

4. Save and then close the workbook.

Continuing Projects

Project 1: Producing Subtotals

Open the Cape Sales and Marketing worksheet (Chap0907) and save it as **Real Estate 9**. Create a report that shows subtotals for the sum of Price of listings The subtotals should be grouped by Suburban Location. Print two copies of the report (one to keep and one to turn in to your instructor). Save and then close the workbook.

Project 2: Consolidating a Monthly Budget

Open the Kipper Industries workbook (Chap0908) and save it as **Employee 9**. In the Quarterly Report sheet, consolidate the monthly budgets into a monthly budget. Save the workbook; print two copies and then close it.

Project 3: Creating Links

Open the Coastal Sales Motor Pool worksheet (Chap0909) and save it as **Vehicle Mileage 9**. Create a link, using a workbook name Vehicle Mileage 9-2 that contains the Grand Total from Vehicle Mileage 9. Print two copies of Vehicle Mileage 9-2. Verify that the link works by changing the value in D6 to 94. Does the Vehicle Mileage 9-2 reflect the change? Save and then close the workbook.

9

Chapter 10

Analyzing Worksheet Data

What-if analysis
A form of data analysis in which you change key variables to see the effects on the results of the computation.

Decision-making is frequently a difficult task. You have many factors to consider and many alternatives to examine and compare. You also need to understand the implications of selecting one alternative over another and the effects of changing business conditions on the desirability of an alternative. Excel can help with this problem because it has the built-in capabilities to compare alternatives and perform *what-if analyses* quickly and accurately.

In this chapter, you learn to use one-input and two-input data tables to compare alternatives. Then you learn how to set up a forecasting model in a worksheet in order to examine more complex business situations. Forecasting worksheets enables you to play out various business scenarios to see the future implications of decisions you make now. In the last section of this chapter, you learn how to use Excel's Scenario Manager to create and organize business scenarios.

If you need to leave your computer before you complete your work in this chapter, be sure to save your work and close the file you have been using. You can then reopen the file with the saved changes when you want to continue this chapter.

Objectives

By the time you have finished this chapter, you will have learned to

1. Use a One-Input Table
2. Use a Two-Input Table
3. Set Up a Forecasting Worksheet
4. Use the Scenario Manager

Objective 1: Use a One-Input Table

Excel makes possible rapid what-if analysis. Worksheets provide immediate feedback to such questions as "What if we reduce costs by 5 percent?" "What if we sell 11 percent more?" Sometimes, however, you want to see the results of calculating a formula for a whole series of input values. For example, "What would be the results of this formula for interest rates from 5 percent to 7 percent in increments of .10 percent?" Answering that question would require you to enter 21 different values. If you also wanted a printout of the results for each value, you would soon start looking for a better way to find the answers you need.

One-input table
A table produced when a series of different values is used in place of one variable in a formula.

Whenever you need to substitute (plug in) a series of values into a cell in one or more formulas, Excel's data tables are the best solution. When you need to substitute values for only one variable (one cell) in a formula, you use a *one-input table*. Excel can create a table that shows the inputs you want to test and the test results so that you don't need to enter all the possible inputs at the keyboard. You can have more than one data table in a worksheet, enabling you to analyze different variables in different areas of the worksheet.

Calculating a Table Using One-Input Cell and One or More Formulas

One of the most frequently used examples of a one-input data table is a table that calculates the loan payments for a series of different interest rates. The single-input data table described in this section creates a list (a table) of monthly payments, given a range of different loan interest rates. The series of different interest rates is the one input that produces the table of results.

Before you create a data table, you need to build a worksheet that solves your what-if problem. For example, a worksheet that calculates a payment on a house or car loan must use the principal, interest rate, and term of the loan. Then in the worksheet, you use the PMT function to produce the amount of the monthly payment for the loan (see Chapter 4, "Using Functions," for a review of the PMT function).

Tip

Drag the AutoFill handle (at the lower-right corner of the selected cell or range) across a series to fill in incremental numbers for input values.

In the following tutorial, you create a worksheet that calculates the loan amount for one input value. In the second tutorial, you set up a one-input data table to produce payment results for a series of interest rates.

Creating the Loan Calculator Worksheet

To create a worksheet used as the basis for the data table, follow these steps:

❶ Click the New button on the Standard toolbar to create a new workbook.

❷ Enter the data shown in Figure 10.1. In cell D7, enter the formula
=PMT(D4/12,D5*12,D3)

The PMT function arguments are explained in Chapter 4. The first argument is the monthly interest rate; the second is the number of monthly payments, and the third argument is the amount of the loan.

Figure 10.1
The Loan
Calculator
worksheet.

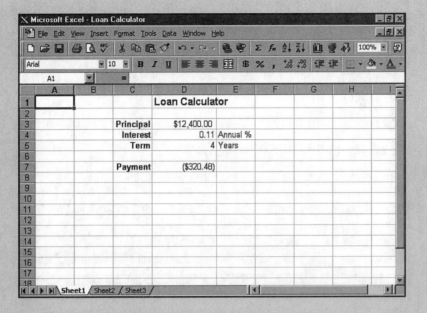

❸ Format cells D3 and D7 to Currency.

> **Note**
>
> Payments are negative numbers in this worksheet because the cash is going out.

❹ Save the workbook (but don't close it) with the name **Loan Calculator**.

Keep the workbook open for the next tutorial.

Next, you enter the series of different values you want to be used as inputs (plugged in) to the formula. You can enter the series of inputs in either a row or a column.

Creating the Loan Data Table

To create the data table in the Loan Calculator workbook, follow these steps:

❶ In cell C10, enter **Interest** and format it as boldface text.

❷ In cell D10, enter **=D7**. Cell D7 contains the formula to produce the result.

> **Note**
>
> You can also type a formula rather than reference a formula located elsewhere.

Cells C11:C17 will contain the interest rates (10 percent to 13 percent) to be used as the one input variable.

❸ In cell C11, enter **.10**.

(continues)

Creating the Loan Data Table (continued)

4 In cell C12, enter **.105**.

5 Select cells C11:C12.

6 Drag the fill handle down to cell C17.

7 Format cells C11:C17 as Percentage with two decimal places.

8 Format cells D10:D17 as Currency.

Your worksheet should now look like Figure 10.2.

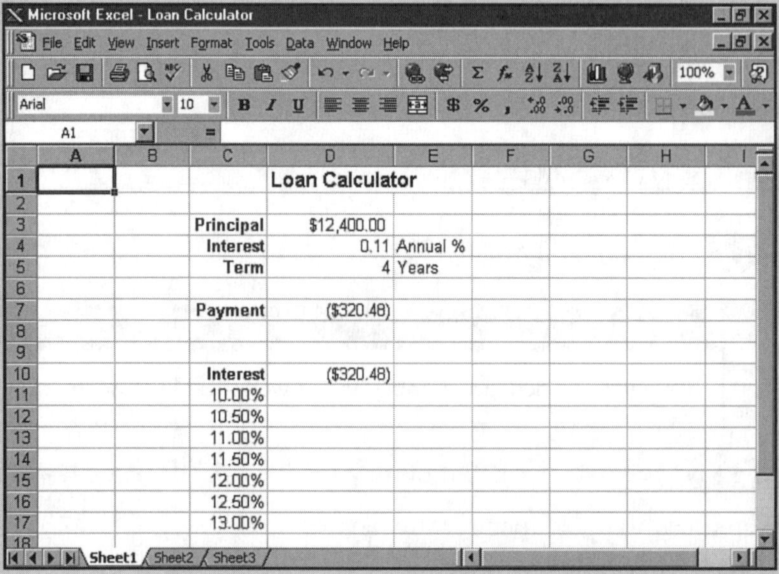

Figure 10.2
The Loan
Calculator
worksheet ready
for the **D**ata,
Table command.

	A	B	C	D	E	F	G	H	I
1				Loan Calculator					
2									
3			Principal	$12,400.00					
4			Interest	0.11	Annual %				
5			Term	4	Years				
6									
7			Payment	($320.48)					
8									
9									
10			Interest	($320.48)					
11			10.00%						
12			10.50%						
13			11.00%						
14			11.50%						
15			12.00%						
16			12.50%						
17			13.00%						
18									

Note

To see the results of other formulas in the table, you enter these formulas in other cells across the top of the table. For example, you can enter additional formulas in cell E10, F10, and so on.

9 Select C10:D17. These are the cells that will make up the table.

10 Choose **D**ata, **T**able to display the Table dialog box (see Figure 10.3).

Figure 10.3
The Table
dialog box.

The one-input variable (the values to be substituted in the formula) is interest rate. The series of interest rates are stored in the column of cells C11:C17. The cell in the PMT formula that you want this column of values plugged into is D4.

10

⓫ In the **C**olumn input cell text box, enter **$D$4** and click OK.

The data table fills with the payment amounts that correspond to each interest rate in the table (see Figure 10.4).

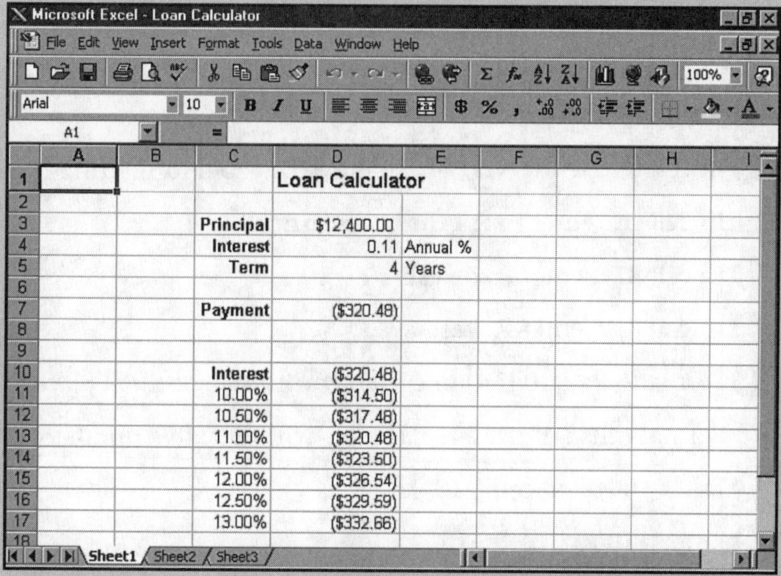

Figure 10.4
The completed table, with results in column D for each value in column C.

⓬ Save and print the worksheet.

Keep the workbook open for the next tutorial.

If you have problems... For most students, deciding which cell to use as the input cell is the most confusing part of setting up a table. Ask yourself, "If I want to calculate payment amounts manually, in which cell do I type all the changing values?" That cell is the input cell. In the Loan Calculator worksheet, you type these interest rates into cell D4. By entering $D$4 into the **C**olumn input cell, you are instructing Excel to test each interest rate in the left column of the table by moving that rate into cell D4. The resulting payment that is calculated for each interest rate (shown in column C) is then placed in the corresponding cell in column D.

Objective 2: Use a Two-Input Table

Two-input table
A table produced when a series of different values are used in place of two variables in a formula.

Sometimes, you may want to see a table that shows the results when two input variables (in two different worksheet cells) are plugged into a formula. To do this, you set up a *two-input table*. In a two-input table, you use both a **R**ow input cell and a **C**olumn input cell. In the following tutorials, you create a data table that changes twoinput values—interest and principal. The worksheet calculates the result of the PMT function for all combinations of those values. The top row of the table contains the different principal amounts to be substituted for the **R**ow input cell, and the left column of the table contains the sequence of interest rates to substitute in the **C**olumn input cell.

When you use two different input values, you can test the results from only one formula. The formula, or reference to the formula, must be in the top-left corner of the table. In the first of the following tutorials, you modify the Loan Calculator worksheet to prepare it for use as a two-input table.

Modifying the Loan Calculator Worksheet

To modify the Loan Calculator worksheet so that it can be used as a two-input table, follow these steps:

1 In cell C10, enter **=D7** and remove the bold formatting.

2 In cell D9, enter **Principal Amounts**.

3 In cell B11, enter **Interest**.

4 In cell B12, enter **Rates**.

5 Format cells D10:H10 to currency with two decimal places.

6 Format cells D11:H17 to currency with negative numbers in parentheses.

7 Enter **10000** in cell D10.

8 Enter **11000** in cell E10.

9 Select cells D10:E10 and drag the fill handle to cell H10.

10 Adjust the column widths so that the numbers you entered in row 10 can be displayed.

Now your worksheet should look like Figure 10.5.

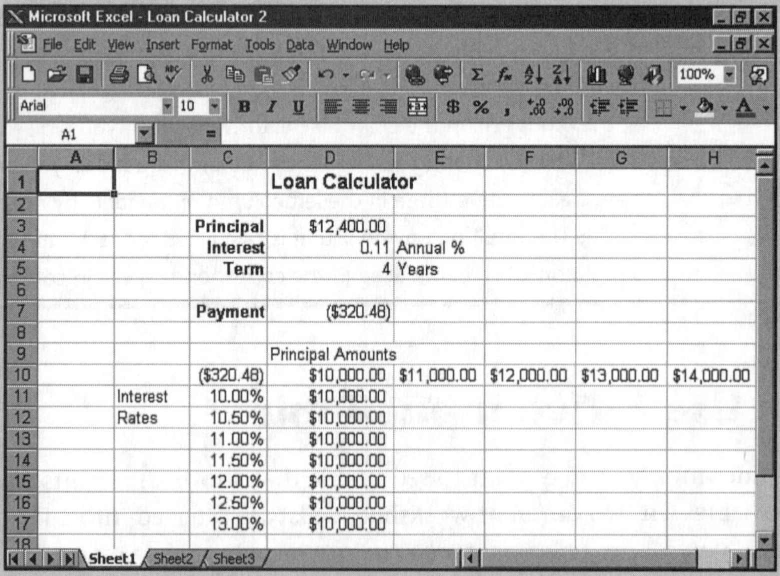

Figure 10.5

The Loan Calculator worksheet modified for use as a two-input table.

11 Save the workbook with the name **Loan Calculator 2**.

Keep the workbook open for the next tutorial.

In the next tutorial, you create a two-input data table to calculate and display your results when both the interest rate and the principal change.

Creating the Two-Input Loan Data Table

To set up the two-input table in the Loan Calculator 2 workbook, follow these steps:

❶ Select cells C10:H17.

❷ Choose **D**ata, **T**able to display the Table dialog box (refer to Figure 10.3).

The principal values are in the top row of the table area, and the principal input cell in the worksheet is cell D3. Interest is still in the column at the left of the table area, and the column input cell is D4.

❸ In the **R**ow input cell text box, type **$D$3**.

❹ In the **C**olumn input cell text box, type **$D$4**.

❺ Click OK.

Figure 10.6 shows the results of the two-input data table. Each dollar value is the amount you pay on a loan with this principal amount and annual interest rate. Because each monthly payment represents a cash outflow, the results appear in parentheses to show that the amounts are negative.

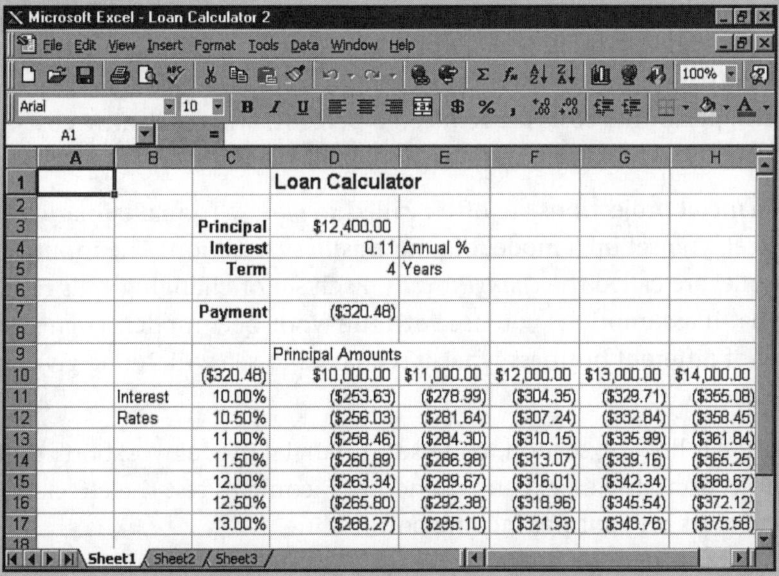

Figure 10.6
The completed data table with the results of combinations from two input values (interest and principal).

❻ Save and print the workbook before closing it.

After the data table is complete, you can change any worksheet values on which the data table depends. Excel recalculates the table using the new values. In Loan Calculator 2, typing a new term amount in cell D5 causes new payment amounts to reappear. You can also change the numbers in the rows and columns of input values and see the resulting change in the data table. In the example worksheet, you can type new numbers or choose **E**dit, **F**ill, **S**eries to replace the numbers in C11:C17 or in D10:H10. The table will be automatically updated.

Objective 3: Set Up a Forecasting Worksheet

Excel worksheets are most frequently used for budgeting. The second most frequent use of Excel worksheets is forecasting. In business, you need to have a good feel for the influence of key financial factors. Because these factors determine the future success or failure of your business, you must be able to project changes in these factors.

Worksheet model
A worksheet with formulas that represent real-world business operations and can be used to create scenarios.

With a worksheet, you can create a financial model of your business. This *worksheet model* will contain certain facts about your business. The worksheet will also contain assumptions you make about how your business functions financially now and in the future. These assumptions are represented by formulas in the worksheet.

A model, whether it be financial or weather, uses certain key inputs to produce outputs (results). As the inputs change, the results change. Weather models require inputs such as temperature, humidity, and wind direction. Financial models use such inputs as tax rates, interest rates, costs of goods sold, and advertising costs. Just as the accuracy of weather forecasts depends on the validity of the weather model used, the accuracy of your financial forecasts depends on the validity (in terms of realism) of your model.

Because a business is never affected by just one factor, financial models have multiple inputs. The interaction of these inputs can be complicated and difficult to keep in mind when you think about your business. For this reason, Excel worksheets are often used to perform what-if analyses, to answer questions, such as "What if sales increase by 5 percent, costs of goods sold increase by 2.5 percent, personnel costs are reduced 6 percent, and marketing costs jump 3 percent? What will the bottom line look like then?"

Scenario
A projected sequence of possible future events; a set of changing input values and their results.

Financial projections are often called *scenarios*. To make financial projections in Excel, you set up a model of your business situation. The input cells of the model are called the *changing cells*. Each set of changing cells represents a set of what-if assumptions you use with the worksheet model. Then you can play out a set of different business what-if scenarios to see which one gives you the best result.

Changing cells
The input worksheet cells in a scenario.

In the following section, you use a financial model workbook that produces a projection of sales, expenses, and net income to test the effects of changing sales and costs on your net income bottom line.

Examining a Modeling Worksheet

The Chap1001 workbook contains an example of a modeling worksheet that could be used by Nole Enterprises in what-if scenarios (see Figure 10.7). The worksheet uses growth percentage estimates for Sales, Cost of Goods Sold (COGS), General and Administrative Costs (G&A), and Marketing Costs (Mktg). These four percentages are the changing cells in the Nole Enterprises scenario. By changing the values in these cells, which are the key inputs to Nole Enterprises' business model, you change the results of the model. These results are for a period of five years. Net Income and Total Income are the results that would be of most interest to the management of Nole Enterprises.

Figure 10.7

A simple financial modeling worksheet.

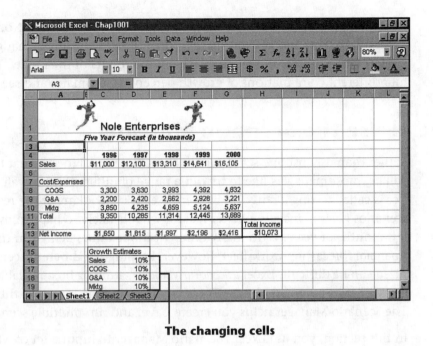

The changing cells

The projections used in forecasting model worksheets usually start with known data for the first time period. This data is used as the starting value to estimate the projected value for the next time period. In this example, Nole Enterprises knows the results of 1996. The annual growth rate estimates in cells D16:D19 are then used to calculate the results for the next time period. For example, sales for 1997 are estimated by multiplying 1996 sales by 110 percent (1+$D$16) to give a 10 percent growth in sales. Sales for 1998 are estimated in the same way using the 1997 value. Take a moment to look at the formulas in cells D5:G10 so that you can understand how the model estimates growth.

This worksheet is, of course, a very simple model, and the growth estimates may not be realistic. The worksheet does, however, illustrate the principles and the techniques used in creating financial forecasting models. In the following tutorial, you enter new values (growth estimates) in the input cells (the changing cells) and see the results.

Entering New Input Values for the Model

To enter new values in the changing cells of the Nole Enterprises worksheet, follow these steps:

1 Open Chap1001 and save it as **Scenario 1**.

2 Change the sales growth estimate in cell D16 to 20 percent.

Note the change in the results of the forecast.

3 Change the G&A costs growth rate to 12 percent.

4 Save and print the worksheet.

Keep the workbook open for the next tutorial.

Now you are ready to do some simple what-if analyses yourself. Notice closely the results of the changes you make in the following tutorial. Change the growth rate estimates to see the effects on the results of the model. Try three or four different combinations of growth percentage estimates and see the results.

Objective 4: Use the Scenario Manager

Scenario Manager
An Excel feature that creates and saves different sets of data as separate scenarios.

Rather than use just one set of input values in a model to see what the results will be, most managers like to try out a range of different input values. This practice is called testing a range of different scenarios. Looking at the results of the scenarios gives managers a better feel for what is likely to happen over the next few months or years. With many different input values being run through a financial forecasting worksheet, however, keeping the different scenarios organized can be difficult. Excel's *Scenario Manager*, a dialog box available through the Scenarios command in the **T**ools menu, is designed to make this task easier. The Scenario Manager helps you create, save, and run multiple scenarios.

In this section, you use Excel's Scenario Manager to input a set of what-if assumptions into your worksheet model and see how the results of the model are affected. The Scenario Manager enables you to define changing cells for your worksheet. You then create different scenarios using these changing cells. The Scenario Manager enables you to store multiple scenarios in the worksheet so that you don't need to save multiple copies of your data.

Testing Multiple Solutions with Scenarios

Worksheets are ideally suited for what-if analysis. You enter values into key cells and watch what happens to the results. Although this procedure enables you to enter new alternatives, reentering previous sets of values is often tedious. In many situations, you need to look at many alternatives, a need that requires entering many different sets of input values (changing cells).

Excel's Scenario Manager can manage multiple scenarios by storing different values for input data cells in scenarios to which you assign different names. These values are stored in the worksheet and saved when you save the worksheet. You can keep many versions—or scenarios—of input values and switch easily among them. When you want to view the results from a different scenario of input values, you just choose a different named scenario in the Scenario Manager dialog box.

A model with named scenarios should have a clear set of one or more key input values and a clear set of one or more result values that change based on the inputs. The Scenario 1 worksheet meets both of these criteria. When you enter new numbers for the growth estimates in cells D16:D19, the Net Income figures adjust automatically, and you see the new Total Income in cell H13. You have a clear set of input values as well as a clear result value. You use the Scenario 1 workbook to create scenarios with the Scenario Manager by saving different named sets of input values for the changing cells. These values are the input values saved by the Scenario Manager.

Before running a what-if scenario with the Scenario Manager, you should give names to the input cells. Excel does not require that the input cells have names, but if they do, the dialog boxes and reports in the Scenario Manager will display the names rather than the difficult-to-understand cell addresses.

Naming the Input and Result Cells

To name the input and result cells for the Scenario 1 worksheet, follow these steps:

1. Select cells C16:D19.

2. Choose **I**nsert, **N**ame, **C**reate.

3. In the Create Names dialog box, make sure that a check mark appears in the **L**eft Column check box.

4. Click OK.

5. Select cells H12:H13.

6. Choose **I**nsert, **N**ame, **C**reate. In the Create Names dialog box, click the **T**op Row check box if a check mark doesn't already appear.

7. Click OK.

This process uses the labels in the left column (column C) to create names for the cells in the right column (column D). Steps 4 and 5 name the final result cell Total_Income by using the label in cell I12.

> **Note**
>
> The Scenario Manager uses a name instead of a cell reference if a name applies specifically to just that cell. If a name applies to more than the single cell, the Scenario Manager ignores the name. To determine whether a cell has a name, select the cell. If a name has been assigned, it will appear in the name box at the extreme left of the formula bar. Otherwise, the name box will display the cell reference. To display a list of names in the worksheet, click the arrow adjacent to the name box in the formula bar.

Displaying the Scenario Manager Dialog Box

To open the Scenario Manager dialog box in the Scenario 1 worksheet, follow these steps:

1. Select the input cells (the changing cells), C16:D19. Keep these cells selected.

When you create your scenario, Excel uses the currently selected cells with their current values as the default changing cells.

(continues)

Displaying the Scenario Manager Dialog Box (continued)

❷ Choose **T**ools, S**c**enarios to display the Scenario Manager dialog box (see Figure 10.8). No scenarios have been stored yet.

Figure 10.8
The Scenario Manager dialog box.

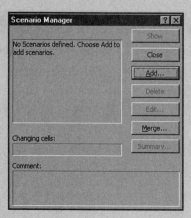

❸ Drag the Scenario Manager dialog box up so that you can see the input cells and the result cell. Excel will remember where you want the dialog box displayed whenever you use the worksheet.

Keep the workbook and the Scenario Manager dialog box open for the next tutorial.

The Scenario Manager dialog box offers you many options for dealing with your scenarios. Table 10.1 explains the functions of the elements of Scenario Manager dialog box.

Table 10.1 Elements of the Scenario Manager Dialog Box

Element	Function
Boxes	
Scenarios	Lists the names of any defined scenarios in the active worksheet; if there are no scenarios, the box is empty.
Changing Cells	Displays the cells containing the data that is to change in each named scenario.
Comment	Displays the date a scenario was created or edited, the name of the individual who created or modified the scenario, and any text you type as a comment.
Buttons	
Show	Displays in the worksheet the changing cell values for the scenario selected in the Scenarios box. The worksheet is recalculated to reflect the new values.
Close	Closes the Scenario Manager dialog box.
Add	Enables you to add a new named scenario.
Delete	Immediately deletes the scenario you have selected in the Scenarios box.
Edit	Displays the Edit Scenario dialog box, enabling you to edit a scenario.

Adding Named Scenarios Using the Scenario Manager

Suppose that you need to create four scenarios for this model: the original values, a most-likely estimate, a best-case estimate, and a worst-case estimate. These estimates will enable you to get a sense of the range of options for the future.

Adding Your First Named Scenario

To create a scenario in the Scenario 1 worksheet with the Scenario Manager, follow these steps:

1 Make sure that the input cells C16:D19 are selected and that the Scenario Manager dialog box is displayed on your screen.

2 Click **A**dd.

The Add Scenario dialog box is displayed (see Figure 10.9).

Figure 10.9
The Add Scenario dialog box.

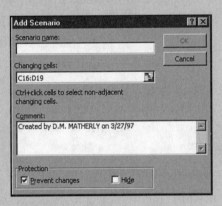

3 In the Scenario **n**ame text box, type **Original**.

Scenario names can be up to 255 characters in length and can contain spaces and numbers.

4 Click OK.

5 The Scenario Values dialog box is displayed with a listing of the values in the changing cells (see Figure 10.10).

Figure 10.10
The Scenario Values dialog box.

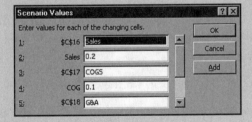

6 Click OK. The Scenario Manager dialog box is displayed.

7 Click Close.

(continues)

Adding Your First Named Scenario (continued)

You now have a single scenario stored in the worksheet. Behind the scenes, Excel saves the set of values in the input cells as the Original scenario.

❽ Save your changes and keep the workbook open for the next tutorial.

You can have several scenarios for each worksheet. In the following tutorial, you create three more scenarios.

Adding Other Named Scenarios

To add the most-likely, best-case, and worst-case scenarios to the Scenario 1 worksheet using the Scenario Manager, follow these steps:

❶ Enter the following most-likely scenario numbers into the worksheet's input (changing) cells: **15%** for Sales, **15%** for COGS, **12%** for G&A, and **17%** for Mktg.

❷ After changing the input values, select the input cells C16:D19.

Keep these cells selected. When you create your scenario, Excel uses the currently selected cells with their current values as the default changing cells. If you forget to do this, you can always enter the changing cells in the Scenario Manager's Changing Cells text box.

Now you can use the Scenario Manager to add the new scenario.

❸ Repeat the steps you followed in the preceding tutorial except type **Most-likely**, the name of the scenario, in the Scenario **n**ame text box.

Next, you add the best-case, and then the worst-case scenarios.

❹ Use the following values for the input cells (D16:D19) in the worksheet:

Best-case scenario: **20%** for Sales, **18%** for COGS, **18%** for G&A, **19%** for Mktg.

Worst-case scenario: **12%** for Sales, **14%** for COGS, **18%** for G&A, **20%** for Mktg.

❺ After you have chosen OK to accept the Worst-case scenario. The Scenario Manager dialog box reappears—this time, with all four named scenarios listed (see Figure 10.11).

❻ Click Close to close the Scenario Manager dialog box.

You now have all four scenarios on the worksheet ready to review.

Figure 10.11
The Scenario Manager after adding the four scenarios.

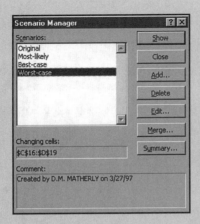

⑦ Save the workbook and keep it open for the next tutorial.

Because the named scenarios are stored in hidden names in the worksheet, when you save the workbook, you save the scenarios you have just created. Saving the workbooks helps prevent you from losing your scenarios if you accidentally make a mistake. When you save the workbook, the input (changing) cells for the scenarios, as well as the scenario names and values, are stored with the worksheet.

Now that you have some named scenarios in the worksheet, you can quickly switch the model from one scenario to another. Simply choose a different scenario from the Scenario Manager dialog box. The values for the scenario you choose appear in the changing cells, and the worksheet is recalculated.

Switching between Named Scenarios

To switch between scenarios in the Scenario 1 workbook using the Scenario Manager, follow these steps:

❶ Choose **T**ools, Sc**e**narios to display the Scenario Manager dialog box.

The current scenario (the one from which you are making the switch) is selected.

❷ If necessary, move the dialog box up to reveal more of the screen so that the input and result cells are visible.

❸ Double-click the name of a different scenario in the Scenarios list box.

(Alternatively, you can select a scenario from the Scenarios list box, and choose **S**how.)

The values for the scenario you choose appear in the changing cells, and the worksheet is recalculated.

❹ When you finish examining the scenarios, select the scenario you want to display and then choose Close.

Keep the workbook open for the next tutorial.

After you have named scenarios in your worksheet, you can go back and change the values for any given scenario. With this capability, you can have a great many scenarios without the tedious work of reentering numbers.

Editing a Scenario

To edit a scenario in Scenario 1 with the Scenario Manager, follow these steps:

1 Choose **T**ools, Sc**e**narios to display the Scenario Manager dialog box.

2 Select the Most-likely scenario.

3 Click the **E**dit button to display the Edit Scenario dialog box (see Figure 10.12).

Figure 10.12
The Edit
Scenario
dialog box.

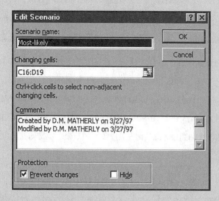

4 To specify different changing cell values, you must edit the contents of the Changing **c**ells text box. To do so, choose OK.

5 The Scenario Values dialog box is displayed (refer to Figure 10.10).

6 Make the following changes in the appropriate text boxes:

Sales: **0.18**; COG **0.15**; G_A **0.11**; and Mktg **0.16**; then choose OK.

7 In the Scenario Manager, choose **S**how to make the worksheet reflect the changes.

8 Choose Close to close the dialog box.

Do not save your changes. Keep the workbook open for the next tutorial.

Eventually, you will finish exploring a particular named scenario. Usually, you won't want to keep the scenarios you no longer use. You can easily delete a named scenario by using the Scenario Manager.

Deleting Named Scenarios

To delete a named scenario in Scenario 1, follow these steps:

1 Choose **T**ools, Sc**e**narios to display the Scenario Manager dialog box.

2 Click Worst-case, the name of the scenario you want to delete in the Scenarios list box.

3 Click the **D**elete button.

The Worst-case scenario is immediately deleted.

4 Close your workbook without saving the changes.

Chapter Summary

In this chapter, you have learned to use a worksheet in a new way. You have also learned how to do a simple comparison of alternatives using one-input and two-input tables. You have learned how to set up a worksheet to run financial projections and test what-if alternatives. Finally, you have learned how to use the Scenario Manager to create, run, edit, and delete scenarios. In Chapter 11, "Hyperlinks in Excel 97," you learn to create hyperlinks between Excel workbooks and between Excel and other Microsoft 97 documents.

Checking Your Skills

True/False

For each of the following, circle *T* or *F* to indicate whether the statement is true or false.

T   F   **1.** The changing cells in an Excel scenario are the result cells.

T   F   **2.** Clicking the **D**elete button in the Scenario Manager dialog box displays the Delete Scenario dialog box.

T   F   **3.** The command that enables you to name one or more cells is found in the **T**ools menu.

T   F   **4.** The top row of a one-input data table consists of one or more formulas or references to formulas.

T   F   **5.** A forecasting worksheet contains a model of an aspect of your business.

T   F   **6.** A scenario name cannot contain spaces.

T   F   **7.** You can have a maximum of three scenarios in a worksheet.

T   F   **8.** You can use formulas when setting up a one-input data table, but you cannot use functions.

T   F   **9.** The input variables to a two-input table must appear in two adjacent columns.

T   F   **10.** When you use two different input values in a two-input table, you can test the results from only one formula in the table.

Multiple Choice

In the blank provided, write the letter of the correct answer for each of the following.

1. To display the changing cell values on a worksheet for the selected scenario, click the _____ button in the Scenario Manager dialog box.

   a. Calculate

   b. Display

   c. Edit

   d. none of the above

2. To leave the Scenario Manager dialog box and return to the active worksheet, click the _____ button in the Scenario Manager dialog box.

   a. Close

   b. Exit

   c. Quit

   d. none of the above

3. The Scenario Manager dialog box is accessed through the _____ menu.

   a. Edit

   b. Tools

   c. View

   d. Data

4. A _____ table is produced when you use a series of different values in place of one variable in one or more formulas.

   a. one-way table

   b. two-way table

   c. database

   d. both a and b

5. A worksheet _____ contains formulas that represent real-world business operations.

   a. data table

   b. result area

   c. model

   d. none of the above

6. The command that enables you to edit a scenario is available through the _____ menu.

   a. Format

   b. Edit

   c. Window

   d. Data

7. A scenario name can consist of up to _____ characters.

   a. 8

   b. 20

   c. 33

   d. 255

8. The command to create a name for a range of cells is accessed through the _____ menu.

   a. Insert

   b. Edit

   c. File

   d. Tools

9. The _____ button in the Scenario Manager dialog box enables you to add a new named scenario.

   a. Add

   b. Include

   c. Edit

   d. Merge

10. Excel saves the set of values in the _____ cells as a scenario.

   a. input

   b. changing

   c. data

   d. what-if

Fill in the Blank

In the blank provided, write the correct answer for each of the following statements.

1. A(n) _____ table is produced when you use a series of different values in place of two variables in a formula.

2. The command that enables you to create tables of results is found in the _____ menu.

3. An Excel _____ is a named set of input values that you can substitute in a worksheet model.

4. You should give a(n) _____ to the input cells in a scenario.

5. To create a scenario using the Scenario Manager, you click the _____ button in the Scenario Manager dialog box.

6. _____ analysis is a form of data analysis in which you change key variables to see the effects on the results of the computation.

7. A(n) _____ is a projected sequence of possible future events.

8. Named scenarios are stored in _____ names in a worksheet.

9. Before you build a data table, you need to build a(n) _____ that solves a what-if problem.

10. Financial projections are often called _____.

Applying Your Skills

Review Exercises

Exercise 1: Using a One-Input Loan Analysis Table

In this exercise, you create a one-input table.

1. Open a new workbook. Setup the format for a one-input analysis table that calculates the monthly payments on a principal of $10,000.00 for interest rates of 5 percent through 9 percent in increments of 0.5 percent.

2. The loan must be paid off in 5 years.

3. Use the **Date**, **T**able command to display the Table dialog box in which you will enter the address of the input cell.

4. Print two copies (one to keep and one to turn in to your instructor); then save the workbook with the name **Loan 1**.

Exercise 2: Using a Two-Input Loan Analysis Table

In this exercise, you create a two-input table.

1. Open a new workbook. Create a two-input analysis table that calculates the monthly payments for principals of $10,000.00, $12,000.00, $14,000.00, and $16,000.00. The interest rates are 7 percent through 12 percent in increments of 0.5 percent.

2. The loan must be paid off in 6 years.

3. Use the **D**ate, **T**able command to display the Table dialog box in which you will enter the addresses of the input cells.

4. Print two copies (one to keep and one to turn in to your instructor); then save the workbook with the name **Loan 2**.

Exercise 3: Setting Up a One-Input Depreciation Schedule

In this exercise, you create a one-input table.

1. Open a new workbook. Create a one-input analysis table that prints a depreciation schedule using the double-declining balance method (use Excel's DDB function). Assume that the new piece of equipment costs $5,000.00 and has a lifetime of 7 years.

2. The salvage value of the machine is $600.00.

3. Use the **D**ate, **T**able command to display the Table dialog box in which you will enter the address of the input cell.

4. Print two copies (one to keep and one to turn in to your instructor); then save the workbook with the name **Depreciation 1**.

5. Keep the workbook open for the next exercise.

Exercise 4: Setting Up a Two-Input Depreciation Schedule

In this exercise, you create a two-input table.

1. Open a new workbook. Modify the Depreciation 1 worksheet you created in Review Exercise 3 so that the table shows a depreciation schedule for a new piece of equipment if the cost ranges from $5,000.00 to $6,000.00 in increments of $100.00.

2. Use a lifetime of 7 years and a salvage value of $600.00.

3. Use the **D**ate, **T**able command to display the Table dialog box in which you will enter the addresses of the input cells.

4. Print two copies (one to keep and one to turn in to your instructor); then save the workbook with the name **Depreciation 2**.

Exercise 5: Using the Scenario Manager

In this exercise, you use the Scenario Manager to create several scenarios for a workbook.

1. Open Chap1002 and save it as **Strawberry Scenario**.

2. For a Best-case scenario, enter the following values in cells C25:C31: Sales: **20**; Cost of Sales: **18**; Payroll **12**; Supplies: **6**, Advertising: **6**; Rent: **10**; Other: **5**.

3. Print two copies of the worksheet—one to keep and one to turn in to your instructor.

4. For a Worst-case scenario, enter the following values in cells C25:C31: Sales: **15**; Cost of Sales: **20**; Payroll **15**; Supplies: **6**, Advertising: **9**; Rent: **15**; Other: **7**.

5. Print two copies of the worksheet.

6. For a Most-likely scenario, enter the following values in cells C25:C31: Sales: **18**; Cost of Sales: **19**; Payroll **12**; Supplies: **6**, Advertising: **7**; Rent: **12**; Other: **5**.

7. Print two copies of the worksheet.

8. Save and then close the workbook.

Continuing Projects

Project 1: Forecasting the Future for Cape Sales and Marketing

The owners of Cape Sales and Marketing have asked you to set up best-guess, best-case, and \
case five-year scenarios for their business. You have met with the owners and have a copy of \
simplified income statement for 1997 (Chap1003). Using this information, set up a workbook
project the statement over four more years. Name the new workbook **Real Estate 10**.

Assume that the percent increases will be consistent for all five years of the projection. Use the S\
nario Manager to produce your own percent increases for all three scenarios. You should include \
inputs Percent Increases for Sales, COGS, G&A, and Mtkg. Print each case scenario (the best-guess
worksheet, the best-case worksheet, and the worst-case worksheet) that result from these scenarios.
Save and then close the workbook.

Project 2: Forecasting Future Sales and Expenditures for Kipper Industries

Set up a forecasting worksheet for Kipper Industries using Chap1004 to represent sales for the next
three quarters. Include the Gross Sales, Freight, Cash Discounts, Cost of Sales—Var, Fixed (Excl
Depr), Depreciation, Selling Expense, Advertising, Administrative, and Bad Debt Provision After
developing the forecasting analysis, test it by trying different combinations of sales and expendi-
tures percentage estimates. Save the workbook as **Employees 10**. Print two copies (one to keep and
one to turn in to your instructor); then close the workbook.

Project 3: Creating a Two-Input Table for Coastal Sales

Coastal Sales needs to purchase more vehicles for its motor pool. Set up a two-input table that calculates the monthly automobile payments for principals of $10,000, $12,000, $13,000, and $14,000.
The interest rates are 7 percent through 12 percent in increments of 0.5 percent. The term of the
loan is five years. If necessary, refer to Figure 10.5 in setting up the worksheet. Save the workbook as
Motor Pool. Print two copies (one to keep and one to turn in to your instructor); then close the
workbook.

Chapter 11

Hyperlinks in Excel 97

Hyperlink
Underlined or otherwise emphasized text or graphics that, when clicked with the mouse, displays another document.

Imagine having the ability to work with documents containing buttons and other active elements that enable you to move to another location in the document or to a different document entirely, with the click of a mouse. Not only would you save time by not having to retrieve separate files, you would not need to worry about the name of the files referred to in the document, just click the *hyperlink*.

Excel 97 hyperlinks enable you to jump to other Excel 97 worksheets or to documents in other Office 97 applications. Hyperlinks also enable you to set up a navigational course for those reading your worksheet. For example, you might create a hyperlink in a cell in your document that refers to a Word document. To get more information about the document, you can click the link and be able to view the document or be connected to the site.

If you need to leave your computer before you complete your work in this chapter, be sure to save your work and close the file you have been using. You can then reopen the file with the saved changes when you want to continue this chapter.

Objectives

By the time you have finished this chapter, you will have learned to

1. Identify the Relationship between the World Wide Web, Hyperlinks, and Excel 97

2. Create Hyperlinks to Other Excel 97 Workbooks

3. Create Hyperlinks to Office 97 Documents

4. Create Button Hyperlinks

5. Edit and Delete Hyperlinks

Objective 1: Identify the Relationship between the World Wide Web, Hyperlinks, and Excel 97

Intranet
A network within an organization that uses Internet technologies (such as HTTP or FTP protocols). You can use an intranet to navigate between documents, pages, or objects by using hyperlinks.

HyperText Markup Language (HTML)
A system of marking up, or tagging a document so that it can be published on the World Wide Web. Documents prepared in HTML include reference graphics and formatting tags. You use a Web browser (such as Microsoft Internet Explorer) to view these documents.

Web browser
Software that interprets HTML files posted on the WWW, formats them into Web pages, and displays them to the user. Web browsers can also play sound or video files embedded in Web documents if you have the necessary hardware.

You can use Microsoft Excel 97 to open workbooks on your company's local Web or *intranet*. If you have a connection to the Internet, you can also open workbooks on the Internet such as FTP (File Transfer Protocol) and HTTP (HyperText Transfer Protocol) servers.

You can also use Microsoft Excel 97 to open and create World Wide Web (WWW) files stored in *HTML* (*HyperText Markup Language*), the format used to create pages on the World Wide Web.

Some of the ways individuals and companies are using hyperlinked documents include the following:

- A simple web involving hyperlinks between Excel worksheets and Word documents that help you switch between documents you update frequently

- A simple hyperlink from an Excel expense statement to a Web site on the Internet containing currency exchange rates

- A web of hyperlinked Excel worksheets that compose an Executive Information System. Names and graphics are linked to Web sites on the Internet so executives can read competitors' business profiles, their latest Web ads, and stock analysis

- An intranet for traveling salespeople built from Excel sales forecasts saved as HTML documents; sales proposals in native Word files so they can be edited; and product information exported to HTML documents from an Access database

- An intranet for clients to track their sales orders; the Internet Assistants for Excel and Access export order tracking information as HTML documents on the intranet. (Because the documents are in HTML, clients with any type of computer system can view their order information with a *Web browser*.)

Even if you are not connected to an intranet or the Internet, you can still create a web of Office 97 documents linked together by hyperlinks. Such a web enables you to quickly jump between related documents. For example, you can create pages of product, service, and ordering information by inserting hyperlinks. After hyperlinks have been created, you can use the Excel 97 Web toolbar to control Web navigation and navigation between existing hyperlinks between Excel worksheets, Excel workbooks, and other Office 97 documents. You learn more about the Web toolbar later in this chapter.

Objective 2: Create Hyperlinks to Other Excel 97 Workbooks

You can create hyperlinks to other files on your system, your network, or the Internet, or to other locations within the current workbook in one of three ways.

You can enter or copy text in a cell or range and make the text a hyperlink. The text appears blue and underlined. When you click the text, you jump to the destination file or location. You can also draw or insert a graphic and make the graphic a hyperlink. The graphic can have any appearance you want, such as the clip art stored in the Microsoft Clip Gallery. When you click the graphic, you jump to the destination file or location. The graphics used as hyperlinks are often called button hyperlinks. A third way to create hyperlinks is to create custom hyperlinks by using a worksheet function. For example, a hyperlink can jump to different destinations depending on what you type in another cell.

In the following tutorials, you learn to create hyperlinks to other Excel 97 workbooks.

11

Creating Hyperlinks to Other Workbooks

To create hyperlinks to other Excel workbooks, follow these steps:

❶ Open the following files and save them using the file names as shown:

Existing File Name	Save as
Chap1101	**Summary Links**
Chap1102	**Northern**
Chap1103	**Southern**
Chap1104	**Western**
Chap1105	**Eastern**

❷ Using the Summary Links workbook, select cell A6 (Eastern).

❸ Click the Insert Hyperlink button on the Standard toolbar. The Insert Hyperlink dialog box is displayed (see Figure 11.1).

Figure 11.1
The Insert Hyperlink dialog box.

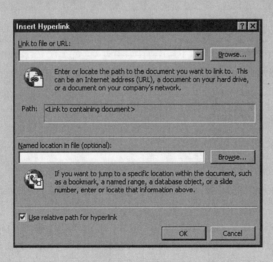

Uniform Resource Locator (URL)
The form of the site address that reveals the name of the server in which the site's files are stored, the file's directory path, and its file name.

❹ Click the **B**rowse button to the right of the **L**ink to file or *URL* text box to display the Link to File dialog box (see Figure 11.2). Note that your file list will differ from that shown in the figure.

(continues)

Creating Hyperlinks to Other Workbooks (continued)

Figure 11.2
The Link to File dialog box displays a list of files in the active folder.

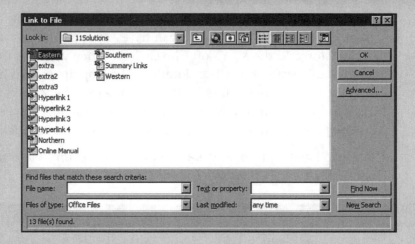

⑤ Select Eastern and then click OK to close the Link to File dialog box.

⑥ Click OK to close the Insert Hyperlink dialog box.

⑦ The hyperlink appears in cell A6 as blue, underlined text. Once you use the link, the text changes color to purple.

⑧ Position the pointer over cell A6. When the pointer changes to a hand symbol, the destination address for the hyperlink appears below the hand symbol (see Figure 11.3). Note that the figures do not show the hand.

Figure 11.3
The destination address for a text hyperlink.

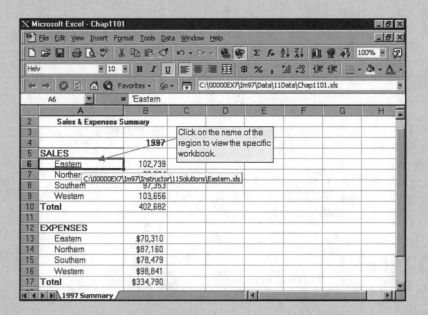

⑨ Click the Eastern hyperlink. The Eastern workbook is displayed (see Figure 11.4). After hyperlinks have been created, you can use the Excel 97 Web toolbar to control Web navigation and navigation between existing hyperlinks between Excel worksheets, Excel workbooks, and other Office 97 documents.

Figure 11.4
The Eastern
workbook.

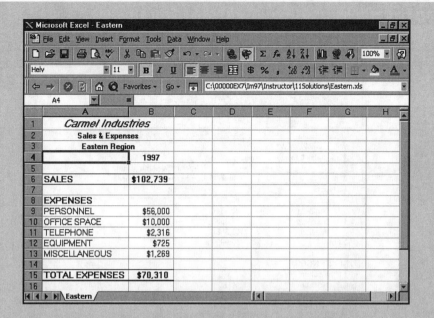

11

Note

If Excel prompts you to save the workbook, select Yes.

---

⑩ Switch to the Summary Links workbook.

⑪ Repeat the preceding steps to create hyperlinks in the Summary Links workbook to the Northern, Southern, and Western workbooks.

⑫ Test each hyperlink. Note that hyperlinked text is blue and underlined. Once you click a hyperlink, it changes to purple.

⑬ Print and save the Summary Links workbook and keep it open for the next tutorial. The completed Summary Links workbook should resemble Figure 11.5 with colored, underlined text in cells A6:A9.

(continues)

Creating Hyperlinks to Other Workbooks (continued)

Figure 11.5
The completed
workbook.

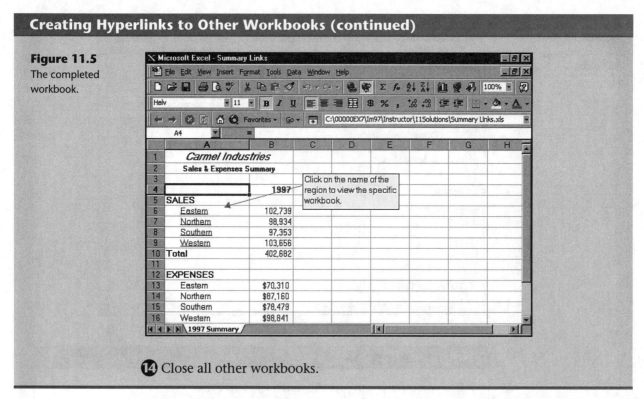

14 Close all other workbooks.

After hyperlinks have been created, you can use the Web toolbar (see Figure 11.6) in Excel to control Web navigation and navigation between existing hyperlinks between Excel worksheets, Excel workbooks, and other Office 97 documents.

Figure 11.6
The Web
toolbar.

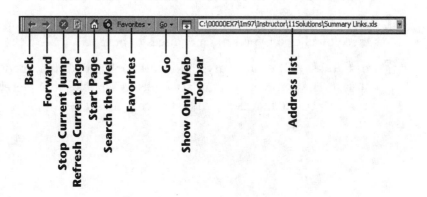

Address
The path to an object, document, file, page, or other destination. An address can be a URL (address to an Internet address) or a UNC network path (address to a file on a local area network).

To display the Web toolbar, click the Web Toolbar button on the Standard toolbar. To remove the toolbar from your screen, click the Web Toolbar button on the Standard toolbar. The Web toolbar enables you to move forward or backward through the hyperlink history or jump to any point within the history of hyperlinks. The history list contains a list of the last 10 files you jumped to using hyperlinks. In addition to using the history buttons, you can use the *Address* list (see Figure 11.7) to quickly move to recently used hyperlinked files.

Figure 11.7
The Address list on
the Web toolbar.

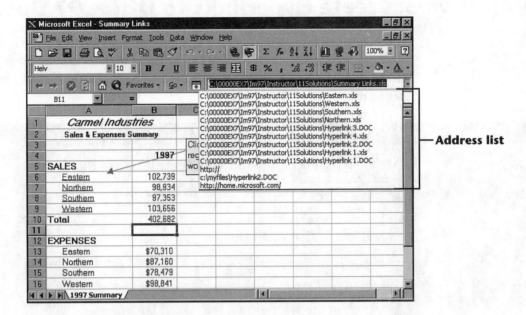

— **Address list**

11

To select a text hyperlink without jumping to the destination, the following three methods are available:

- Click a cell next to the cell that contains the hyperlink and then use the arrow keys to move onto the cell that contains the hyperlink

- Click the cell that contains the hyperlink, hold the mouse button down for at least one second and then release the button

- With the right mouse button, click the cell that contains the hyperlink; then point to Hyperlink in the shortcut menu that is displayed

Navigating Hyperlinks

To use the Web toolbar History buttons and the Address list button to move among recently browsed (hyperlinked) files, follow these steps:

 ❶ Be sure that the Summary Links file is open and that the Web toolbar is displayed. If it isn't, click the Web toolbar button on the Standard toolbar.

 ❷ To open the previous document in the history list, click the Back button on the Web toolbar.

 ❸ To open the next document in the history list, click the Forward button on the Web toolbar.

❹ Click the Address text drop-down arrow and select Western from the history list. The Western workbook file opens.

❺ Save, then close all workbooks

Once you select a hyperlink, you can edit the text or delete the link. You learn more about these activities in Objective 4.

Objective 3: Create Hyperlinks to Office 97 Documents

Whether or not you are connected to the Internet, Microsoft Excel has the capability to navigate between linked Office 97 documents. In the following tutorial, you open an Excel 97 workbook and paste hypertext links to a Word 97 document.

Creating Hyperlinks to a Word 97 Document

To create hyperlinks to a Word 97 document, follow these steps:

1 Open Chap1106 and save it as **Excel Link 1**.

2 Use the Windows 95 Start menu to open Word 97; then open Chap1107 and save it as **Word Link**.

3 In the Excel worksheet, Excel Link 1, select cell G10; then choose **E**dit, **C**opy.

4 Switch to the Word document, Word Link 1.

5 Position the insertion point at the end of the first sentence after the word over. Choose **E**dit, Paste as **H**yperlink to create a hyperlink between the Excel worksheet and the Word document. Your Word document should resemble Figure 11.8.

Figure 11.8
The Word document after inserting a hyperlink at the end of the first sentence.

Hyperlink ——

6 Position the mouse pointer over the value. When the pointer changes to a hand symbol, the destination address for the hyperlink appears above the hand symbol (see Figure 11.9).

Figure 11.9
The destination address for a hyperlink.

7 Click on the hyperlinked value in the Word document. Note that the Excel Link 1 workbook is displayed with the hyperlinked cell selected (see Figure 11.10).

Figure 11.10
The hypertext link after returning to Excel Link 1.

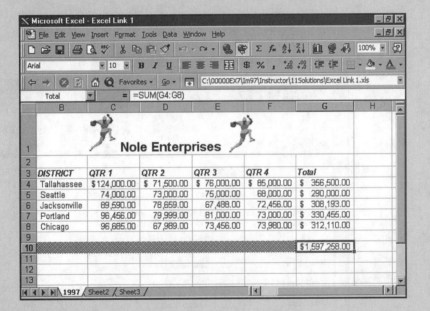

8 In the Excel Link 1 worksheet, select cell G4; then choose **E**dit, **C**opy.

9 Switch to the Word document, Word Link 1.

10 Position the insertion point at the end of the second paragraph—after the word 1997; then choose **E**dit, Paste as **H**yperlink to create a second hyperlink between the Excel worksheet and the Word document (see Figure 11.11).

(continues)

Creating Hyperlinks to a Word 97 Document (continued)

Figure 11.11

The Word document after inserting a hyperlink at the end of the second sentence.

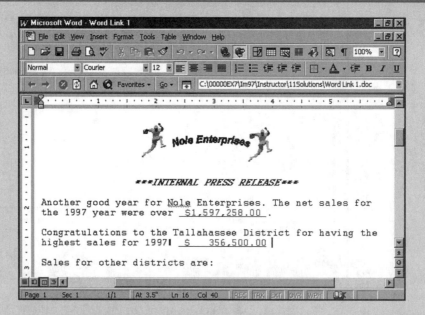

⑪ Repeat the copy and paste procedures previously described to create hyperlinks for Seattle, Jacksonville, Portland, and Chicago annual sales.

⑫ Verify that each hyperlink works by selecting the value in the Word document and clicking it. When completed, Word Link 1 should resemble Figure 11.12.

Figure 11.12

The Word document after inserting several hyperlinks.

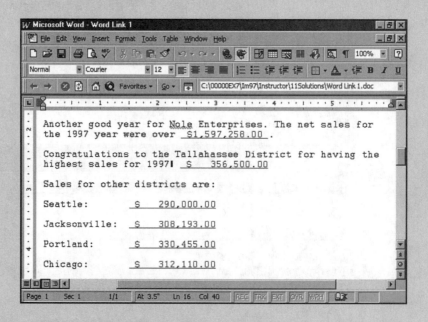

⑬ Print two copies of Word Link 1—one to keep and one to turn in to your instructor; then save and close both Word Link 1 and Excel Link 1.

Objective 4: Create Button Hyperlinks

You have already learned how to create text hyperlinks. In this section, you learn how to create graphic hyperlinks. The ability to create graphic hyperlinks is helpful for visually displaying information and making the hyperlinks more attractive. The only difference between a text hyperlink and a graphic hyperlink is that with a graphic hyperlink, instead of clicking on text, you click on a graphic image. This objective contains two tutorials—one for adding a graphic hyperlink to an Excel worksheet and another in which you add a graphic hyperlink to a Word document. In this objective, you learn to create a graphic hyperlink in both a Word document that returns the reader to an Excel worksheet, and in an Excel worksheet that returns the reader to a Word document.

Adding a Hyperlink Graphic to an Excel Worksheet

To create a hyperlink graphic to connect an Excel workbook with a Word 97 document, follow these steps:

1 In Word 97, open Chap1108 and save it as **Word Link 2**.

2 In Excel 97, open Chap1109 and save it as **Excel Link 2**.

3 In the Excel Link 2 worksheet, select the football player to the left of the company name by clicking it so that handles appear (see Figure 11.13).

Figure 11.13
A selected
graphic.

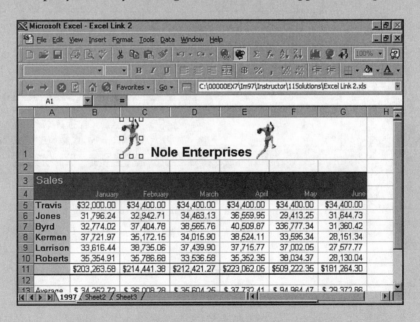

4 Click the Insert Hyperlink button to display the Insert Hyperlink dialog box (refer to Figure 11.1).

5 In the **Link** to file or URL box, type **Word Link 2** and click OK.

(continues)

Adding a Hyperlink Graphic to an Excel Worksheet (continued)

6 To test the hyperlink, first deselect the graphic of the football player. Next, move the mouse pointer over the graphic. When the pointer changes to a hand symbol, the destination address for the hyperlink appears below the hand symbol (see Figure 11.14). Remember that the textbook figures do not show the hand.

Figure 11.14
The destination address for a hyperlink graphic.

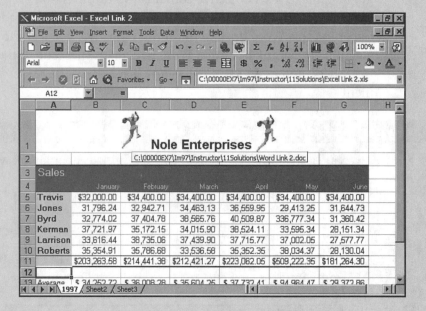

7 Click the hyperlink graphic. The Word Link 2 document is displayed (see Figure 11.15).

Figure 11.15
The Word Link 2 document.

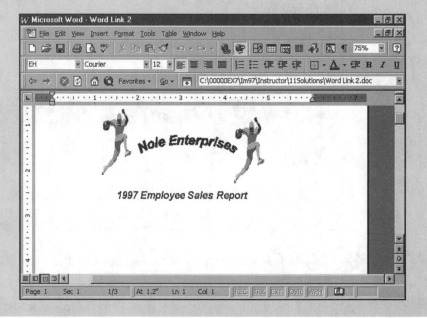

> **Note**
>
> If Excel prompts you to save the workbook, choose **Y**es.

8 Save both files and keep them open for the next tutorial.

In addition to using a hyperlink to connect Excel to Word, you can also create a hyperlink in the destination file to return to the source file.

Adding a Hyperlink Graphic to a Word Document

To create a hyperlink graphic to connect a Word 97 document with an Excel 97 worksheet. Be sure that the Word Link 2 Word document is displayed; then follow these steps:

1 Choose the **V**iew, **P**age Layout view.

2 In the Word Link 2 document, scroll down to display page 3 on your screen.

3 Select the graphic of the football player at the bottom of the page (see Figure 11.16).

Figure 11.16
The selected graphic.

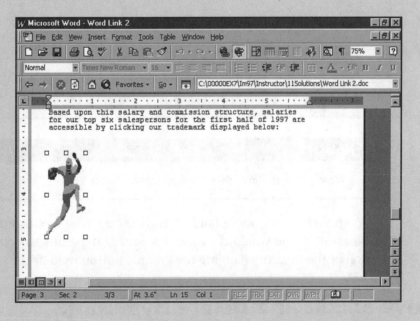

4 Click the Insert Hyperlink button. The Insert Hyperlink dialog box is displayed (refer to Figure 11.1).

5 In the **L**ink to file or URL box, type **Excel Link 2** and click OK.

(continues)

Adding a Hyperlink Graphic to a Word Document (continued)

6 To test the hyperlink, first deselect the graphic. Next, move the mouse pointer over the graphic. When the pointer changes to a hand symbol, the destination address for the hyperlink appears above the hand symbol (see Figure 11.17). Remember, that the hand symbol does not appear in the figures.

Figure 11.17
The destination address for a hyperlink graphic.

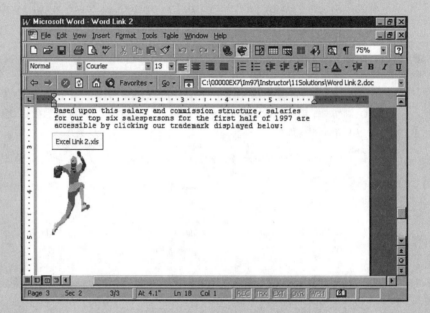

7 Click the hyperlink graphic. The Excel Link 2 worksheet is displayed.

8 Save your changes and keep the workbook open for the next tutorial.

Note

If Word prompts you to save the document, choose **Y**es.

When you become more familiar with Excel's Web toolbar and its hyperlink capabilities, you will find reasons for editing hyperlinks by changing the location of the links or changing the graphic button used in the link.

Objective 5: Edit and Delete Hyperlinks

After hyperlinks have been used, you may decide to change the text or graphic for the hyperlink; you may decide to change the destination of a hyperlink; and you may decide that a link is no longer necessary and you want to delete the hyperlink. In this objective, you are introduced to the methods for accomplishing these activities.

Changing the Graphic for a Hyperlink

To change the graphic for a button hyperlink in the Excel Link 1 workbook, follow these steps:

1 Select the graphic on the left side of the heading by holding down Ctrl while you click the graphic. Handles appear around the graphic.

2 Double-click the graphic to display the Microsoft Clip Gallery 3.0.

3 Select a graphic from the Sports and Leisure category; then click the **Insert** button. The new graphic image appears in the Excel worksheet with handles surrounding it.

> **Note**
>
> If Sports and Leisure graphics are not available, select any graphic image.

4 Click elsewhere on the worksheet to deselect the graphic.

5 Click the new graphic hyperlink to test the link. You should see the Word Link 1 document on your screen.

6 Save your changes and keep the file open for the next tutorial.

In addition to changing the appearance of a hyperlink graphic, you can also change the destination of a hyperlink, which you learn to do in the following tutorial.

Editing Hyperlinks

To change the destination of a hyperlink using the Excel Link 1 workbook, follow these steps:

1 In the Excel Link 1 workbook, select the graphic on the left side of the heading by holding down Ctrl and clicking the graphic. Handles appear around the graphic

2 Click the Insert Hyperlink button to display the Edit Hyperlink dialog box (see Figure 11.18).

(continues)

Editing Hyperlinks (continued)

Figure 11.18
The Edit Hyper-
link dialog box.

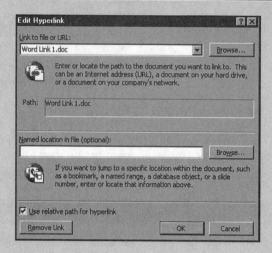

③ Click the **B**rowse button to the right of the **L**ink to file or URL text box to display the Link to File dialog box. This dialog box contains a list of files in the active folder (refer to Figure 11.2).

④ Select Word Link 2 and then click OK to close the dialog box.

⑤ Test the hyperlink by clicking the graphic in the Excel Link 1 workbook. The Word Link 2 document should appear on your screen.

⑥ Save your changes and keep the file open for the next tutorial.

Hyperlinks can be deleted from either the hyperlink source file or the hyperlink destination file. Although a link can be removed by deleting the button or text that is used to make the link, a better, less drastic approach is to simply remove the link. In the following tutorial, you delete a hyperlink.

Removing Hyperlinks

To delete a hyperlink using the Excel Link 1 workbook, follow these steps:

① Using the Excel Link 1 workbook, select the hyperlink graphic (the graphic on the left side of the heading) by holding down Ctrl and clicking the graphic. Handles appear around the graphic.

② Click the Insert Hyperlink button to display the Edit Hyperlink dialog box.

③ In the Edit Hyperlink dialog box, click the **R**emove Link button located on the lower-left side of the dialog box.

④ Click OK to close the Edit Hyperlink dialog box.

⑤ Click the former hyperlink graphic. Notice that nothing happens—the link has been removed.

⑥ Print two copies of Excel Link 1—one to keep and one to turn in to your instructor; then save and close the workbook.

Chapter Summary

In this chapter, you have been introduced to one of the newest and most dynamic features of Excel 97—the capability to create hyperlinks between other workbooks, other Office 97 files, and with World Wide Web pages. You now know how to create both text and graphic hyperlinks and how to find additional graphic images that you can use for your link buttons. Lastly, you learned how to edit and remove hyperlinks.

Checking Your Skills

11

True/False

For each of the following, circle *T* or *F* to indicate whether the statement is true or false.

T   F   **1.** You cannot use an Intranet to navigate between documents.

T   F   **2.** You can use Microsoft Excel 97 to create World Wide Web pages.

T   F   **3.** HMM is the language used to create pages on the World Wide Web.

T   F   **4.** Use a Web viewer to view WWW documents.

T   F   **5.** You must use the Web Link program to create hyperlinks to other files on your system.

T   F   **6.** URLs are used to store hyperlinks.

T   F   **7.** Use the Hypertext toolbar to move between existing hyperlinks.

T   F   **8.** An address can be a URL.

T   F   **9.** You cannot edit a hyperlink entry.

T   F   **10.** The **E**dit, **P**aste command is used to create a hyperlink.

Multiple Choice

In the blank provided, write the letter of the correct answer for each of the following.

1. When working with hyperlinks, the mouse pointer changes to a _____ symbol when selecting the hyperlink.

    a. double-headed arrow

    b. white cross

    c. hand

    d. finger

2. A(n) _____ is the path to an object, document, file, page, or other destination.

    a. address

    b. trail

    c. link

    d. bus

3. Which of the following is *not* a way to create hyperlinks?

    a. You can enter or copy text in a cell or range and make the text a hyperlink.

    b. You can use a workbook function.

    c. You can draw or insert a graphic and make the graphic a hyperlink.

    d. All are ways to create hyperlinks.

4. Hyperlinked text appears in the color _____.

    a. yellow

    b. blue

    c. green

    d. red

5. When the mouse pointer changes to a hand, you are probably selecting a _____.

    a. grammatical error

    b. misspelled word

    c. graphic

    d. hyperlink

6. The history list on the Web toolbar contains a list of the last _____ files you jumped to in the current program session.

    a. 5

    b. 10

    c. 15

    d. 20

7. To select a hyperlink graphic without activating the hyperlink, hold down _____ and click the graphic.

    a. ⬆Shift

    b. Ctrl

    c. Tab⇄

    d. Alt

8. A company's internal Internet is called a(n) _____.

    a. browser

    b. address

    c. telephone

    d. intranet

9. World Wide Web documents are prepared in _____.

    a. HTML

    b. HLTX

    c. HTTP

    d. FTP

10. A _____ is software that interprets HTML files posted on the World Wide Web.

    a. hypertext

    b. FTP

    c. HTTP

    d. browser

Fill in the Blank

In the blank provided, write the correct answer for each of the following statements.

1. _____ enable(s) you to jump to other documents and objects in Office 97 applications.

2. A(n) _____ is a network within an organization.

3. A(n) _____ is the path to an object.

4. When using the Web toolbar, use the _____ feature to display the 10 previous Web sites from the current session.

5. If text appears in blue and is underlined, it is probably a(n) _____.

6. To open the previous document in the history list, click the _____ button on the Web toolbar.

7. A large selection of clip art is stored in the Microsoft Clip _____.

8. _____ is the form of the site address that reveals the name of the server in which a site's files are stored.

9. To open the next document in the history list, click the _____ button on the Web toolbar.

10. _____ enable you to set up a navigational course for those reading your worksheet.

Applying Your Skills

Review Exercises

Exercise 1: Connecting Office 97 Files with Hyperlinks

In this exercise, you create a hyperlink between an Excel workbook and a Word document.

1. Open the Chap1110 workbook and save it as **Sun Beach Summary**.

2. Open the Chap1111 Word document and save it as **Sun Beaches.**

3. Use the **C**opy and Paste as **H**yperlink commands to link the worksheet with the Word document using the quarterly sales amounts for each city.

4. Test the hyperlinks.

5. Print two copies of both files (one to keep and one to turn in to your instructor).

6. Save and then close both documents.

Exercise 2: Connecting Office 97 Files using a Graphic Hyperlink

In this exercise, you create a graphic hyperlink between an Excel workbook and a Word document.

1. Open the Chap1112 workbook and save it as **Universal Sales**.

2. Open Chap1113 document and save it as **Universal Report**.

3. In the Word document, create a hyperlink between the graphic image at the end of the document to the Universal Sales workbook.

4. Test the hyperlink.

5. Print two copies of both files—one to keep and one to turn in to your instructor.

6. Save and then close both files.

Exercise 3: Creating Hyperlinks Between Excel Workbooks

In this exercise, you create a hyperlink button between Excel worksheets within a workbook.

1. Open the Chap1114 workbook and save it as **AQN Detail**.

2. Open the Chap1115 workbook and save it as **AQN Summary**.

3. Use the graphic on the right of the title in the AQN Summary workbook to create a hyperlink to the AQN Detail workbook.

4. Test the hyperlink.

5. Print two copies of both workbooks; then save and close both workbooks.

Exercise 4: Creating Hyperlinks Between Excel Worksheets within a Workbook

In this exercise, you create a hyperlink button between Excel worksheets within a workbook.

1. Open the Chap1116 workbook and save it as **Reliable Data**.

2. Open the Chap1117 workbook and save it as **Reliable Summary**.

3. Use the graphic on the right of the title in the Reliable Summary workbook to create a hyperlink to the Reliable Data workbook.

4. Test the hyperlink.

5. Save and print two copies of both workbooks. Keep both workbooks open for the next exercise.

Exercise 5: Deleting Hyperlinks

In this exercise, you delete a hyperlink button between Excel workbooks.

1. Make sure that the Reliable Summary workbook is open.

2. Select the hyperlink graphic.

3. Choose **E**dit, Clea**r**, **A**ll.

4. Save and print two copies of the workbook before closing it.

Continuing Projects

Project 1: Creating a Hyperlink between Office 97 Applications

Establish a graphic hyperlink between a Cape Sales and Marketing announcement and a real estate listing. Open Chap1118 and save it as **Real Estate 11**. Open the Word file, Chap1119, and save it as **Real Estate 12.doc**. Using the house graphic at the bottom on the Real Estate 12 document, create a hyperlink to the Real Estate 11 worksheet. Print two copies of both documents (one to keep and one to turn in to your instructor). Then save and close both files.

Project 2: Creating Hyperlinks between Worksheets in a Workbook

Use hyperlinks in a Kipper Industries workbook to connect information on a summary sheet with data from related worksheets in the workbook. Open the Chap1120 workbook and save it as **Employee 11**. Using the summary figures on the Employee Summary worksheet, hyperlink each total with its corresponding worksheet. For example, on the Employee Summary sheet, create a hyperlink between the Accounting Salary Costs figure and the Accounting worksheet. When you are done, you should be able to click on any of the totals on the summary sheet and jump to the corresponding worksheet. Test the links. Print two copies of the Employee Summary worksheet (one to keep and one to turn in to your instructor). Save and then close the workbook.

Project 3: Using Graphic Hyperlinks between Worksheets in a Workbook

Use hyperlinks in a Coastal Sales Industries workbook to connect information on a summary sheet with data from related worksheets in the workbook. Open Chap1121 and save it as **Vehicle Mileage 11**. Using the graphics in row 5 on the Summary worksheet, hyperlink each graphic with its corresponding weekly worksheet. For example, on the Summary worksheet create a hyperlink between the graphic in cell B5 with the Week 1 worksheet. When you are done, you should be able to click on any of the graphics on the summary sheet and jump to the corresponding worksheet. Test the links. Print two copies of the Summary sheet (one to keep and one to turn in to your instructor). Save and then close the workbook.

Working with Windows 95

Graphical user interface (GUI) A computer application that uses pictures, graphics, menus, and commands to help users communicate with their computers.

Microsoft Windows 95 is a powerful operating environment that enables you to access the power of DOS without memorizing DOS commands and syntax. Windows uses a *graphical user interface* (GUI) so that you can easily see on-screen the tools you need to complete specific file and program management tasks.

This appendix, an overview of the Windows 95 environment, is designed to help you learn the basics of Windows.

Objectives

By the time you finish this appendix, you will have learned to

- Start Windows 95
- Use a Mouse
- Identify the Elements of a Window
- Understand the Start menu
- Exit the Windows 95 Program

Objective 1: Start Windows 95

The first thing you need to know about Windows is how to start the software, and in this lesson, you learn just that. Before you can start Windows, however, it must be installed on your computer. If you need to install Windows, refer to your Windows manual or ask your instructor for assistance.

In most cases, Windows starts automatically when you turn on your computer. If your system is set up differently, you must start Windows from the DOS prompt (such as C:\>). Try starting the Windows program now.

Starting Windows

Desktop
The background of the Windows screen, on which windows, icons, and dialog boxes are displayed.

1. Turn on your computer and monitor.

Most computers display technical information about the computer and the operating software installed, and then Windows 95 starts automatically. If Windows 95 starts, you can skip step 2. Otherwise, you will see the DOS prompt (C:\>) in the upper-left corner of the screen.

2. At the DOS prompt C:\>, type **win** and then press ⏎Enter.

When you start the Windows program, a Microsoft Windows 95 banner displays for a few seconds; then the *desktop* appears (see Figure A.1).

Figure A.1
The Windows 95 desktop appears a few seconds after a Windows 95 banner.

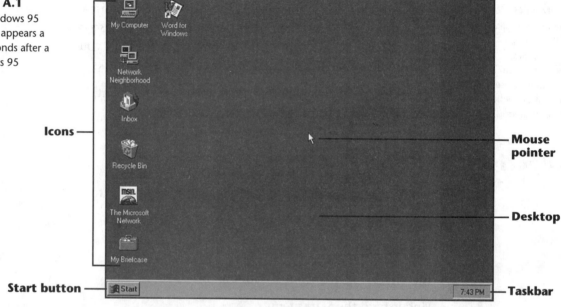

Icon
A picture that represents an application, a file, or a system resource.

Program *icons* that were created during installation (My Computer, Recycle Bin, Network Neighborhood) are displayed on the desktop. Other icons may also appear, depending on how your system is set up. *Shortcuts* to frequently used objects (such as documents, printers, and network drives) can be placed on the desktop. The *taskbar* appears along the bottom edge of the desktop. The *Start button* appears at the left end of the taskbar.

Objective 2: Use a Mouse in Windows

Shortcut
Gives you quick access to frequently used objects so you don't have to look through menus each time.

Windows is designed to be used with a *mouse*, so it's important that you learn how to use a mouse correctly. With a little practice, using a mouse is as easy as pointing to something with your finger. You can use the mouse to select icons, to make selections from *pull-down menus* and *dialog boxes*, and to select objects that you want to move or resize.

Taskbar
Contains the Start button, buttons for each open window, and the current time.

Start button
A click on the Start button opens the Start menu.

Mouse
A pointing device used to make choices, select data, and otherwise communicate with the computer.

Pull-down menus
Menus that cascade downward into the screen whenever you select a command from the menu bar.

Dialog box
A window that opens on-screen to provide information about the current action or to ask the user to provide additional information.

Mouse pointer
A symbol that appears on-screen to indicate the current location of the mouse.

Mouse pad
A pad that provides a uniform surface for a mouse to slide on.

In the Windows desktop, you can use a mouse to:

- Open windows

- Close windows

- Open menus

- Choose menu commands

- Rearrange on-screen items, such as icons and windows

The position of the mouse is indicated on-screen by a *mouse pointer*. Usually, the mouse pointer is an arrow, but it sometimes changes shape depending on the current action.

On-screen the mouse pointer moves according to the movements of the mouse on your desk or on a *mouse pad*. To move the mouse pointer, simply move the mouse.

There are four basic mouse actions:

- *Click* To point to an item, and then press and quickly release the left mouse button. You click to select an item, such as an option on a menu. To cancel a selection, click an empty area of the desktop. Unless otherwise specified, you use the left mouse button for all mouse actions.

- *Double-click* To point to an item, and then press and release the left mouse button twice, as quickly as possible. You double-click to open or close windows and to start applications from icons.

- *Right-click* To point to an item, and then press and release the right mouse button. This opens a Context menu, which gives you a shortcut to frequently used commands. To cancel a Context menu, click the left mouse button outside the menu.

- *Drag* To point to an item, and then press and hold down the left mouse button as you move the pointer to another location, and then release the mouse button. You drag to resize windows, move icons, and scroll.

If you have problems... If you try to double-click but nothing happens, you may not be clicking fast enough. Try again.

Objective 3: Understand the Start Menu

Program folder
Represented by an icon of a file folder with an application window in front of it, program folders contain shortcut icons and other program folders.

The Start button on the taskbar gives you access to your applications, settings, recently opened documents, the Find utility, the Run command, the Help system, and the Shut Down command. Clicking the Start button opens the Start menu. Choosing the Programs option at the top of the Start menu displays the Programs menu, which lists the *program folders* on your system. Program folders are listed first, followed by shortcuts (see Figure A.2).

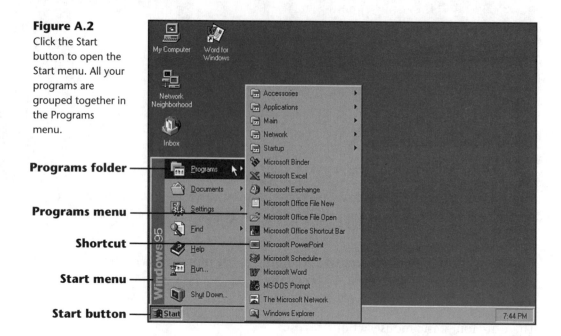

Programs folder

Programs menu

Shortcut

Start menu

Start button

When the Start menu is open, moving the mouse pointer moves a selection bar through the menu options. When the selection bar highlights a menu command with a right-facing triangle, a submenu opens. Click the shortcut icon to start an application. If a menu command is followed by an ellipsis, clicking that command opens a dialog box.

Objective 4: Identify the Elements of a Window

In the Windows program, everything opens in a window. Applications open in windows, documents open in windows, and dialog boxes open in windows. For example, double-clicking the My Computer icon opens the My Computer application into a window. Because window elements stay the same for all Windows applications, this section uses the My Computer window for illustration.

The Title Bar
Across the top of each window is its title bar. A title bar contains the name of the open window as well as three buttons to manipulate windows. The Minimize button is for reducing windows to a button on the taskbar. The Maximize button is for expanding windows to fill the desktop. The Close button is for closing the window.

The Menu Bar
The menu bar gives you access to the application's menus. Menus enable you to select options that perform functions or carry out commands (see Figure A.3). The File menu in My Computer, for example, enables you to open, save, and print files.

Title bar   Minimize   Maximize   Close
button   button   button

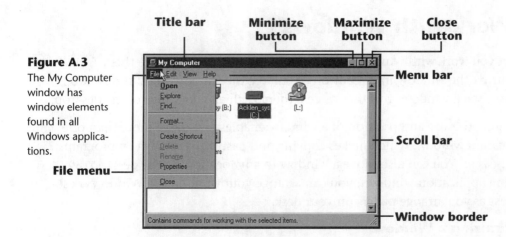

Figure A.3
The My Computer
window has
window elements
found in all
Windows applica-
tions.

File menu

Menu bar

Scroll bar

Window border

Some menu options require you to enter additional information. When you select one of these options, a dialog box opens (see Figure A.4). You either type the additional information, select from a list of options, or select a button. Most dialog boxes have a Cancel button, which closes the dialog box without saving the changes; an OK button which closes the dialog box and saves the changes; and a Help button, which opens a Help window.

Figure A.4
You can use the
options in the
Find dialog box
to search for a
file.

Type the
name of the
file here

Click here
to select
this option

Click here to
choose from
a list

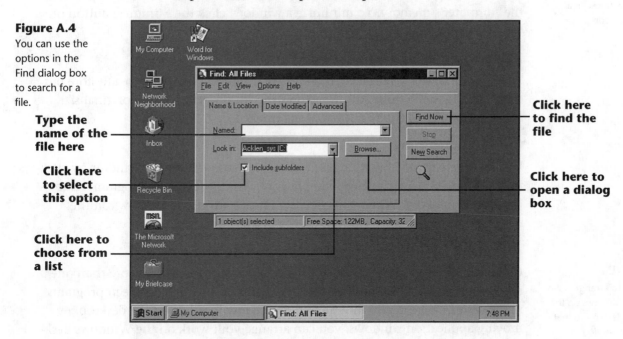

Click here
to find the
file

Click here to
open a dialog
box

Scroll Bars

Scroll bars appear when you have more information in a window than is currently displayed on-screen. A horizontal scroll bar appears along the bottom of a window and a vertical scroll bar appears along the right side of a window.

The Window Border

The window border identifies the edge of the window. In most windows, it can be used to change the size of a window. The window corner is used to resize a window on two sides at the same time.

Objective 5: Work with Windows

When you work with windows, you need to know how to arrange them. You can shrink the window into a button or enlarge the window to fill the desktop. You can stack windows together or give them each an equal slice of the desktop.

Changing the size and position of a window enables you to see more than one application window, which makes copying and pasting data between programs much easier. You can also move a window to any location on the desktop. By moving application windows, you can arrange your work on the Windows desktop just as you arrange papers on your desk.

Maximizing a Window

Maximize

To increase the size of a window so that it fills the entire screen.

You can *maximize* a window so it fills the desktop. Maximizing a window gives you more space to work in. To maximize a window, click the Maximize button on the title bar.

Minimizing a Window

Minimize

To reduce a window to a button.

When you *minimize* a window, it shrinks the window to a button on the taskbar. Even though you can't see the window anymore, the application stays loaded in the computer's memory. To minimize a window, click the Minimize button on the title bar.

Restoring a Window

When a window is maximized, the Maximize button changes into a Restore button. Clicking the Restore button restores the window back to the original size and position before the window was maximized.

Closing a Window

When you are finished working in a window, you can close the window by clicking the Close button. Closing an application window exits the program, removing it from memory. When you click the Close button, the window (on the desktop) and the window button (on the taskbar) disappear.

Arranging Windows

Tile

To arrange open windows on the desktop so that they do not overlap.

Cascade

To arrange open windows on the desktop so that they overlap, with only the title bar of each window (behind the top window) displayed.

Changing the size and position of a window enables you to see more than one application window, which makes copying and pasting data between programs much easier. You also move a window to any location on the desktop. By moving application windows, you can arrange your work on the Windows desktop just as you arrange papers on your desk.

Use one of the following options to arrange windows:

- Right-click the taskbar, then choose *Tile* Horizontally.

- Right-click the taskbar, then choose Tile Vertically. See Figure A.5 for an example.

- Right-click the taskbar, then choose *Cascade*. See Figure A.6 for an example.

- Click and drag the window's title bar to move to the window around on the desktop.

- Click and drag a window border (or corner) to increase or decrease the size of the window.

Figure A.5
The windows are tiled vertically across the desktop.

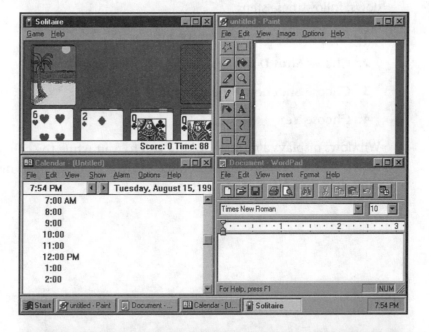

Figure A.6
The windows are cascaded on the desktop.

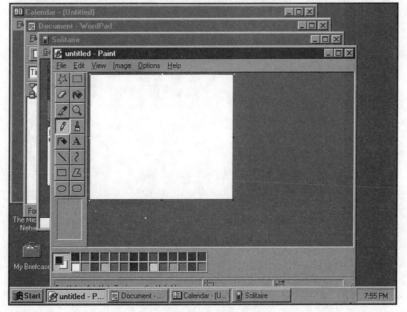

Objective 6: Exit the Windows Program

In Windows 95, you use the Shut Down command to exit the Windows program. You should always use this command, which closes all open applications and files, before you turn off the computer. If you haven't saved your work in an application when you choose this command, you'll be prompted to save your changes before Windows shuts down.

Exiting Windows

You should always exit Windows before turning off your computer. To exit Windows, follow these steps:

1. Click the Start button on the taskbar.

2. Choose Sh**u**t Down.

3. Choose **S**hut down the computer.

4. Choose **Y**es.

Windows displays a message asking you to wait while the computer is shutting down. When this process is complete, a message appears telling you that you can safely turn off your computer now.

Glossary

Absolute cell reference A cell reference that remains the same when copied or moved.

Active cell The worksheet cell receiving the data you type, surrounded by a thick border.

Annuity calculations Calculations based on a series of even payments over a specified time.

Argument The number(s), cell(s), or named range(s) that a function uses in its calculations.

Array A rectangular range of values or formulas treated as one group.

AutoComplete feature If the first few characters you type in a cell match an existing entry in that column, Microsoft Excel fills in the remaining characters for you. Excel completes only those entries that contain a combination of text and numbers; entries that contain only numbers, dates, or times are not completed by Excel.

Automate To create a Visual Basic Procedure (a macro) to perform repetitive worksheet tasks automatically.

AutoSum button Clicking this button, which is Located on the Standard toolbar, is an efficient way to total rows or columns in your worksheet.

Best Fit A command that automatically adjusts the column width or row height to the widest cell in the column.

Cascade To arrange open windows on the desktop so that they overlap, with only the title bar of each window (behind the top window) displayed.

Cell The intersection of a column and a row in a spreadsheet.

Cell address Location of a cell based on the intersection of a column and row.

Cell Comment An explanatory note or comment added to the worksheet. It can be displayed, edited, and printed.

Cell pointer A cross-shaped white marker; the shape the mouse pointer takes when it is on the worksheet.

Chart object An item on a chart (such as an arrow) that can be moved, sized, and formatted.

Chart sheet A workbook sheet that contains a chart but not a worksheet.

Chart Wizard A charting tool used to guide you through creating, formatting, and modifying a chart.

Clipboard A part of memory set aside for storing information or formulas you want to move or copy to another location.

Consolidated report A report in which data from multiple source areas (usually different worksheets) is gathered into one worksheet.

Consolidation function The function (like SUM or AVERAGE) that Excel is to use when it consolidates your data.

Criteria Specified tests for the contents of the fields in a record; test conditions used to find records in a database.

Cursor The blinking line in the formula bar, indicating the point of insertion.

Data form Displays field names, text boxes, and buttons for adding, deleting, and finding records in your database.

Data series A collection of data from a worksheet; the data your chart represents.

Database A collection of related information about a subject organized in a useful manner.

Default An automatic setting that the computer uses unless you specify another setting.

Default chart type The chart that Excel automatically creates based on the selected data.

Dependent workbook A workbook containing an external reference (a link) to another (source) workbook and therefore dependent on the other workbook for data.

Desktop The background of the Windows screen, on which windows, icons, and dialog boxes are displayed.

Destination area The range of cells you select to hold data summarized by the Consolidate command.

Dialog box A window that opens on-screen to provide information about the current action or to ask the user to enter additional information to complete an action.

Drag-and-drop A mouse procedure enabling you to move or copy data.

External reference formula A reference to a cell or range in another Excel workbook, also called an external reference.

Field A column in a database; each column contains one type of information.

Field names Labels (the column headings) that identify the contents of a column in a database.

File The area on a disk in which workbooks are saved.

Fill handle The black square at the lower-right corner of a selected cell or range.

Filter The criteria that tell Excel which database records to display.

Font One complete collection of letters, punctuation marks, numbers, and special characters with a consistent and identifiable typeface, weight (roman or bold), posture (upright or italic), and type size.

Footer Text, date, page numbering, and formatting in the bottom margin of each page of a document.

Formula bar Area near the top of the Excel screen in which you enter and edit data.

Formula palette Used to edit functions in formulas or to create formulas in functions.

Function A predefined formula consisting of a name and one or more arguments.

Graphical User Interface (GUI) A computer application that uses pictures, graphics, menus, and commands to help users communicate with their computers.

Gridlines The intersecting horizontal and vertical lines on a worksheet.

Header Text, date, page numbering, and formatting in the top margin of each page of a document.

Icon A picture that represents an application, a file, or a system resource.

Key field A field that can be used to find a particular record in a database because each record contains a unique value in that field.

Legend A guide, displayed near the chart, that identifies the data in the chart.

Link A one-way data connection from the source workbook to the dependent workbook.

Macro A stored list of commands and keystrokes that are automatically executed by Excel.

Manual page break Determines the end of a page, inserted with a command.

Marquee Moving dashes outlining the area cut or copied to the Clipboard.

Maximize To increase the size of a window so that it fills the entire screen.

Minimize To reduce a window to a button.

Mixed cell reference A single cell address that contains a relative and an absolute reference.

Modules Where Excel places the recorded commands. Modules can be viewed through the Visual Basic Editor.

Mouse A pointing device used to make choices, select data, and otherwise communicate with the computer.

Mouse pad A pad that provides a uniform surface for the mouse to slide on.

Mouse pointer A symbol that appears on-screen to indicate the current location of the mouse.

Order of precedence The order mathematicians have established for performing arithmetical operations in a formula.

Paste area The new location in the worksheet where selected data will be moved or copied.

Paste function A sequence of dialog boxes that aid in the entry of functions in your worksheet.

Plot area The area on the chart containing the pie, lines, columns, or bars.

Point size One point equals 1/72 inch. In Excel, font size and row height are measured in points. The larger the point size, the larger the font size.

Predefined formats Standardized formats that come with Excel.

Print area Section of worksheet defined to be printed.

Print Preview mode Mode in which you see an overview of the print area showing you what the page will look like when printed.

Procedure A macro; a series of Visual Basic statements you create using the Macro Recorder and store together.

Program folder Represented by an icon of a file folder with an application window in front of it, program folders contain shortcut icons and other program folders.

Pull-down menu Menu that cascades downward into the screen whenever you select a command from the menu bar.

RAM Stands for random-access memory. A temporary memory area in a computer.

Range One or more blocks of cells that can be formatted, moved, copied, or referred to as a unit.

Range name A meaningful name you give to a cell or range of cells.

Record A row of cells containing fields of related information in a database.

Relative cell reference A cell reference that adjusts to its new location when copied or moved.

Serial number A date expressed as a number. Days are numbered from the beginning of the 20th century.

Shortcut   Provides quick access to frequently used commands so that you don't have to look through menus.

Sizing handles   The black squares on the border enclosing a selected chart.

Sort field   The field specified to control the reordering of a database.

Source area   The cell ranges from which the Consolidate command draws data.

Source workbook   A workbook that supplies data over a link to a dependent workbook.

Spell check   A feature enabling you to check for misspelled words, unusual capitalization, and repeated words.

Start button   A click on the Start button opens the Start menu.

Style   A combination of formatting characteristics (such as alignment, borders, font, and number formatting).

Summary report   A list in which data is broken into groups and summarized by group subtotals with an overall total given at the bottom of the list.

Taskbar   Contains the Start button and buttons for each currently open window.

Tile   To arrange open windows on the desktop so that they do not overlap.

Toolbar   A bar across the top of the Excel window containing a series of icon buttons used to access commands and other features.

Unattached text   Text in a text box on a chart that can be selected and moved to different locations on the chart.

Visual Basic for Applications   A programming language; the Excel Macro Recorder creates macros consisting of Visual Basic statements.

Workbook   A collection of related worksheets kept in a single file. A workbook can contain 1 to 255 worksheets.

Worksheet   One page (or sheet) of your work in an Excel workbook consisting of columns and rows in which you enter text, numbers, and formulas.

X-axis   The horizontal (category) axis on a chart.

Y-axis   The vertical (value) axis on a chart.

Index

H-I-J

Q-R

S

X-Y-Z